A Practitioner's Guide to Cannabis

A Practitioner's Guide to Cannabis

Win Turner
Center for Behavioral Health Integration
School of Social Welfare, Stony Brook University
Montpelier, Vermont
US

Joseph Hyde
JBS International, Inc.
School of Social Welfare, Stony Brook University
North Bethesda, Maryland
US

Copyright © 2023 by John Wiley & Sons, Inc. All rights reserved.

Published by John Wiley & Sons, Inc., Hoboken, New Jersey.
Published simultaneously in Canada.

No part of this publication may be reproduced, stored in a retrieval system, or transmitted in any form or by any means, electronic, mechanical, photocopying, recording, scanning, or otherwise, except as permitted under Section 107 or 108 of the 1976 United States Copyright Act, without either the prior written permission of the Publisher, or authorization through payment of the appropriate per-copy fee to the Copyright Clearance Center, Inc., 222 Rosewood Drive, Danvers, MA 01923, (978) 750–8400, fax (978) 750–4470, or on the web at www.copyright.com. Requests to the Publisher for permission should be addressed to the Permissions Department, John Wiley & Sons, Inc., 111 River Street, Hoboken, NJ 07030, (201) 748–6011, fax (201) 748–6008, or online at http://www.wiley.com/go/permission.

Trademarks: Wiley and the Wiley logo are trademarks or registered trademarks of John Wiley & Sons, Inc. and/or its affiliates in the United States and other countries and may not be used without written permission. All other trademarks are the property of their respective owners. John Wiley & Sons, Inc. is not associated with any product or vendor mentioned in this book.

Limit of Liability/Disclaimer of Warranty: While the publisher and author have used their best efforts in preparing this book, they make no representations or warranties with respect to the accuracy or completeness of the contents of this book and specifically disclaim any implied warranties of merchantability or fitness for a particular purpose. No warranty may be created or extended by sales representatives or written sales materials. The advice and strategies contained herein may not be suitable for your situation. You should consult with a professional where appropriate. Neither the publisher nor author shall be liable for any loss of profit or any other commercial damages, including but not limited to special, incidental, consequential, or other damages. Further, readers should be aware that websites listed in this work may have changed or disappeared between when this work was written and when it is read. Neither the publisher nor authors shall be liable for any loss of profit or any other commercial damages, including but not limited to special, incidental, consequential, or other damages.

For general information on our other products and services or for technical support, please contact our Customer Care Department within the United States at (800) 762–2974, outside the United States at (317) 572–3993 or fax (317) 572–4002.

Wiley also publishes its books in a variety of electronic formats. Some content that appears in print may not be available in electronic formats. For more information about Wiley products, visit our web site at www.wiley.com.

Library of Congress Cataloging-in-Publication Data
Names: Turner, Win, author.
Title: A practitioner's guide to cannabis / Win Turner, Joseph Hyde.
Description: Hoboken, New Jersey : John Wiley & Sons, [2023] | Includes bibliographical references and index.
Identifiers: LCCN 2022047010 (print) | LCCN 2022047011 (ebook) | ISBN 9781119634218 (paperback) | ISBN 9781119634232 (pdf) | ISBN 9781119634201 (epub)
Subjects: LCSH: Cannabis--United States. | Cannabis--Health aspects--United States.
Classification: LCC HV5822.C3 T87 2023 (print) | LCC HV5822.C3 (ebook) | DDC 362.29/50973--dc23/eng/20221123
LC record available at https://lccn.loc.gov/2022047010
LC ebook record available at https://lccn.loc.gov/2022047011

Cover Image: © fizkes/Shutterstock
Cover Design: Wiley

Set in 9.5/12.5pt STIXTwoText by Integra Software Services Pvt. Ltd, Pondicherry, India
SKY10043892_030623

v

Contents

1 Introduction *1*

2 What is Cannabis? *5*
The Geographical and Historical Origins of Cannabis *6*
History of the Medicinal Use of Cannabis *7*
Recent US History of Cannabis Use *9*
Factors Influencing Cannabis Legalization in the United States *10*

3 The Chemistry of Cannabis *13*
Psychoactive Chemicals in Cannabis *13*
Synthetic Cannabinoids *15*
Cannabinoids and the Human Body *17*
The Changing Chemistry of Cannabis and Synthetics *19*

4 Cannabis Use in the United States *20*
Potential Effects of Legalization of Cannabis in the United States *20*
Risks and CUD *22*
Risks Pertaining to Cannabis Delivery Methods and Potency *24*

5 Cannabis, its Recreational Use, and its Effects *27*
Recreational Use of Cannabis *29*
Pregnancy *31*
Highway Safety *33*
Cognitive Impairment *33*

vi | *Contents*

6 Cannabis as Medicine and the User's Experience *35*
Multiple Sclerosis *36*
Chronic Pain *36*
Epilepsy *38*
Cancer *38*
Psychiatric Conditions *39*
Medical Cannabis Patients Describe Their Experiences *39*
Positive Experiences *40*
Negative Experiences *41*
Recommendations *41*
Summary *41*

7 A New Approach to Cannabis Screening *42*
Universal Screening for Substance Use Disorders *42*
Rationale for a Cannabis Screener *43*
Cannabis Intervention Screener *44*
Development of the CIS *45*
Summary of CIS Evaluation Findings *46*
Cannabis Use Vs. Misuse Vs. Abuse *48*
Implications from CIS Study Findings *51*

Orientation to Clinical Interventions Addressing Cannabis Use Disorder *53*
Motivational Interviewing and Motivational Enhancement Therapy *53*
Brief MI Interaction for Cannabis Misuse *54*
Cognitive Behavioral Therapy *55*
Intrapersonal Skills Training *57*
CBT Introduction *58*
The Structure of a Session Delivery: "Law of Thirds" *59*
Session 1. Eliciting the Life Movie *64*
Clinician Preparation *65*
Session 1 Outline and Overview *66*
Session 1 Protocol with Scripts *68*
Session 1. Eliciting Life Movie and Change Plan Handouts *78*
Treatment Information Sheet *79*
Eliciting the Life Movie: MI Conversation *81*
A Change Plan—Optional *84*

Contents | **vii**

Learning New Coping Strategies (Handout) *85*
Session 2. Enhancing Awareness *89*
Clinician Preparation *90*
Session 2 Outline and Overview *91*
Session 2 Protocol with Scripts *94*
Session 2. Enhancing Situational Awareness Handouts *102*
Review of Progress and Between-Session Challenges *103*
Alcohol/Cannabis use Awareness Record *104*
Alcohol/Cannabis use Awareness Record Example *105*
Planning to Feel Good (Optional) *106*
Session 3. Learning Assertiveness *107*
Clinician Preparation *108*
Session 3 Outline and Overview *109*
Session 3 Protocol with Scripts *111*
Session 3. Learning Assertiveness Handouts *120*
Review of Progress and Between-Session Challenges *121*
Communication Styles *122*
Between-Session Challenge Assertiveness *124*
Session 4. Supporting Recovery through Enhanced Social
Supports *126*
Enhancing Social Support *128*
Session 4 Outline and Overview for Enhancing Social
Support *129*
Session 4 Protocol with Scripts *132*
Session 5. Supporting Recovery through Healthy Replacement
Activities *136*
Clinician Preparation *137*
Session 5 Outline and Overview for Enhancing Healthy
Replacement Activities *138*
Session 5 Protocol with Scripts *140*
Session 5. Supporting Recovery Through Healthy Replacement
Activities Handouts *143*
Review of Progress and Between-Session Challenges *144*
Social Support *145*
My Social Atom *146*
Plan for Seeking Support *147*
Increasing Pleasant Activities *148*
Engaging in Replacement Activities *149*

viii | *Contents*

Session 6. Problem Solving *150*
Clinician Preparation *151*
Session 6 Outline and Overview *152*
Session 6 Protocol with Scripts *155*
Session 6. Problem Solving Handouts *163*
Review of Progress and Between-Session Challenges *164*
Problem Solving *165*
Session 7. Handling Urges, Cravings, and Discomfort
(urge Surfing) *167*
Clinician Preparation *168*
Session 7 Outline and Overview *169*
Session 7 Protocol with Scripts *172*
Session 7. Handling Urges, Cravings, and Discomfort
Handouts *186*
Coping with Cravings and Discomfort *187*
Daily Record of Urges to Use *189*
Urge Surfing *190*
Session 8. Making Important Life Decisions *192*
Clinician Preparation *194*
Session 8 Outline and Overview *195*
Session 8 Protocol *197*
Session 8. Making Important Life Decisions Handouts *201*
Clinician's Quick Reference to Session 8 *202*
MI Skills and Strategies *204*
Readiness-to-Change Ruler *205*
Values Exploration *206*
My Values *208*
Decision-Making Guide *209*
Decision-Making Guide Example *211*
Thinking About My Use Option 3 *213*
Session 9. Enhancing Self-awareness *214*
Clinician Preparation *215*
Session 9 Outline and Overview *216*
Session Protocol *217*
Session 9. Enhancing Self-Awareness Handouts *227*
Clinician's Quick Reference to Session 9 *228*
Alcohol/Cannabis Use Awareness Record *229*
Alcohol/Cannabis Use Awareness Record (continued) *231*
Alcohol/Cannabis Use Awareness Record Example *232*

Contents ix

Future Self Letter *233*
Relaxation Practice Exercise *234*
Session 10. Mindfulness, Meditation, and Stepping Back *235*
Clinician Preparation *238*
Session 10 Outline and Overview *239*
Session Protocol *240*
Session 10. Mindfulness, Meditation, and Stepping Back
Handouts *246*
Clinician's Quick Reference to Session 10 *247*
Mindfulness Meditation Instructions *248*
Meditation Exercise: On the Riverbank *249*

References *250*
Index *267*

1

Introduction

Half a century ago, the United States was in the grips of a marijuana panic. It was 1969, the year George Harrison was arrested for marijuana possession and Richard Nixon, chief architect of what would soon be called the War on Drugs, entered the White House. In October of that year, *LIFE* magazine devoted a cover story to the drug debate. The cover displayed an ominous close-up of a hand clutching a shriveled blue joint. "MARIJUANA," declared the accompanying text. "At least 12 million Americans have now tried it. Are penalties too severe? Should it be legalized?" [1].

The answer, back then at least, seemed to be a resounding no. Sure, stoned flower children and drug-addled rock stars sucked up most of the media attention, but public opinion on marijuana policy more closely reflected Nixon's "silent majority" of disapproving conservatives. In 1969, Gallup surveyed Americans for the first time on whether they believed the use of marijuana should be made legal. Only 12 percent of respondents favored legalization. Although that number rose to 28 percent during the 1970s, it remained well under half of Americans, and pro-legalization sentiment entered a lull during the Reagan and Bush Sr. era.

Fifty-one years later, everything has changed. While popular opinion often shifts at a glacial pace, US public policy surrounding cannabis use has revolutionized in just a few years. In 2012, Washington and Colorado became the first two states to pass ballot initiatives legalizing recreational use of marijuana, despite the federal government's disapproval [2]. By the spring of 2018, seven more states—as well as the District of Columbia—had legalized recreational use of marijuana, and

A Practitioner's Guide to Cannabis, First Edition. Win Turner and Joseph Hyde.
© 2023 John Wiley & Sons, Inc. Published 2023 by John Wiley & Sons, Inc.

1 Introduction

29 states altogether had either decriminalized or allowed medical marijuana use [2]. That same year, Vermont legalized marijuana through the legislative process, another national first. 2018 and 2019 were both pivotal years for the legalization movement, and the momentum is unlikely to slow in the new decade. (Things have moved even faster in Canada, which legalized marijuana nationwide, ending nearly a century of prohibition, in 2018.) Concurrently, Americans no longer disapprove of the puffy cloud in overwhelming numbers. A 2018 Gallup poll found that 66 percent of US adults approve of marijuana legalization—the highest percentage since Gallup began asking the question in 1969. Much of the shift in public opinion occurred relatively fast: Support for legalization rose by a staggering 30 percent between 2005 and 2018 [3, 4].

This legal revolution has been accompanied by a subtler and less quantifiable cultural shift. Think back again to the '60s and early '70s: Pot—or "grass" —was the preferred creative lubricant of Bob Dylan and Jerry Garcia, the healing herb of Bob Marley, the necessary concession which thousands of hippie festivalgoers brought to Woodstock, the onscreen vice of Dennis Hopper and Peter Fonda in *Easy Rider* (1969). It was the subject of admiring odes like The Beatles' "Got to Get You Into My Life" and Black Sabbath's "Sweet Leaf," which famously opens with the sound of guitarist Tony Iommi coughing after a particularly strong hit from a joint [5]. For decades to come, fictitious pot-smokers of the cinema world would still be portrayed as bumbling, jobless slackers and dimwitted goofs—Cheech & Chong, for instance, or Jeff Spicoli, the stoner character portrayed by Sean Penn in *Fast Times at Ridgemont High*.

Yet, in 2022, marijuana is hardly a countercultural concern. For many users, cannabis has become as ordinary and routine as yoga, or a glass of wine with dinner. "It's Official: Weed's Not Cool Anymore," states a 2019 *Observer* headline. "The exclusive cool kids club of cannabis is over," the article declared. "Moms use it, Elon Musk uses it, Canada says most of its police can use it (off-duty, of course). The number of Baby Boomers who have used it has doubled since 2006. ... Every demographic you previously wouldn't have dared suspect of using cannabis is now experimenting with the plant" [6].

Indeed, cannabis is no longer the purview of societal outlaws and troublemaker teens. It has been normalized among virtually every demographic: An estimated 128 million Americans have tried it. People use it to self-medicate for a wide variety of ailments, as evidenced by a 2019 Reddit thread asking users to share how cannabis impacted their health or mentality. One user wrote: "It reduces the pain and stress from my bowel disease and I definitely have less severe symptoms." Another said that cannabis gave them "better sleep, no more depression." And yet another respondent wrote: "Helps with insomnia, anxiety, PTSD, physical pains, adds pleasure to senses, strokes of creative thought, imagination. Makes me healthier" [7].

Yet, 50 years after that *LIFE* cover story, there remains much that we don't know about the plant. While it's possible that low doses of cannabis may help some people's depression, some studies also suggest that it *increases* depressive symptoms. And dosage matters enormously when it comes to cannabis: Marijuana use generally has a biphasic effect, which means that it can have one effect at low doses and the opposite effect at higher doses. For instance, a low dose can encourage sleep and reduce pain, while high dosages can induce anxiety. (One study even found that daily use of high-potency cannabis correlates with an increased risk of psychosis. An estimated one in five new cases of psychosis were linked to daily cannabis use. One in 10 were linked to use of high potency cannabis [8].)

Of concern, researchers have never comprehensively studied high-dose cannabis (much of the legal weed now available falls into that category). Unlike alcohol, it can be difficult to assess equivalent doses of smoked THC. The challenge for practitioners is that patients frequently don't verbalize reasons for changing their use or varying dosage. And in a market-driven setting, slick branding drives the conversation and dominates the perception: Consumer understanding of dosage is more heavily influenced by marketing and ad copy than reliable science. Meanwhile, researchers have cause for concern. Roughly one in six cannabis users meet the criteria of cannabis use disorder (CUD). Although rates in youth of cannabis use remain high, the Healthy Kids Colorado Survey (HKCS) results indicate no significant change in the past 30-day use of marijuana by middle and high school-aged youth between 2013 (19.7%) and 2019 (20.6%) [9].

In this dramatically shifting universe of cannabis use, old models no longer make sense and the conventional wisdom is as stale as last week's pot brownie. Health care providers and practitioners of all stripes— social workers, psychologists, alcohol and drug counselors, and care providers—need to meet the post-legalization moment proactively with relevant and timely information instead of antiquated twentieth-century perceptions of marijuana use. In other words, it's crucial for practitioners interacting with users to have what we call "Cannabis Clinical Competencies." Experts need to understand patterns of use and disorder in today's shifting cannabis culture and must be equipped with tools to see through the proverbial smoke of misinformation and marketing.

This book aims to provide new tools for understanding patients' use, a heightened awareness of the complexities of cannabis science, and informed strategies for effective intervention. Throughout these nine chapters, we'll provide case illustrations, interview summaries with cannabis patients, intervention sample scripts, clinical algorithms, and evidence-based brief treatment for substance use disorders. We'll begin by summarizing the history of cannabis stretching back thousands of years, then delve into the chemistry of the drug and seek a thorough understanding of its medicinal and recreational uses. From there, we'll introduce the Cannabis Intervention Screener (CIS)—a new cannabis-specific screening tool that stratifies risk with important clinical utility—and suggest a guide for evidence-based treatment for cannabis use disorder. And we'll provide suggestions for how to talk to patients about cannabis use meaningfully and effectively.

The goal is to synthesize decades of swift transformation in cannabis culture with a thorough understanding of the challenges facing practitioners in the burgeoning legalization era. Cannabis has come a long way since 1969. Fifty years ago, Americans responded to cannabis with panic and policies that misunderstood addiction science and ultimately did more harm than good. Today's users—legal or otherwise—deserve a more mindful and informed approach from practitioners.

2

What is Cannabis?

The herbaceous flowering plant *Cannabis sativa* is from the family Cannabaceae, which is native to Central Asia and India. It is known by many names—*marijuana, pot, grass, weed*—and can be smoked, vaporized, and consumed orally through edible products. Cannabis contains both medicinal and psychoactive properties and in its nontoxic form, hemp, can be used to make rope, textiles, clothing, paper, and biofuel. Cannabis contains more than 100 chemical compounds, called cannabinoids; the two most commonly known are delta-9-tetrahydrocannabinol (THC) and cannabidiol (CBD). THC is highly potent and primarily accounts for the psychoactive response from cannabis (e.g., euphoria, heightened sensory awareness, creativity, altered sense of time and space, enhanced appetite, increased sexual desire, drowsiness), whereas CBD is generally not psychoactive and instead is often used as an anti-inflammatory agent and analgesia.

Cannabis has a long and circuitous history of sanctioned and unsanctioned use by civilizations and societies dating back to ancient times. Understanding this history can help shed light on current attitudes toward and perspectives on cannabis use in the United States, which directly impact cannabis use behaviors. This chapter will briefly discuss the geographic and historical origins of cannabis, the recent history of its use in the United States, and ideological/sociocultural factors that account for the growing increase in its acceptance and availability in the United States (For a brief summary of the chemical and botanical properties of cannabis, see Chapter 3.)

A Practitioner's Guide to Cannabis, First Edition. Win Turner and Joseph Hyde.
© 2023 John Wiley & Sons, Inc. Published 2023 by John Wiley & Sons, Inc.

The Geographical and Historical Origins of Cannabis

Cannabis has been used in one form or another since the prehistoric ages and is widely believed to have originated in the steppes of Central Asia in approximately 12,000 BCE. In early human societies, it played a role in textile manufacturing (e.g., basketry, fishing nets), medicine, food (i.e., the seeds), and as a part of shamanic rites and religious rituals [10].

Its cultivation for fibers is estimated to have started around 4000 B.C. [11]. Some of the oldest evidence of its use for psychoactive purposes comes from the excavation of a shamanic tomb in China in 2700 B.C. [12]. Ancient Chinese texts also make reference to and praise the cultivation and use of cannabis and its byproduct, hemp.

Cannabis use migrated from China to Korea and Japan around 200 B.C., largely in the form of hemp (e.g., used for rope, clothing), and into the South Asian subcontinent around 2000 B.C. to 1000 B.C. [13]. Its use flourished in India, where it was often taken for psychoactive and medicinal purposes, such as during weddings and religious celebrations (e.g., Holi). Cannabis is mentioned in the Hindu scripture the *Bhagavad-Gita* and is associated with the Hindu god Ganga (giving rise to the term *ganja*). From India, the plant migrated to Tibet and Nepal in the 7th Century, where it was used as part of Tantric practices.

Cannabis appeared in the Middle East likely between 2000 B.C. and 1400 B.C. via nomadic Indo-European traders and warriors. It then moved into Russia and Ukraine, eventually spreading into Eastern Europe around 3000 B.C. to 2000 B.C. Throughout the 5th Century, cannabis was used across Germany, Britain, Scotland, and France, generally for sails, rope, paper, clothing, and nets. From the Middle East or Europe, cannabis then diffused into Greece and Rome, where it was used medicinally, as a psychotropic, and as a source of fiber. In at least the 15th Century, it likely made its way into Eastern Africa via trade routes from Egypt and Ethiopia and spread throughout Africa largely through coastal migrant settlements. There, it was often used to treat snake bites, malaria, fever, blood poisoning, anthrax, asthma, and dysentery [11]. Cannabis later arrived in South America in the 16th Century, where it became a part of religious rituals and was provided for physical ailments like toothaches and menstrual cramps [11]. Its recreational use in South and Central America did not appear until the 19th Century and during construction of the Panama Canal in the 20th Century [13].

The popularity of cannabis fibers among the British extended to the United States via British colonization [13]. Hemp was grown on the estates of George Washington and Thomas Jefferson, and the US Constitution was written on paper made from hemp. In 1619, the Virginia Assembly passed a law requiring all farmers to grow hemp, which was considered legal tender in Pennsylvania, Virginia, and Maryland. Domestic production decreased after the Civil War, with the advent of the cotton gin offering a cheaper alternative to hemp. Strictly recreational use likely was not introduced until much later, during the early 20th Century, as a product of Mexican immigration [14].

History of the Medicinal Use of Cannabis

As noted here, ancient civilizations, including those in Egypt and China, are known to have medicalized cannabis for disease such as fatigue, rheumatism, and malaria [10]. Numerous other societies, including those in India, the Middle East, Southeast Asia, South Africa, and South America, have documented histories of using cannabis as a medicine for a wide range of maladies, such as pain, malaria, constipation, fever, rheumatism, sleeplessness, dysentery, poor appetite, slow digestion, headache, female reproductive disorders, labor/childbirth pain, skin inflammation, depression, and cough [11, 15].

The medicalization of cannabis was greatly influenced by the work of Irish physician William Brooke O'Shaughnessy [11]. While working in India in the 1840s, O'Shaughnessy wrote prolifically about the medicinal benefits of cannabis (which was commonly used in India) and provided detailed records of his numerous animal and human experiments in treating cholera, rheumatism, hydrophobia, tetanus, rabies, and convulsions. His research, published in The *Bengal Dispensatory* in 1842 and The *Bengal Pharmacopoeia* in 1844, led to a surge in the medical field's interest in the potential ameliorative effects of cannabis, and the republication of his findings in British and European medical journals helped pioneer scientific inquiry into the plant. Indeed, more than 100 articles on the medical use of cannabis appeared in medical journals from 1840 and 1900. By then, the British had adopted cannabis as an

2 What is Cannabis?

effective analgesic, anti-inflammatory, antiemetic, and anticonvulsant [10]. Nonetheless, its psychoactive properties led to public fear of misuse and addiction, and cannabis was removed from the *British Pharmacopoeia* by 1932 [10].

On the heels of O'Shaughnessy's pivotal research, cannabis began to be recognized and used by Western medicine around the mid-19th Century, including its listing in the United States Dispensatory in 1854 [15]. In the US, commercial cannabis was available in drugstores and pharmacies, and doctors often prescribed it for sedative or hypnotic purposes, as an analgesia, and for other miscellaneous uses (e.g., poor appetite, gastric upset, vertigo) [11]. Increasing research in the United States and United Kingdom throughout the late 19th Century shed light on its utility in controlling pain, anxiety, migraines, poor appetite, and restlessness [15]. However, medicinal cannabis use began to decline around 1890, replaced by the advent of synthetic (and more stable and reliable) drugs like aspirin, chloral hydrate, and barbiturates.

At the start of the 20th Century, efforts to regulate cannabis, such as through the Pure Food and Drug Act, underscored a growing concern about the plant's safety. Consequently, from 1914 to 1925, 26 states made cannabis illegal [14]. By the 1930s, public perception in the United States had solidly shifted, mirroring that of Britain and Europe [10] and fed in part by massive economic and job losses during the Great Depression. No longer embraced as a potentially powerful medicinal tool, cannabis was now deemed harmful, addictive, and a moral blight on civilized society. This was reflected in the passage of the Uniform State Narcotic Act in 1932, which gave states the ability to control the sale and use of narcotics (and cannabis). Among its most vocal supporters and lobbyists was Harry Anslinger, Commissioner of the Federal Bureau of Narcotics, who also was a central figure in the adoption of the Marijuana Tax Act of 1937. The first federal government regulation of cannabis, the Marijuana Tax Act provided an additional barrier to the research and use of cannabis for medical purposes by taxing physicians and pharmacists using cannabis medicinally. And although it technically did not criminalize cannabis, it essentially did so by making the sale and possession largely illegal. Its passage was intended to (and indeed did) dissuade the general public from recreational use, as Anslinger was an outspoken critic who claimed cannabis led to addiction, violent crime, psychosis, and mental dysfunction.

Having now effectively made the medical use and study of cannabis not only more difficult but costly and socially taboo, the federal government in 1942 had the plant removed from the *United States Pharmacopeia and National Formulary* [16], and in 1951 and 1956, enacted legal penalties for the possession of cannabis via the Boggs Act and the Narcotic Control Act, respectively. Cannabis was finally criminalized at the federal level under the Comprehensive Drug Abuse Prevention and Control Act of 1970. It should be noted that that significant political factors influenced the federal criminalization of marijuana [17].

Recent US History of Cannabis Use

The placement of cannabis in the most restrictive schedule under the Comprehensive Drug Abuse Prevention and Control Act (i.e., Schedule 1) meant physicians and researchers had limited access to study its therapeutic effects (interested researchers must seek licensing from the Drug Enforcement Agency (DEA) and permission from the National Institutes of Drug Abuse). But despite this, interest in medical cannabis grew throughout the 1970s, primarily through citizen activism and lobbying at the state level [18]. During this time, Oregon, Alaska, and Maine decriminalized cannabis, and the rise of activist groups, like the National Organization for the Reform of Marijuana Laws, helped further fuel grassroots efforts to sanction therapeutic cannabis [18]. National professional societies, like the American Medical Association, American Bar Association, American Public Health Association, and National Education Association, followed suit and passed declarations in support of decriminalizing the drug [14].

However, not everyone endorsed this growing movement, and a backlash against the legalization of medical cannabis eventually gave rise to highly punitive policies throughout the 1980s and early 1990s under Presidents Reagan and Bush, such as the "War on Drugs," "mandatory minimums," and the "Three Strikes" life sentencing laws for repeat drug offenders [14], laws which disproportionately impacted persons of color.

But by 1996, a milestone piece of legislation was passed in California that would reverberate across US law and culture for decades and help fuel the swing in public attitudes toward decriminalization—Proposition

2 What is Cannabis?

215 (the Compassionate Use Act). Under this law, patients were protected from state prosecution for cultivating, possessing, and using cannabis for preapproved medical purposes. It also allowed physicians to recommend medical cannabis without reprisal. The federal government under President Clinton vehemently opposed the controversial new law, threatening to target California physicians who recommended cannabis to their patients, revoke their registration with the DEA, and block them from participating in Medicare and Medicaid. But to no avail; within 10 years, an additional 22 states, Washington D.C., and Guam followed in California's footsteps, and a national conversation about the widespread legalization of medical cannabis was already underway [19].

Support for medical cannabis helped usher in legislation on nonmedical use. On January 1, 2014, Colorado became the first state to permit recreational cannabis use and distribution. As of June 2019, 33 states and Washington D.C. had passed laws broadly legalizing cannabis in some form (all 33 states plus Washington D.C. have decriminalized cannabis for medical use, and 11 states plus Washington D.C. have decriminalized cannabis for both medical and recreational use) [20]. But what factors have given rise to this dramatic shift toward more liberal views of cannabis use and legalization? And what does this mean for public health moving forward?

Factors Influencing Cannabis Legalization in the United States

Since the early 1990s, the percentage of people in the United States favoring legalization of cannabis has increased approximately 1.5 percentage points a year, representing a dramatic fluctuation over a relatively short period of time [21]. The American publics' views of cannabis has changed as state legislation has similarly become more accepting, suggesting, at least to some extent, the latter and the former are synergistic. The legalization of cannabis and regulated dispensaries and "grow warehouses" has also given birth to a new industry, creating jobs and revenue streams that help "normalize" cannabis in the eyes of many Americans, particularly college-aged and young adults [22].

But a host of other political, ideological, and sociocultural factors are driving the wave of increased legalization in the United States and signaling the need for greater education efforts to ensure both health-care providers and the general public are aware of the possible risks and outcomes associated with cannabis use. For instance, a decline in punitive attitudes regarding cannabis use and increased media coverage on the medicalization of cannabis has been impactful [21]. State budgets have become increasingly strained by the costs of processing and housing persons charged with nonviolent offenses (including cannabis-related offenses). Concurrently public and medical sentiment and opposition to the incarceration of nonviolent substance users, often persons of marginalized populations have grown. In 2017, the former director of the US Center for Substance Abuse Treatment published an article building the case for decriminalization and legalization [23]. Border state policy diffusion—that is, the adoption (or rejection) of legislation in nearby states that appears to sway attitudes and legislation in remaining states—has played a modest role [19]. And political culture is also relevant, with states having a more liberal citizenry being more likely to adopt medical cannabis legislation than states with more conservative citizenry [19].

Rising interest in criminal justice reform and efforts to address policies that generate racial/ethnic and gender disparities also cannot be discounted. Now more so than ever, coalitions of politicians, legislators, and concerned citizens of all political ideologies are seeking criminal justice reform, and this dovetails directly with efforts to decriminalize cannabis. Data indicate that enforcement of cannabis laws tends to be unequal across racial/ethnic groups, with African Americans and Latinos being significantly more likely than Whites to be arrested despite comparable rates of use across ethnicities [24–26]. Vocal proponents of criminal justice reform see decriminalization or legalization of cannabis as a flagship issue and foundational opportunity to finally turn the page on the failed "War on Drugs," expunge cannabis-related convictions, reduce the number of justice-involved persons in the system (specifically, African American and Latino persons), and lower costs associated with court proceedings and incarceration.

Coupled with the documented decrease in the perceived risks of cannabis use [27], increased attitudes of permissiveness and the trend toward greater legalization efforts all raise concerns about the American public's access to and understanding of cannabis. Cannabis is a heterogenous plant with variable strengths, methods of consumption, delivery devices, strains, and cannabinoid concentrations, any of which could affect outcomes like level of intoxication, dependency severity, and addiction potential. The recent surge in cannabis potency over the past two decades (i.e., a 300% increase from 1995 to 2014) [28] alone suggests widespread education about the harms, risks, toxicity, and addiction liability of cannabis/cannabis-derived products is critical and in fact may be a sensible prevention and harm reduction strategy. But healthcare providers need more education and guidance in how to have balanced discussions with patients addressing both the legalization of—and thus access to—cannabis as well as its adverse effects, addiction potential, rapidly changing delivery methods, concentration levels, and, as needed, options for addiction treatment and recovery.

3

The Chemistry of Cannabis

The chemical components of the biologically active cannabis plant have been the subject of extensive research for decades. Its chemistry is notably complex and marked by more than 500 constituents (and the copious potential interactions that can occur between them) as well as more than 700 varieties (e.g., indica, ruderali, sativa) [29]. Cannabis contains a plethora of chemically active compounds, including cannabinoids, terpenes (terpenoids), flavonoids, and numerous hydrocarbons, sugars, amine/amide functions, carbohydrates, phytosterols, and fatty acids [30, 31]. As cannabis is one of the most widely used substances around the world, understanding its chemical makeup and mechanisms of action is important to the development of effective prevention and treatment messaging and interventions for healthcare patients and the general public as a whole.

The purpose of this chapter is to briefly orient clinicians to the chemical complexity of cannabis and its spectrum of psychoactivity. This chapter is not intended to be a thorough primer on the botanical and chemical makeup of cannabis. Rather, the aim is to highlight key aspects of cannabis chemistry—including the ways in which cannabis functions in the human body—that may aid in improved understanding the plant's psychoactive effects, therapeutic uses, addiction potential, and other adverse outcomes.

Psychoactive Chemicals in Cannabis

The most chemically active compounds in cannabis, and the ones to which the primary psychotropic properties of cannabis are attributed, are the **cannabinoids**. Cannabinoids occur in one of three

A Practitioner's Guide to Cannabis, First Edition. Win Turner and Joseph Hyde.
© 2023 John Wiley & Sons, Inc. Published 2023 by John Wiley & Sons, Inc.

14 | 3 *The Chemistry of Cannabis*

forms: **Endogenous cannabinoids** (i.e., endocannabinoids) exist in the body naturally, can have neurotransmitter-like effects in the brain, and include anandamide and 2-arachidonyl glycerol.

More than 100 cannabinoids belonging to 11 different classes have been isolated from the cannabis plant, but the two main types are tetrahydrocannabinol (Δ^9-THC) and cannabidiol (CBD). Δ^9-THC is highly abundant, widely studied, and is mainly responsible for the psychoactive effects of the plant, whereas CBD is a secondary, nonintoxicating component of cannabis and is responsible for much of the plant's medicinal/therapeutic effects [32, 33]. The *Cannabis sativa* species that is marked by high levels of Δ^9-THC is primarily used for recreational and medicinal purposes, and the fibrous species (known as hemp) is mainly used for textiles and food and is nearly devoid of Δ^9-THC (but high in CBD).

In terms of therapeutic effects, Δ^9-THC is known to modulate pain, spasticity, appetite, mood, respiration, inflammation, and complications from solid organ transplantation (e.g., graft-versus-host disease) [34]. Δ^9-THC is a partial CB1 and CB2 cannabinoid receptor agonist (see the section "Cannabinoids and the Human Body") and in higher doses can induce anxiety, paranoia, perceptual disturbances, and cognitive dysfunction. CBD has demonstrated anticonvulsive, anti-inflammatory, antioxidant, antipsychotic, and immunosuppressant properties and has shown efficacy in modulating neurological and neurodegenerative symptoms in several disease states, including epilepsy, Parkinson's disease, amyotrophic lateral sclerosis, Huntington's disease, Alzheimer's disease, and multiple sclerosis [34, 35].

Both Δ^9-THC and CBD are biologically active, with variable concentrations throughout the plant (though its concentration is highest in the plant's flowers). Other "minor" cannabinoids that may have therapeutic effects, though less studied than Δ9-THC and CBD, include tetrahydrocannabivarin (THCV), cannabinol (CBN), cannabichromene (CBC), and cannabigerol (CBG) [34, 35]. For instance, CBG has demonstrated anti-inflammatory, antimicrobial, antidepressant, antihypertensive, and analgesic effects in human and animal trials and may be a potent mitigator of methicillin-resistant *Staphylococcus aureus* (MRSA). CBC, also nonpsychoactive, has been implicated as a modulator of analgesic, anti-inflammatory, digestive, antibacterial/antifungal, and neurodegenerative processes. CBN appears to be useful as a sedative, anticonvulsant, anti-inflammatory agent, antibiotic, and as an MRSA treatment. Finally, administration of THCV is associated with weight loss, anticonvulsant effects, and appetite suppression [34, 35].

Beyond cannabinoids, the other primary constituent in cannabis are the **terpenes**—the most common of which are limonene, myrcene, and alpha-pinene [36]. Terpenes are responsible for cannabis' characteristic aromas and tastes and are produced by many different plants (e.g., lemon, orange, pine, hops, lavender, green tea) as a way of attracting pollinators and warding off predators. Myrcene is an anti-inflammatory that has sedative effects; limonene is a potent anxiolytic that also appears to have antibiotic and chemotherapeutic properties; and alpha-pinene—the most widely distributed terpenoid in nature—is an anti-inflammatory, antibiotic, antibacterial, and anxiolytic compound [34]. It is unclear, the role that terpenes play in the pharmacologic outcomes of cannabis [34]. But in animal studies, even low concentrations of terpenes may significantly increase or decrease activity levels, and their effects may extend to those occurring in ion channels, neurotransmitters, and smell and taste receptors.

Cannabinoids and terpenoids are extracted from the bracts and flowers of the cannabis plant chemically (e.g., petroleum ether, ethanol), through high-pressure liquid CO2, or through natural solvents (e.g., olive oil, coconut oil). The extract—called "oil"—can be administered medicinally as an oral spray, pill, or tincture (e.g., Sativex®, a Δ^9-THC/CBD oral spray; Cannador®, a Δ^9-THC/CBD capsule). Terpenoids are hypothesized to work synergistically with phytocannabinoids to modify or enhance each other's effects such that the resulting outcome is stronger than that which would be produced by either alone—a complex interaction known as the **"entourage effect."** This effect may explain why some people report experiencing more of an effect from cannabinoid extracts than from Δ^9-THC alone [33, 35]. For instance, the addition of limonene to Δ^9-THC can greatly enhance euphoria, and adding myrcene to Δ^9-THC increases sedation [34]. However, randomized controlled trials are still needed to compare the efficacy of cannabinoid-terpene combinations with either or alone.

Synthetic Cannabinoids

Although outside of the scope of this guide, the authors recognize the need to briefly summarize some information concerning the category called **synthetic cannabinoids**. These substances were developed first to investigate cannabinoid receptors for research and then introduced into the European consumption market in 2005 and then the United States in 2008. The primary initial organic chemist researcher and developer of synthetic cannabinoids John William Huffman was funded by NIDA to investigate potential for new medicines. Huffman's Clemson university lab produced more than 400 new cannabinoid compounds from 1990 to 2011. Huffman never intended them for public consumption and in an interview Dr. Huffman stated, "synthetic cannabinoids do not belong to the same structural group as THC; they are really dangerous compounds."

By 2010, fake marijuana was cheaply and widely available legally in stores and did not show up on drug tests. The synthetics are chemical compounds dissolved in solvents (e.g., acetone) and then spayed onto dried leaves to resemble cannabis. Plant-Based THC is a partial agonist of cannabinoid receptors vs. synthetics which are full agonists heightening and making the physiological response unpredictable. Cannabis often causes a quick response whereas synthetics can take a while and thus users over-consume trying to get high at the same rate as plant-based cannabis. Additionally, unaware users can overdose when the synthetics are mixed intentionally or unintentionally in the lab with potent opioid additives like fentanyl. Usually sold in small plastic packets often as "potpourri" with "not for human consumption" warning labels the synthetics are often labeled names such as: Spice, K2, King Kong, Scooby Snacks, Laugh Out Loud, and Power Diesel.

The method of use is similar to plant-based cannabis for example, smoking out of a pipe but the effects are dramatically different. Rather than being described by users as a mellow, relaxing high, synthetics are listed by the CDC as potentially causing the following:

Clinical features of synthetic cannabinoid poisoning vary and may include:

- Neurologic signs and symptoms including agitation, sleepiness, irritability, confusion, delirium, dizziness, incoordination, inability to concentrate, stroke, and seizures;
- Psychiatric signs and symptoms including hallucinations, delusions, psychosis, violent behavior, and suicidal thoughts;
- Other physical signs and symptoms including tachypnea, tachycardia, hypertension, severe nausea and vomiting, chest pain and heart attack, rhabdomyolysis, kidney failure, and death.
- The long-term effects of using synthetic cannabinoids are unknown.

Synthetic cannabinoid use can lead to physical and psychological dependence on these drugs. Patients who have used synthetic cannabinoids for long periods and abruptly stop have reported withdrawal-like symptoms, suggesting that the substances are addictive. Overdose can occur when the compound is tainted with fentanyl and other highly potent chemicals [37].

The chemistry of synthetic cannabinoids is a cause of real concern and poses a significant public health risk due to their adverse and potentially dangerous, if not fatal, side effects. Further, overdose of synthetic cannabinoids appears to be more cardiotoxic and neurotoxic than overdose of true cannabis [38]. Authors of this book remind readers, "synthetic cannabis" like K2 should not be confused with real cannabis that is grown.

Synthetic cannabinoids are unregulated and often made outside the US; thus, their exact compositions of chemicals, components, and variations can differ across products, and are continuously changing. Consequently, their precise toxicology, physiology, and consequences are difficult to fully understand or for healthcare providers to predict and respond to during acute crisis [39]. And because these easily accessible products are typically street sourced, it is usually not possible for consumers to know which—or how many—additives a synthetic product contains, increasing the odds of adverse effects such as overdose. In July 2012 a national ban was enacted against the sale of synthetic cannabinoids in the US. Local and state laws also regulate synthetic cannabinoids. While synthetic cannabinoids are illegal in the US, the product may still be sold illegally on the streets and produced in countries outside the US.

Cannabinoids and the Human Body

The human body is replete with cannabinoid receptors designed specifically to respond to cannabis; in combination with the endocannabinoids themselves as well as their metabolic enzymes, the trio is known collectively as **the endocannabinoid system**. Functioning much like a lock-and-key structure, cannabinoid receptors (i.e., "locks") located on various cell membranes throughout several organ systems become activated by cannabinoids (i.e., "keys"), allowing the plant to induce a variety of physiological processes such as those pertaining to appetite, pain, mood, digestion, sensory integration (e.g., balance, sense of space),

3 The Chemistry of Cannabis

stress response, and memory [31]. The human endocannabinoid system also regulates processes like inflammation, immune system functioning, nerve functioning, and metabolism.

Two cannabinoid receptors have been identified and are particularly well-studied: The CB1 and CB2 receptors. CB1 receptors are found in high concentration in various tissues within the brain and throughout the central nervous system but also are located in the lungs, liver, and kidneys. This distribution explains why cannabis can affect functions like heart rate, mood, appetite, motor activity, pain tolerance, learning, memory, and decision making. Further, the paucity of CB1 receptors in the brainstem, which controls breathing and consciousness, explains why cannabis is not linked to life-threatening overdose. CB2 receptors are mainly located on T-cells throughout the immune system (e.g., bone marrow, thymus, spleen, tonsils) but also exist in the gastrointestinal tract, uterus, lung, and bone [31, 34].

Δ^9-THC is a partial agonist that binds to CB1 and reduces excitability by inhibiting the release of neurotransmitters affected by endogenous cannabinoids [34]. It may inhibit the release of GABA, thereby increasing the release of dopamine, glutamate, and acetylcholine. This latter mechanism of action is thought to be the primary factor underlying cannabis' psychoactive effects. Δ9-THC also activates CB2 receptors to reduce immune cell functions, including those that lead to inflammation. CBD, on the other hand, has a low affinity for both receptors and works as an inverse agonist, reducing pro-inflammatory markers like tumor necrosis factor-alpha, inducible nitric oxide synthase, and cyclooxygenase-2.

Δ^9-THC and CBD are activated by heat and light, which results in removal of a carboxyl group (i.e., decarboxylation). The resulting vapor can then be inhaled, resulting in rapid onset and quick peak blood concentration (e.g., immediate onset; 5–10 minutes' peak plasma time). Effects begin to taper off after a few hours. Onset and peak concentration are delayed when cannabinoids are ingested orally (e.g., 30–90 minutes' onset; 1–6 hours peak plasma time), but they last longer compared with inhalation, tapering off in 4–8 hours. Similarly, the bioavailability (that is, the amount of the drug entering the blood stream once administered) of Δ^9-THC and CBD is much higher when inhaled (2–56%) versus oral administration (<20%). Both cannabinoids are mainly metabolized by the group of liver enzymes known as cytochrome P450, which help the body to excrete the drug.

The Changing Chemistry of Cannabis and Synthetics

Levels of Δ^9-THC concentration appear to be increasing over time, since the mid-1980s. Consequently, the public is increasingly being exposed to a more potent product and potentially without their awareness [28]. In an analysis of samples provided by regional laboratories of the Drug Enforcement Administration between 1995–2014 [28], hash oil preparation had the highest concentration of Δ^9-THC, followed by hashish and lastly cannabis. Data clearly showed an increase in potency over time, from about 4% in 1995 to 12% in 2014, whereas CBD appeared to have declined over the last decade, from about 0.5% in 2004 to < 0.2% in 2014 [28]. These patterns are consistent with a similar analysis performed by a certified cannabis lab in Colorado [40] that found not only increased potency over time but concentration levels as high as 30% in some samples. Both analyses also mirror findings from Europe showing a marked increase in resin potency from 2006–2016 [41]. All of these data underscore the importance of ramping up public health, patient education, and physician/clinician education efforts about the risks and side effects of cannabis, particularly Δ^9-THC. It should be noted that some of these increases are due to changes in growing procedures and that what is sold on the market today are the cannabis flowers which have the highest concentration of THC. In the 80s and 90s, what was commonly sold was a mix of flowers, leaves, and stems.

Misperceptions about the use of cannabis—including the myth that synthetic cannabinoids are safer than cannabis and other noncannabinoid illicit drugs—persist both within healthcare populations and in the general public. To help offset knowledge gaps and potentially reduce cannabis use, it is critical that healthcare providers understand the basic chemistry of cannabis and its constituents and particularly what those mean for its abuse liability, addiction potential, and other adverse outcomes.

4

Cannabis Use in the United States

Cannabis is the most widely used substance in the United States and remains classified by the US Food and Drug Administration as a Schedule I drug. The Substance Abuse and Mental Health Service Administration's (SAMHSA) 2018 National Survey on Drug Use and Health (NSDUH) finds that 43.5 million Americans aged 12 and older reported using cannabis in the previous year, which is roughly equivalent to 16% of the US population [42]. This represents a notable increase from 2002 to 2017. Further, between 2001–2002 and 2012–2013, the percentage of Americans who reported using cannabis in the past year more than doubled [43]. The segment of the US population reporting cannabis use is largely accounted for by young people ages 18–25 [42].

Problematic cannabis use—primarily in the form of cannabis use disorder (CUD)—should be a major concern to behavioral health service providers given the known potential harms and comorbidities accompanying the disorder—many of which could exacerbate existing psychiatric conditions and symptoms [44]. This chapter will offer a snapshot of the current use of cannabis in the United States by discussing the incidence and correlates of CUD, and what clinicians need to know about rapidly evolving methods of cannabis delivery in terms of potency and possible harms to patients.

Potential Effects of Legalization of Cannabis in the United States

As of 2022, 40 US states and the District of Columbia have legalized medical cannabis use, and 17 states and the District of Columbia have

A Practitioner's Guide to Cannabis, First Edition. Win Turner and Joseph Hyde.
© 2023 John Wiley & Sons, Inc. Published 2023 by John Wiley & Sons, Inc.

legalized cannabis for recreational use by adults. As the legal landscape of permissible or decriminalized medical and recreational cannabis use has expanded in the United States (see Chapter 2: What Is Cannabis? for a cursory review on the history of cannabis decriminalization and legalization in this country), so, too, have societal perceptions of and attitudes toward cannabis use. Large-scale national surveys indicate the US public has become increasingly accepting of cannabis use since the 1960s, and that perceptions of its risk/safety profile are also becoming more positive, especially among adolescents [27, 45, 46].

Although increases in cannabis use have occurred throughout time periods in which states are also increasing legal access to cannabis for medical and nonmedical reasons, it is unclear whether the relaxation of medical and recreational marijuana laws are directly affecting actual use behaviors and, if so, to what extent. For instance, Dilley and colleagues found no increase in cannabis use among youth following legalization of recreational cannabis in Washington state and in fact found that use actually declined among eighth graders and tenth graders [47]. This is in direct contrast to Cerdá et al., who reported an increase in cannabis use among eighth graders and tenth graders in Washington state following legalization of nonmedical cannabis use but no change in use behaviors among youth in Colorado [48]. Dilley et al. opine that this discrepancy could be due to the two studies using different surveys (one providing state-specific estimates and the other national and regional estimates) and to possible differences in sampling error [47].

Further, despite the documented increase in cannabis use from 2002 to 2014 (i.e., prevalence increased from 10.4% to 13.3%) [49], rates of CUD held steady at about 1.5% during this same time, raising uncertainty about whether legalization is actually leading to an increase in cannabis use disorder. Additionally, Davenport, using data from the NSDUH, observed declining rates of cannabis dependence among people with heavy use (26.5% in 2002–2004 to 16.1% in 2014–2016) [50]. However, this may be in part a byproduct of inadequate widespread screening for CUD among healthcare patients and underscores the utility of clinicians asking patients about their quantity and frequency of cannabis use as a part of routine clinical care or clinical interview [51].

Some researchers have cogently argued that the key focus should not be on whether legalization is increasing cannabis use but whether it is increasing problematic, harmful use (i.e., CUD [52]). This answer likely will require additional research to better understand conversion rates of nonproblematic cannabis use to CUD that coincide with periods of legalization and increased access to cannabis [53], given that current data are conflicted on whether CUD has truly been on the rise [54] or has stabilized [26]. Earlier research from Cerdá et al. found nearly double the odds of past-year cannabis use and CUD among states with legal medical use compared with states without legal medical use; however, the prevalence of CUD among cannabis users was similar between states with and without medical legalization [55]. This suggests that although legalization may increase access and thus the prevalence of people using cannabis, data are equivocal on whether conversion to problematic cannabis use is a true byproduct of this legislation.

If future analyses do confirm an increase in CUD resulting from cannabis legalization, this would suggest an urgent need for better screening, diagnosis, and treatment approaches. Current CUD prevention and treatment programs have shown limited efficacy and require greater research funding and clinical trial activity [52]. This could be complicated by emergent public perceptions that cannabis is not harmful, which would logically decrease the likelihood of treatment seeking or willingness to accept a clinician's offer for services, education, and/or resources to aid in cannabis cessation. As such, greater patient and public health outreach strategies are needed to ensure adequate understanding of the known risks and potential harms of cannabis. Of note: Common definition of "harms" appears misaligned when cannabis harm is considered in the same conversation with harms of fentanyl and methamphetamine. Cannabis harms seem to more commonly cluster in the domains of psychosocial functioning, learning, and potential exacerbation of psychiatric symptoms or conditions. While harms of fentanyl and methamphetamine for instance, cluster in areas of overdose death, HIV and HCV exposure and other physical and medical harms.

Risks and CUD

The annual prevalence of cannabis use in the United States is high, estimated to be around 30% [54] and 18% in 2015 by the Center for Disease Control/Marijuana and Public Health (https://www.cdc.gov/marijuana/data-statistics). According to the CDC approximately 30% of cannabis users will have (or develop) a cannabis use disorder. Although cannabis is not known to lead to fatal overdose, the National Institute on Drug Abuse (2020) warns of harms due to cannabis' potential harms, such as the development of CUD—a condition classified in the fifth edition of Diagnostic and Statistical Manual of Mental Disorder that characterizes risky behavior and continued use despite the presence of risky psychological, physical, or social negative consequences [56]. As with other illicit substances, cannabis can induce craving and withdrawal symptoms and—also similar to other substance use disorders (SUDs)—CUD is associated with increased likelihood of having a comorbid psychiatric condition, including other SUDs (especially cannabis use disorder and tobacco use disorder), mood disorders, personality disorders (mostly borderline and schizotypal personality disorders), and generalized anxiety disorder [57].

Although widely perceived by the general public to be mostly benign, there are notable risks associated with cannabis use, including use disorder potential (i.e., CUD); withdrawal syndrome; psychomotor impairments, which poses an additional risk to safety, such as driving impairment; possible dysfunctions in or loss of interpersonal relationships; declining academic performance and/or reduced work performance; and—when exposure occurs during critical periods of brain development (e.g., in utero, infancy, childhood, adolescence)—chronic cannabis use may contribute to neurodevelopmental deficits and intellectual difficulties [45, 52]. Cannabis use and/or CUD are correlated with an increased risk of respiratory disease, such as asthma and pneumonia [58]; suicide attempt when co-occurring with bipolar disorder [59], youth suicide attempt [60], and post-deployment suicide attempt among veterans [61]; and prescription opioid use disorder [62]. Cannabis use during pregnancy may result in adverse effects to the developing fetus (e.g., low birthweight, maternal anemia, neonatal intensive care placement) [63]. **Readers are reminded that correlation is not causality.**

From 2006 to 2014, cannabis-related emergency department visits among people in the United States aged 12 and older increased each year by 7%, with publicly insured individuals 40% more likely than privately insured individuals to have a cannabis-related visit (Shen et al., 2019). Visits were most common among people ages 12–17 but showed an increasing trend among people age 45 and older [64]. Similar findings were reported from the Nationwide Inpatient Sample

4 Cannabis Use in the United States

of hospitalized adults age 18 and older who were admitted with cannabis abuse/dependence [65]. Data showed a 260% increase in such admissions from 2002 to 2011 and an increasing trend among people aged 50 and older [65]. Cannabis abuse/dependence in this sample was associated with chronic conditions, including cannabis use disorder, chronic respiratory disease, psychosis, depression, congestive heart failure, liver failure, pulmonary hypertension, and cancer [65]. Taken together, these studies suggest the need for better patient education, appropriate screening, and treatment/referral when indicated not only for adolescents, who are a well-known at-risk population, but middle-aged and older adults as well [66].

Risks Pertaining to Cannabis Delivery Methods and Potency

Another area of concern involves increased exposure to the primary psychoactive component of cannabis—delta-9-tetrahydrocannabinol (THC), concentrations of which have dramatically increased over time. Recreational cannabis in the 1960s–1980s is thought to have had a THC concentration of 3–4%; and by 2017 ranged from 17%–28% [67]. Moreover, high-concentration edibles, dab, "shatter," and oil may have THC levels as high as 95% [67]. These products increasingly comprise a notable share of the cannabis market. For instance, in Washington state, high-potency cannabis extracts (e.g., wax, shatter, hash) increased their share of the market by 145% from 2014 to 2016, comprising more than one-fifth of state cannabis expenditures; the mean potency for these products was 68.7% [68]. Although there is a lack of widespread data available on how higher concentrations of THC affect the prevalence of use and risk for CUD, preliminary findings thus far are troublesome. For instance, as concentrations of THC have increased, risk of developing full dependence (i.e., CUD) also appears to increase [57]. as does the risk of acute side effects, like psychotic symptoms and loss of consciousness [69].

Cannabis concentrates are increasingly popular recreational products with exceedingly high amounts of THC (approximately 39%–69% versus the 12%–20% typically present in the cannabis plant). Concentrates where the THC has been extracted via the use of solvents are even more potent (i.e., over 80% concentration) compared with nonsolvent-based concentrates [69]. There is a growing concern about the use of these products particularly among adolescents, as the majority of adolescents who report use of cannabis may be using cannabis concentrates, placing them at higher risk of CUD, cannabis-related psychosis, and cognitive impairment [69]. Youth who use cannabis concentrates also may be more likely than those who use cannabis but not concentrates to have co-occurring SUDs, use cigarettes and/or e-cigarettes, have a lower perceived risk of harm from cannabis use, experience family conflict, have low family attachment, demonstrate academic decline, and have a low commitment to school [69].

There are also growing concerns about novel methods of cannabis consumption (e.g., vaping, consuming edibles, or "dabbing"). For instance, edibles (i.e., drink, food, and lozenges infused with THC) are often perceived by youth to be low risk, but their pharmacokinetic profiles are hard to determine because of variations in edible products' bioavailability (which can range from 4% to 20%), which itself can differ from person to person [70]. Although blood concentrations of THC are comparatively lower from edible products versus smoking or vaporizing, some studies have shown THC effects can still have a rapid onset and, among occasional users, may produce stronger effects relative to regular users [70].

Other methods of consumption pose risks to health and increase the odds of negative side effects [70]. Vaporizing lacks the toxic byproducts seen with combustible products but still results in rapid absorption of THC by the lungs and can induce cognitive and psychomotor impairment [70]. Vape pens are popular vehicles for use with high-potency cannabis concentrates and thus more commonly used by adolescents than adults [71]. They are associated with a lower perceived risk of use, younger onset of use, greater frequency of use, and increased risky behavior (e.g., vaping while operating a vehicle) [72]. Vaping may also expose users to cannabis oils containing harmful chemicals, like propylene glycol and polyethylene glycol, which, when heated, produce acetaldehyde and formaldehyde (the former of which is highly toxic and carcinogenic and the latter of which is a "probable carcinogen" in humans) [73]. Cannabis purchased off the street poses the greatest risk for toxin exposure as these products are "home grown" or brought in from outside the US. State licensed growing facilities are routinely required to use independent labs to test for a range of contaminants includes toxins, mold, fungus, and heavy metals. Finally, dabbing—a form of vaporizing cannabis concentrates—may be associated with an increased risk of tolerance, withdrawal symptoms, respiratory failure, memory dysfunction, loss of consciousness, acute psychotic symptoms, poor academic or work performance, and difficulties with interpersonal relationships when used with butane hash oil [70, 74–76]. It should be noted that in nearly all legal states, cannabis products that you purchase from a licensed facility are required to undergo a series of chemical tests by a state-accredited lab. These lab tests are designed to assure that products are safe to consume and accurately labeled. Lab tests for safety include residual pesticides, unwanted contaminants, and the presence of mycotoxins like mold and mildew. As this cannabis industry has grown, so has the regulatory over states. ISO/IEC 17025:2017 accreditation services to Medical and Recreational Cannabis Testing Laboratories is considered by many the "gold standard." For a state-by-state review, readers are suggested to review either specific state regulations or review summaries publicly available on website such as www.leafly.com. *Leafly provides: Cannabis testing regulations: A state by state guide.*

Moving forward, more research will be needed to better understand the effects of cannabis use (including that of alternative consumption methods [e.g., "dabbing"] and high-potency products) and its short- and long-term harms, such as accidental poisoning, acute psychosis, driving impairments, and cannabis dependence/CUD. The development and implementation of public and professional education efforts to increase knowledge about the effects of cannabis use and of high-potency cannabis exposure, as well as to mitigate harms from acute and chronic cannabis use are sorely needed and become more so each year.

5

Cannabis, its Recreational Use, and its Effects

People are motivated to use cannabis for a variety of desired recreational, medicinal, or psychosocial effects. Understanding the cannabis user's experience including the physiological and psychological impact is essential to all healthcare providers. The need for this understanding now is even more pronounced given the current increase in access to all forms of cannabis, the methods to use, the legality and the high prevalence of use in the US. As described in previous chapters, cannabis is a complex substance with a multitude of alkaloids (plant substances that impact physiology) affecting humans who choose to use any of the chemovars (varieties of cannabis) now available (chemovares) [77].

The method, the frequency, the dose of specific cannabis psychotropic chemicals involved, the specific cannabis product all impact the individual's experience [78–80]. The complexity in understanding the effect of cannabis is further illustrated by how the form of cannabis that is, the cannabinoid type and potency as well as the terpenes alters the human physiological response. Cannabis ethnobiologists describe an "entourage effect" gained through consuming the variety of chemicals in the whole plant-based substance (100 distinct cannabinoid compounds) versus an isolated cannabinoid chemical for example, THC or CBD [77, 81].

Additionally, a cannabis user's experience is also significantly influenced by their interpretation or meaning of the event. Meaning is impacted by a host of factors including the current culture's understanding, the setting, the individual's psychology, their social network, one's medical/psychological knowledge, research findings, myths, legal regulations, and even the amount of exposure to current cannabis marketing. In fact, clinical studies examine this influence of our own "meaning" on

A Practitioner's Guide to Cannabis, First Edition. Win Turner and Joseph Hyde.
© 2023 John Wiley & Sons, Inc. Published 2023 by John Wiley & Sons, Inc.

substance use through studies which "trick" users into thinking they are using when in essence they are not. We often call this a "placebo" effect which can be influenced by the expectancies we all bring into an experience. As Metrik et al. surmise, "The belief that individuals have about the drug content (stimulus expectancy) activates their outcome expectancies about the effects that the drug is likely to have on them, producing the placebo effects (changes in mood, behavior)" [82, 83].

Why I use: Quotes from Reddit

The Best Cannabis Subreddits of 2020 UPDATED

https://extractmag.com/cannabis-subreddits

I smoke weed for the same reason anyone has a beer. Sometimes you just want to kick back and relax.

I smoke weed and meditate. It gives me a unique perspective.

Four nights ago, I had an edible with my friend; probably too much of it but I digress.

It was my friend's first time and she felt normal the next day. I've smoked and ingested many times before, but I feel like the high hasn't really gone away. I feel like I'm not in my own body, when I itch or touch my face it feels like it's numb or not really happening and I'm just slightly dizzy.

For this reason and also because it helps me think abstractly, I didn't realize I loved physics and nature until the barriers fell while sitting in my house wondering how to fill my time. That's the weird thing about living alone, you have to find ways to fill large periods of alone time; for someone struggling with his identity, lost in a myriad of relationships where I feigned interest in a bunch of things, pathetically. I ended up pretty unhappy, until I started smoking and thinking. Then I started my on-going obsession with reality, documentaries, physics, math, nature, whatever. It all fascinates me.

Thus, a broad based, current and nuanced understanding of cannabis use complexities is essential to a practitioner's knowledge because an individual's meaning and physiological effects experienced and expressed can vary significantly from the published and researched findings to date. To validate this fact, one just needs to read the "why I use weed & what happens when I use" conversations in Reddit's cannabis subgroups of which there are many (see text box).

Recreational Use of Cannabis

A practitioner's understanding of a patient's particular motivation helps form a foundation for a more successful motivational intervention. Decades of research have shown consistent patterns of motivation for using cannabis. On self-report surveys, the most common motivations listed by cannabis users are relaxation, euphoria, or access to an altered state, reflection/contemplation, and as a social activity [84, 85]. Common sought-after effects reported by recreational cannabis users include using cannabis to (from Green et al., 2003):

- Stimulate appetite
- Increase concentration
- Spur creativity
- Help in relaxation
- Serve as a socializing activity
- Obtain an enjoyable experience in and of itself
- Enhance sexual pleasure

Our current understanding of the mental health impact from using cannabis is evolving rapidly. The complexity of cannabis, the psychoactive chemicals, the route of administration, the acute/chronic effects, the biphasic effect all matter in trying to tease out the impact on mental health. To date, several biphasic effect profiles have been posited for cannabinoids; that is, a low dose may produce one effect (e.g., reduction in anxiety) and a high dose may cause the opposite effect (e.g., increased anxiety) [86, 87].

Researchers are actively trying to determine if using cannabis or the specific cannabis compounds are either causal or correlate factors for experiencing mental illness, that may impact the course of an illness negatively or positively as a treatment for mental illness. The literature is full of confusion—while one study raises the specter of potential catastrophic risks in a given domain, another study refutes those findings. This confusion can detract from our appreciation of known adverse psychosocial consequences for cannabis use, and this phenomenon also illustrates there is much still to be learned [86, 88].

Any definitive understanding gleaned from past and current cannabis research needs careful interpretation based on the specifics of the population of study (e.g., age, gender, poly substance user), the specifics of cannabis including but not limited to potency, methods of use and frequency of use, and the empirical methods and design of the study itself. In general, due to cannabis being a federal schedule one substance, the allowed potency of approved cannabis strains in US research studies is substantially lower than most users currently experience. Increased THC and decreased CBD in the new cannabis strains, newer methods (dabs, edibles, and vapes) and types of use (concentrates and resins, etc.) are hypothesized to create the most negative impacts across a wide array of domains including mental health symptoms, cognitive performance, executive functioning, inhibitory motor control, and increased desires for continued use. Acute symptoms associated with over-consumption of high potency cannabis (edibles, concentrates) can include rapid heart rate, irritability, panic, nausea, drowsiness, confusion, short-term psychosis, or vomiting [70, 89] What is clearest from findings to date is that most studies are unclear as to the benefits of cannabis use and there are only a limited number of published results demonstrating any significant improvements with medical or non-medical cannabis. A comprehensive review from the National Academies of Sciences, Engineering, and Medicine (2017) on the science to date including the health impact from medical and recreational cannabis use reports some significant positive benefits.

Comorbidity data clearly demonstrates that substance users and/or specifically persons with cannabis use disorder (CUD) have higher rates of comorbidity (CUD 21.4% vs. < 1%) for mental health illnesses [90]. Additionally, there is clear data to illustrate that more frequent use is also linked to the prevalence of comorbidity [91]. Drs. Borodsky and Budney emphasize the scientific literature is clear that the co-occurrence of cannabis use or CUD and major depressive, psychotic, anxiety, posttraumatic stress, and bipolar disorders is disproportionally large when compared to either those who do not use cannabis or to those without mental disorders [91–94]. The National Academy of Sciences, Engineering, and Medicine highlights that cannabis use impacts mental health in significant and negative ways. People who use marijuana regularly are 2x more likely to experience depression or social anxiety; 3x more likely to have suicidal thoughts, 7x more likely to develop schizophrenia if genetically predisposed, and experience increased symptoms of mania and hypomania among people with bipolar disorders.

Again, we need to state these associations are not pronouncing cause and effect. Researchers Drs. Borodovsky and Budney explain, that in both the United States and Canada's current environment of legal medical and or "recreational" cannabis, individuals with mental health disorders receiving psychiatric medications are replacing and/or swapping out their prescribed medicines with cannabis to treat depression, anxiety, and symptoms of psychosis. Not surprising, given the fact that most psychotropic medications for depression and for pain do not yield the effect that were once promised. Additionally, the "cannabis as medication" phenomenon is occurring "despite limited controlled clinical evidence supporting the therapeutic efficacy of cannabis for mental disorders [95] and despite data indicating that medical cannabis patients with a history of psychiatric problems have more problematic cannabis use than medical cannabis patients without a history of psychiatric problems" [88, 96].

In summary, what research findings describe to date is that cannabis impacts on common mental health disorders (i.e., depression, anxiety, schizophrenia, bipolar, PTSD) is complex. On the one hand there are no controlled clinical efficacy trials demonstrating any significant therapeutic effect and yet some studies titrating the dose of THC and or CBD demonstrate it can help those with anxiety, psychosis and PTSD experience symptom relief. Again, the positive and negative nature of findings is in psychosis studies where researchers demonstrate in certain subgroups cannabis plant material can increase the likelihood of developing psychosis and worsening of symptoms in contrast to using CBD alone which might offset the risk. Cannabis and its impact on bipolar disorder fares the worst in both longitudinal studies and meta-analyses where the culmination of findings highlights the negative effects in onset and worsening symptoms [88].

Pregnancy

As legal access to cannabis expands, there has been a growing concern about the effects of prenatal cannabis exposure [97]. Self-report data from the National Survey on Drug Use and Health show a significant increase in the prevalence of reported prenatal exposure to cannabis in the United States [98]. Between 2002 and 2017, past-month cannabis use increased from 3.4% to 7.0% among pregnant women overall and from 5.7% to 12.1% during the first trimester [98]. Percentages for use are higher for women of younger age, lower socioeconomic status

(SES), and those living in urban environments [97]. Recent studies in the United States utilizing toxicology screening suggest that the incidence may be larger than these data suggest. Many women choose not to disclose prenatal cannabis use to providers suggesting that the actual rate of use among pregnant women is higher [99, 100]. Given this new extent of use, providers and the public need to be aware of the known potentials for harm.

Concerns from repeated findings in more recent meta-analyses fall into several primary areas including: (a) anemia in pregnant mothers; (b) decreased birth weight; (c) increased need for neonatal intensive care; and (d) a number of potential neurological, neurocognitive, and neurodevelopmental impacts for newborns that can persist into adolescence. Recent data and meta-analyses suggest effects on fetal developmental trajectories where prenatal exposure leads to higher rates of preterm birth, and greater need for intervention [101, 102]. In a recent example, Corsi and colleagues (2019) used a large matched sample of Canadian women and found a modest increase in the likelihood of several developmental markers including preterm birth, being small for gestational age, placental abruption, and an increased need for neonatal intensive care among women using cannabis during pregnancy. The findings published for newborns and youth list a variety of symptoms: tremors, altered sleep patterns, lower memory scores, attention problems and in adolescence a greater likelihood of emotional and behavioral problems [63]. The authors state the results of these studies "suggest that the endocannabinoid system plays an essential role in the ontogeny of the nervous system during fetal brain development and that early gestational exposure to cannabis is able to induce lasting but subtle neurodevelopmental alterations." Of note, other published meta-analyses do not find the extent of consequences listed above. Methodological limitations in this field of research include a lack of well-controlled studies, confounds such as polysubstance use, tobacco use, SES, and lack of longitudinal data [103]. Still, all emerging data suggest the need for caution. Because of the known and potential concerns with any cannabis use regardless of method, the Association of Obstetrics and Gynecology, strongly recommends that all providers advise their patients to stop using prior, during, and after pregnancy [97].

Highway Safety

Driving under the influence of any substance is a behavior that has received decades of fear-driven national public attention. While certainly no practitioner would ever endorse driving while high, the evidence for cannabis impairment while driving is equivocal. The March 2013 report Cannabis effects on driving skills reported that certain driver skills such as reaction times, divided-attention tasks, and lane-position variability show cannabis-induced impairment [104]. A newer study from the National Highway Traffic Safety Administration finds that drivers who use cannabis are at a significantly lower risk for a crash than drivers who use alcohol [105]. After adjusting for age, gender, race, and alcohol use, drivers who tested positive for cannabis were no more likely to crash than those who had not used any drugs or alcohol prior to driving. Authors concluded that "specific drug concentration levels cannot be reliably equated with a specific degree of driver impairment" [105]. Lastly, a study released in February 2019 by the Society for the Study of Addiction, looked at cannabis-related traffic fatalities in cannabis legal states such as Colorado and Washington. Lane and Hall (2019) documented an increase in cannabis-associated traffic fatalities in the year following legalization at a rate of increase of 1.08 traffic fatalities per million residents in the first year (2014) followed by a trend reduction of −0.06 per month in the year following (2015) [106].

Cognitive Impairment

It is generally accepted that cannabis has a broad array of short-term neurocognitive effects including detriments of learning and memory, executive functioning, and motor control (National Science Foundation, 2017). Further, a number of studies have found a correlation between regular adolescent use of cannabis and an increased likelihood of negative outcomes, such as lower academic attainment and employment instability [60, 107]. However, whether the relationship is causal remains controversial, as social determinants and genetic factors may play a disproportionately influential role in life trajectory. Until recently, a study by Zalesky et al. (2012) has been cited as evidence of enduring cognitive decline due to cannabis use [108]. However, in the past year, a large cross-sectional study of associations between cannabis use and cognitive functioning of adolescents and young adults indicates abstinence of longer than 72 hours diminishes most of the cognitive deficits associated with cannabis use [109]. Results indicated that previous studies of cannabis in youth may have overstated the magnitude and persistence of cognitive deficits associated with use [109].

There is strong medical consensus (AMA 2020) that no cannabis use should occur during vulnerable periods of human development including prior, during and after pregnancy and throughout childhood, adolescence and into young adulthood. Yet, our patients convincingly report they feel better across a wide range of physical and mental health symptoms. The answers as to why they feel this way are slowly emerging as we learn more about the endocannabinoid system but there are vast inconsistencies in findings amplifying the need to further understand our patients with refined cannabis specific screeners.

6

Cannabis as Medicine and the User's Experience

Research on the medical utility of cannabis is in its infancy. Federal policies have made US research in this area expensive, time consuming, and challenging, making it difficult to provide an analysis of the risks and benefits of medicinal cannabis use. Researchers seeking to conduct studies on cannabis or cannabinoids must navigate multiple review processes, including the National Institute on Drug Abuse, the US Food and Drug Administration (FDA), the US Drug Enforcement Administration, as well as institutional review boards.

Comments from Medicinal Cannabis Users

I'm in my 50s and work in the medical field and am not a recreational pot smoker (or anything else for that matter). The chemotherapy combined with the prescription medications left me so miserable and incapacitated, I was desperate. For me, the medical marijuana was a miracle drug, a lifesaver. I wished I had used it from the beginning because it was so helpful.

Huffington Post, December 2014

Since starting on medical cannabis, I have been able to stop all prescription pain killers.

Reddit

However, due in part to the increasing number of states in which medical cannabis is legal, pressure to provide data has increased. Despite this, only a small number of papers published in 2016 in the United

---

A Practitioner's Guide to Cannabis, First Edition. Win Turner and Joseph Hyde.
© 2023 John Wiley & Sons, Inc. Published 2023 by John Wiley & Sons, Inc.

States considered medicinal outcomes. In recent decades much of the research on medicinal cannabis has taken place outside the United States most notably in Israel and Canada.

Nonetheless, there are indicators that cannabis may have medical benefits. Evidence exists for the utility of cannabis for pain, nausea, and appetite stimulation [110]. Cannabis use or adjunctive use for treatment of other medical conditions may have anecdotal evidence but requires more research.

Evidence for the efficacy of cannabis with some specific disorders is summarized here.

Multiple Sclerosis

The anti-inflammatory effects of cannabinoids have long been known, although whether they translate into clinical efficacy remains an open question for multiple sclerosis (MS) [111]. For people with MS who have treatment-resistant spasticity, cannabis appears to modestly reduce pain and spasticity [112, 113]. Interestingly, smoked cannabis temporarily increases respiratory airflow, perhaps due to the anti-inflammatory effects. Some animal studies have found that cannabis can protect neurons from neuronal damage caused by use of MDMA (ecstasy) [114].

Chronic Pain

Chronic Pain Defined
Chronic pain is defined as pain that persists or recurs for more than three to six months. It may present as headache, musculoskeletal pain, visceral pain, neuropathic pain, pain arising from rheumatic disease, and cancer pain [112].

Pain reduction has been a major source of interest among researchers, as many people with chronic pain report using cannabis to manage their symptoms and reduce their use of opioids and other psychoactive pain medications [115, 116]. Studies on the effects of THC only have not seen an effect on pain perception. However, in studies of THC combined with CBD, results include reduced pain and reduced use of opioid pain medications [117–119]. The growing awareness that cannabis can reduce pain (along with its lack of toxicity and overdose potential) has led some physicians to begin calling for cannabis to be used as an alternative or supplemental to opioid medications in the hopes that it may reduce reliance on these medications [120]. In the recently published review by the Canadian Agency for Drugs and Technologies in Health, the authors describe the evidence of effectiveness for chronic pain [121]. Their findings indicate that the strongest evidence for cannabis use for chronic pain is for neuropathic pain. "However, benefits need to be weighed against harms" [121]. And the writers went on to state: "Findings are inconsistent for effect of cannabis-based medicines in patients with fibromyalgia, musculoskeletal pain, Crohn's disease, and MS" [121].

In the article published in 2015 in the Journal of the American Medical Association, "Use of cannabis for chronic pain, neuropathic pain, and spasticity due to multiple sclerosis is supported by high-quality evidence. Six trials that included 325 patients examined chronic pain, 6 trials that included 396 patients investigated neuropathic pain, and 12 trials that included 1600 patients focused on multiple sclerosis. Multiple trials had positive results, suggesting that cannabis or cannabinoids may be efficacious for these indications" [122]. This article went further to provide guidance to medical providers when considering a patient for medicinal cannabis. See text box.

Practical Considerations for Medical Marijuana

"An appropriate medical marijuana candidate should have 1. A debilitating medical condition that data suggests would respond to medical marijuana pharmacotherapy, such as nausea and vomiting associated with cancer chemotherapy, anorexia from wasting illnesses like AIDS, chronic pain, neuropathic pain, or spasticity associated with multiple sclerosis 2. Failed trials of first- and second-line pharmacotherapies for these conditions 3. No active substance use disorder or psychotic disorder or no unstable mood or anxiety disorder 4. Residence in a state with medical marijuana laws and meets requirements of these laws" [79].

Epilepsy

Epilepsy is considered to be one of the most common neurological diseases especially in the world. Approximately one-third of patients with epilepsy have seizures that are resistant to antiepileptic medications. Clinical trials for the treatment of medically refractory epilepsy have mostly focused on new drug treatments, and result in a significant portion of subjects whose seizures remain refractory to medication. The use of cannabis sativa plant in treating seizures is known since ancient times [123].

A body of literature is emerging on the anti-epileptic (i.e., anticonvulsant) properties of cannabis, particularly CBD-rich cannabis. Clinical reports have provided conflicting data [124]. Results from an FDA-approved study on use of CBD for a severe form of childhood epilepsy suggest a dramatic reduction in seizures in this population [125]. More recently, a study of children and young adults with treatment-resistant epilepsy found that CBD reduced monthly seizures by 36.5 percent [126]. More rigorous studies are needed to clarify the role of CBD in reducing or preventing seizures.

Cancer

A number of in vitro and animal studies have indicated that cannabinoids may help prevent the spread of cancerous cells and lead to cancer cell death in both breast and prostate cancers [127, 128]. Despite the unfiltered and heavily carcinogenic smoke produced by burning cannabis, there has been no consistent link observed between cannabis smoking and lung cancer [129, 130]. These data suggest an anti-cancer effect with cannabis, as comparable levels of tobacco smoking increase the risk of lung and other cancers. More research is necessary to determine whether cannabis (or more specifically the cannabinoids in cannabis) can be useful in cancer treatment, although cannabis is known to reduce some side-effects of chemotherapy by reducing pain and increasing appetite [131].

Psychiatric Conditions

Despite the limited data, an increasing number of states have approved cannabis for use with a large number of medical and psychiatric conditions. Preliminary research on efficacy of cannabis (and especially CBD) in psychiatric disorders, such as psychotic illness and anxiety disorders, contradicts some literature on the negative psychiatric effects of cannabis and suggests a need for a more nuanced understanding of this complex plant [132, 133]. Patient-reported use of medical cannabis for pain, anxiety, and depression symptoms: systematic review and meta-analysis [134]. Anecdotal evidence although mixed, does reflect positive user experience for behavioral health issues. See text extracted from social media.

Extracted from Redditt.com

Pot definitely helped this combat veteran through tough times and I honestly think it's leaps and bounds better than what the VA wanted to prescribe me.

Over time it has eliminated what used to be nearly constant migraines.

But today I want to give you a glimpse of the real reason I smoke every day ... the demons in my head. My childhood and teens were full of abuse and pain.

I'm using weed to treat my anxiety and depression.

Medical Cannabis Patients Describe Their Experiences

More rigorous qualitative studies of medicinal cannabis users have been undertaken and published in recent years which will be summarized below. These published reports align with and support the limited qualitative interviews we have completed during the past three years. The largest single study with 984 respondents was completed by Piper et al 2017 [115]. These findings and findings from other scholars in the field, are generally consistent [135, 136]. Below we will summarize the pluses, minuses, and end-user thoughts about changes described in these studies. But before this discussion, we believe it is important to have a better understanding of who are medical cannabis patients. Demographically, patients are near equally represented by gender; 52% are female and 48% male with an average age of 49. Slightly more than 66% of patients have been diagnosed with a chronic pain condition. Behavioral health conditions were commonly reported including Generalized or Social Anxiety (34.9%), Major Depressive Disorder (31.1%), Post-Traumatic Stress Disorder (25.0%), insomnia or other sleep disorders (22.4%). 80% of patients had completed post-secondary education and 76% of these adults were employed, retired, or disabled. Although approximately half of all patients report smoking cannabis, patients report preferring to use tinctures, edibles, or salves, however costs for these products are described as prohibitive.

> ("It stops the pain." "It changes perception and experience of my chronic pain," "It breaks the cycle of chronic pain," "It's been life changing for my pain."). Some pain responses were more limited "I can tolerate the chronic pain better."
>
> ("It helps me sleep ALL night long." "Help with my insomnia" "This is the first time since I was 8 years old that I have been nightmare free").

Positive Experiences

Positive health benefits were most commonly described include pain relief (36%) and improved sleep.

> "I get to feel normal." "It gives me the ability to function throughout the day," "I am more active and able to do things I want."

A second theme was described related to relative safety when compared to (pain) medications and over-dose potential ("You can't OD," "It will not kill me"). A sub-theme that emerged was the reduced addictive potential, reducing or eliminating narcotic pain medications was referenced as a positive aspect. Improved quality of life is also described.

Negative Experiences

The single most common complaint (30%) was the high cost of purchasing cannabis from a dispensary. The second negative experience described was side effects: the odor of cannabis, coughing, appetite increase, and weight gain, and (occasional) heightened anxiety (bi-phasic effect). The third negative experience was stigma. Especially the negative attitudes held by some employers and members of the medical community. The systematic review article by Gardiner et al. (2019) underscores divergent beliefs and a lack of knowledge by medical providers.

Recommendations

Two general recommendations emerged from this report. First was to reduce cost or develop an allowable way for patients to defer costs such as allowing cannabis as a medical expense. Second was for medical provider education to reduce stigma and bias and increase their knowledge of cannabis use for patients with certain conditions [137].

Summary

Diverging claims of harms and benefits of medicinal cannabis persist as do policy, political, and ideological barriers in the United States impeding true "agnostic" research.

We recommend that (a) providers increase their awareness of their own beliefs and attitudes about cannabis use and how it may affect their practice, and (b) always listen to their patient's experience of use prior to emphasizing preconceived ideas about cannabis use and associated consequences (e.g., impaired driving, cognitive impairment, and mental health concerns) and (c) utilize refined screening and assessment tools specifically developed for cannabis users.

As state and national efforts for legalization continue, practitioners need to be more cognizant of the impacts of cannabis use. We need to build our skills to have thoughtful, non-judgmental, non-fear-based conversations with our patients regarding their cannabis use, so they might make better decisions regarding their psychosocial, emotional, and physical health. We practitioners must also urge patients to be discerning consumers of cannabis-related science.

7

A New Approach to Cannabis Screening

Universal Screening for Substance Use Disorders

The prevalence of cannabis use in the United States provides a strong rationale for implementing universal screening in clinical settings and a targeted approach to intervention. This can be incorporated into the SBIRT (Screening, Brief Intervention, and Referral to Treatment) workflow already used by many practitioners to identify and prevent risky substance use. The rationale for universal screening is simple. Alcohol and other drug use, including cannabis use, is common and can increase the risk for health problems, safety risks, and a host of psychosocial issues. Alcohol and drug use often go undetected and, surprisingly to some, patients are more open to these conversations than clinicians often expect [138–140].

Lessons learned from several large-scale SBIRT projects suggest that framing the entire SBIRT process as a wellness initiative aimed at reducing the risks of preventable disease and injury can help normalize the screening process and ameliorate patient concerns. The SAMHSA-funded SBIRT Tennessee project director described an increase in screening adherence and fewer patient complaints when they posted a statement emphasizing that all patients were being screened for general wellness and preventable risks. A critical lesson learned from both Tennessee and Vermont's SAMHSA-funded SBIRT projects is the importance of beginning the screening with questions that are non-intrusive and lacking in stigma associated with substance use (e.g., questions about seatbelt

---

A Practitioner's Guide to Cannabis, First Edition. Win Turner and Joseph Hyde.
© 2023 John Wiley & Sons, Inc. Published 2023 by John Wiley & Sons, Inc.

use, flu shots, distracted driving). This strategy increases opportunities for population-based risk reduction (e.g., reducing the risk of driving without seatbelts or distracted driving) while also serving as a substance use screening induction method. The approach lessens the potential for patient concerns about being singled out or judged regarding substance use. Like any SBIRT screening protocol, patients endorsing risk for any of the introductory wellness questions are provided with a very brief motivational discussion and information about the associated health risk. Once these introductory questions are completed, patients can then be asked about tobacco, alcohol, or other substance use, and mood.

Common SBIRT alcohol and drug use screening tools used in clinical settings include the Alcohol, Smoking, and Substance Involvement Screening Test (World Health Organization, 2010), the Alcohol Use Disorder Identification Test (AUDIT; World Health Organization, 1982), and the Drug Abuse Screening Test (DAST; Skinner, 1982). These tools can be administered by questioning or patient self-completion of a form (paper or tablet).

Regardless of administration method, the screening tools attempt to elicit from the patient: (1) negative or concerning consequences of use that map onto DSM-5 criteria; (2) screening scores that can be stratified based on the degree of substance use risk; (3) treatment matching as these risk levels can determine need for specialized referral). Importantly, the endorsed responses to screening questions provide the springboard for reflective feedback discussions as part of a brief intervention. That is, the endorsed responses are topics of personal consequence that the practitioner skilled in Motivational Interviewing (MI) can raise with the client, to develop discrepancies and activate patient motivation to reduce risk.

Rationale for a Cannabis Screener

From 2010 to 2018, we interacted with a multitude of different medical settings adopting integrated healthcare; in many of these sites practitioners consistently voiced concerns and frustrations at the challenges of intervening meaningfully with cannabis-using patients. They reported that many patients did not verbalize reasons to change their use and in fact patients stated they felt cannabis was helpful for a variety of mental health and physical symptoms. Practitioner challenges were validated by the dearth of patient-endorsed consequences on the DAST 10-item

7 A New Approach to Cannabis Screening

screening tool. Cannabis-using patients endorsed an average of just 1.3 items, limiting the potential reasons for change that the practitioner could raise as a focus of a brief motivational intervention.

> *For patients with concerning cannabis use, are we asking the right questions?*

The minimal number of consequence items endorsed presented an important question that needed to be addressed. Would the addition of a brief cannabis-specific secondary screening tool increase the number of items of concern patients endorse, consequently increasing the potential for the brief intervention with greater potency and meaningfulness? More specifically, if patients are presented with items specific to potential negative personal impact of marijuana use versus general drug use consequences, will they endorse more of these items? In doing so, will their interest in discussing the item content increase? Will this lead to more robust opportunities to develop discrepancies and elicit change talk, increasing the intervention potency from an MI perspective?

Cannabis Intervention Screener

To build a more robust cannabis intervention strategy, our solution was to create the Cannabis Intervention Screener (CIS) as part of a targeted approach for triage, secondary screening, and motivational interventions based on endorsed concerns.

The CIS can be used in medical and social service settings to identify individuals using cannabis at levels that may adversely impact their health or social functioning. The CIS is unique in that it was specifically developed to help practitioners stratify individual risk and to elicit and provide opportunities for motivational interventions with cannabis users; a patient population often presenting with lack of reasons (motivation) to examine the impact of their use [141].

The CIS is comprised of three sections:

- A (two-part) single item pre-screen cannabis use frequency measure (triage)
- Five items eliciting methods of cannabis use and reasons for use
- Ten items assessing negative impacts of cannabis use in the past year
- The complete CIS is provided in Appendix A.

Development of the CIS

Our clinical team reviewed cannabis literature and found six validated marijuana assessment tools from which items were selected to create the CIS; the new tool is not as lengthy as the predecessor assessment tools. In the pilot conducted, patients completed the initial cannabis frequency item (CIS triage) as part of routine intake and initial screening. Patients endorsing a frequency of use of several times per week or more were administered the full CIS and, for comparison, the DAST 10. In the initial pilot of the CIS, medical providers recommended setting an initial (triage) screening cut-off based on consumption, similar to the AUDIT-C scoring. This would identify potential cannabis risk based on frequency of consumption and signal need for further screening. The initial cut-off chosen was "several days per week" (interpreted as two or more) on the CIS single-item triage. The medical providers based this cut-off recommendation on three critical factors: (1) the lack of clear medical evidence that less-frequent cannabis use leads to significant health risks; (2) the limited time availability of providers in clinical settings (i.e., Emergency Departments, Federally Qualified Health Centers) for addressing less-frequent cannabis use; and (3) the lack of patient readiness/willingness to discuss their cannabis use when they are likely to perceive no concerns because that use is minimal.

If a patient scored as engaging in risky cannabis use based on CIS questions 1–10, the SBIRT practitioners would engage in a brief intervention and related follow up. The practitioners would utilize responses from the CIS to inform and guide the brief intervention. Brief intervention had two possible goals: to negotiate a commitment to reduce or cease cannabis use, or to negotiate a referral for further assessment and CUD treatment services.

At the time of the cannabis screening tool validation study, we included three states reflecting three different landscapes of marijuana public policy: (1) Washington state where recreational use was legal; (2) Iowa where use was illegal; and (3) Vermont which de-criminalized cannabis use. All three states approved cannabis use for specific medical purposes. Participating sites included diverse practice settings including community health centers, emergency departments, college health services, and routine primary care practices.

As part of the study, practitioners involved completed a survey, to elicit their perspectives on the quality of the brief interaction with the patient and the degree to which motivational indicators were present. Initial pilot data were collected on 215 patients endorsing cannabis use. Overall, initial pilot data indicated that patients significantly endorsed more items on the CIS versus the DAST (449 items vs. 225 respectively; t = 2.3, p < .05 representing twice the number of endorsements). Fifteen percent of patients verbally shared they used cannabis to cope with negative affect and sleep, while two percent of patients verbally shared they use marijuana to cope with physical pain.

Summary of CIS Evaluation Findings

Data from the validation study confirmed the use of this initial cannabis triage frequency cut-off. Of 76,365 Vermont adult patients screened in healtcare settings (see Exhibit 7.1), 18 percent reported using cannabis in the past year. Cannabis use was most prevalent for young adults, 18–24 years of age. Eight percent (6,005) reported using two or more times per week, with two-thirds of those individuals (approximately 6 percent) reporting using four times a week or more and about 8 percent indicated use several days a week or daily, meeting the criteria for full screening. In the multistate sample of cannabis users, 34 percent endorsed less than weekly use, while 66 percent endorsed weekly or more use. Of those using weekly or more, 41 percent (of the 66 percent) endorsed daily or almost daily use. This represents approximately 26% of persons who acknowledged using cannabis, reported using daily or near daily. Patients endorsing greater than weekly use had significantly elevated CIS impact scores.

Methods of cannabis use were compared using of the entire sample across all three states. It is important to note that patients were asked to identify all methods of cannabis use versus their single preferred method

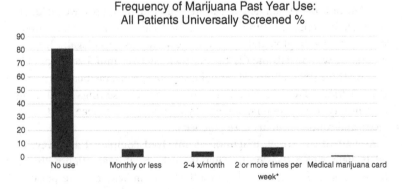

Exhibit 7.1 Frequency of Marijuana Use among Vermont Patients Endorsing past Year Use (N = 76,365).

as patients may have selected more than one method. Exhibit 7.2 illustrates that the primary method of use among this sample of cannabis users was smoking, followed by edibles, dabbing, and vaping. Seventy-three percent of patients reported only one method of use, with the vast majority of all patients (93 percent) endorsing smoking as their primary method. More frequent use was associated with engaging in multiple methods of use. Patients who endorsed using at least several days a week or more were more likely to vape or consume edibles in addition to smoking. Additionally, if patients endorsed using weekly or greater, they were more likely to also endorse dabbing.

As indicated earlier, the CIS collects data on impacts and/or consequences an individual may experience as a result of using cannabis. The CIS exhibit 7.3 below illustrates the frequency of specific concerns

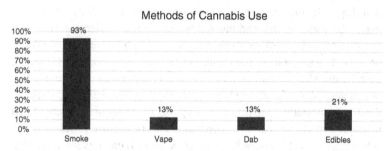

Exhibit 7.2 Primary Methods of Cannabis Use.

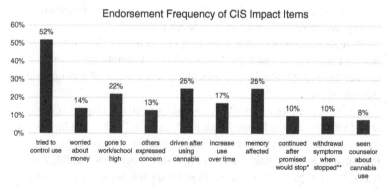

Exhibit 7.3 Endorsement Frequency of CIS Impact Items. Note: Two items had substantial amounts of missing data as respondents could indicate if they felt the item was not applicable to them (*38% missing data; **17% missing data).

endorsed. This information is essential for making decisions on how to best to engage and interact with cannabis users. The four most endorsed items were: trying to control use, driving, memory impairment, and using at school and work.

Cannabis Use Vs. Misuse Vs. Abuse

Categorizing cannabis use in categorical terms (use vs. misuse vs. abuse) that help both users and health providers discuss, prevent, and/or limit negative consequence is an important endeavor. In 2014, the American Psychiatric Association's (APA) latest version of the diagnostic criteria guide the DSM 5 evolved beyond defining distinct categories for substance use disorders and instead moved toward a continuum method to defining risk (low, moderate, or severe). While frequency of use is a partial indicator of risk and harm it is the adverse consequences of that use that primarily defines a use disorder within a framework of DSM-5 or ICD 10. Research on the matching of negative consequences to the severity of risk demonstrates that 5 of the 11 criteria are most indicative of a severe SUD including (1) experiencing withdrawal symptoms; (2) desire and/or inability to reduce or stop use; (3) forfeiture of recreational or other activities because of substance use; (4) failure to fulfill major role obligations at home, school, or work; and (5) craving, strong desire, or urge to use a substance. These criteria define an apparent "loss of control" indicated by a multitude of linked negative consequences. For those with less severe use often a few distinct risk factors are endorsed illustrating less negative impact on a person's life [142].

Ultimately, accurate stratification of cannabis risk during the screening and assessment process is critical for determining the potential impact of an individual's use and the development of a collaborative treatment plan.

Exhibit 7.4 indicates how CIS consequence items map to DSM-5 criteria [56]. Prevalence for each risk level, as found in the validation evaluation, is also indicated in the figure. Exhibit 7.5 aligns practitioner response to levels of risk and to likely DSM5 diagnoses. Exhibit 7.6 portrays the risk pyramid diagram illustrating impact scores on the CIS, prevalence percentages, and the level of risk of persons using cannabis in the validation sample.

Cannabis Use Vs. Misuse Vs. Abuse | 49

Exhibit 7.4 CIS Impact Questions Alignment with DSM-5 Cannabis Use Disorder Criteria.

CIS Questions 1–10	DSM 5 Criteria Items
Prior attempts to control use (Q 1 and Q7)	Attempting to quit or control use
Worried about the amount of money (Q2)	Role obligations
Impact on work or school (Q3)	Role obligations
Impact on social functioning (Q4)	Social/Interpersonal consequences
Driven a car or other vehicle under the influence (Q5)	Hazards associated with use
Memory/cognitive functioning (Q6)	Psychological/physical problems with use
Withdrawal symptoms (Q8)	Withdrawal symptoms
Using greater quantities (Q9)	Using greater quantities
Prior treatment engagement (Q10)	Prior attempt to quit of control use

Exhibit 7.5 CIS Impact Scale Scores, Alignment with DSM-5 Diagnoses and Clinical Intervention.

Impact Cut Off Levels	Suggested Intervention	Estimated Population Percent Per Risk Level	Alignment with DSM-5 Risk Criteria
None (0–1)	Positive Feedback	48%	No risk
Lower (at-risk) (2–3)	Brief Intervention (BI)	32%	At-risk for mild CUD
Moderate (4–5)	BI and Brief Treatment	14%	Moderate CUD
Severe (6 +)	BI and Treatment Referral	6%	Severe CUD

In our study, the correlation between the increased frequency of use and the number of negative impacts endorsed was strong (negative impacts increase as frequency of use increases), which is similar to findings in alcohol screening [143, 144]. There was a significantly elevated chance that patients had tried to control their use when they used more than weekly and multiple times per day. Similarly, patients endorsing

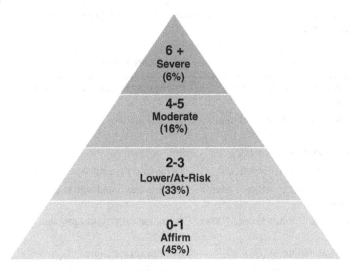

Exhibit 7.6 The Cannabis Risk Pyramid (For Patients Endorsing Any Cannabis Use).

use multiple times per day endorsed all CIS impacts and negative consequences significantly more often when compared with those who endorsed using less frequently. The difference in the rates of endorsed risks based on frequency of use is illustrated in Exhibit 7.7. Among patients who used cannabis less than weekly, only 17 percent fell in the moderate- to high-risk levels, compared with 45 percent of patients who used more frequently (weekly or more frequently).

As indicated in Exhibit 7.8, patients who endorsed using cannabis for mental health reasons or for both mental health and physical reasons were significantly more likely to have moderate to high levels of CIS risk. Thus, it appears that individuals who use cannabis to cope with mental health symptoms are also more likely to endorse negative impacts related to their cannabis use. Perhaps individuals with mental health problems or mental health and co-occurring physical problems who also use cannabis, may have a different outlook on their cannabis use compared to those who use for physical or solely recreational reasons and thus, perceive the impact differently. Although patient endorsements of use for physical health, mental health, or recreational purposes are not scored as part of the CIS, this information provides an opening for practitioner engagement and exploration using motivational interviewing strategies (e.g., pros and cons).

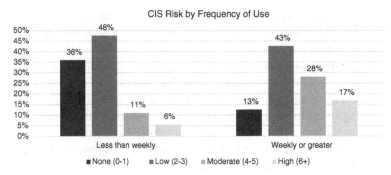

Exhibit 7.7 CIS Risk by Frequency of Use.

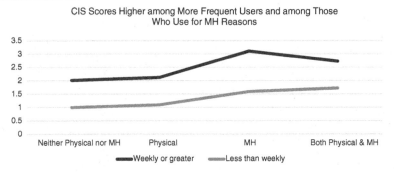

Exhibit 7.8 CIS Scores.

Implications from CIS Study Findings

In summary, the CIS validation study demonstrated that:

- The CIS is a useful screening tool for cannabis screening and intervention.
- Use of the initial frequency prescreen (CIS triage) and the answer of weekly use as the cut off was effective in distinguishing between those who had few if any negative impacts (who do not need further screening) and those with most impact from use (who should receive further screening).
- Patients who used daily or multiple times a day endorsed the most negative impacts; using multiple times daily was associated with the highest CIS impact scores.

52 | 7 A New Approach to Cannabis Screening

- Patients who endorse use for mental health reasons alone or both mental health/physical health may benefit from screening for co-occurring conditions.
- CIS endorsements of reasons for cannabis use can identify the best focus for brief motivational interventions with patients (see following lines). For many patients who report more frequent use of cannabis, trying to control use is a salient discussion topic. Other commonly endorsed items that may be relevant points for discussion include driving under the influence, memory loss, concerns from friends and family, and using during work/school.
- Patients with CIS scores of 4 and higher indicating moderate to severe CUD, should be referred for further assessment and treatment.

Orientation to Clinical Interventions Addressing Cannabis Use Disorder

The treatment approach for cannabis use disorder described in this guide follows a clinical method that draws on innovations and essential elements influenced by screening, brief intervention, and referral to treatment (SBIRT) model, motivational interviewing (MI), motivational enhancement therapy (MET), mindfulness, values-based clinical practices, functional analysis, and cognitive behavioral therapy (CBT). Current approaches to understanding the treatment of cannabis use, mental health, and co-occurring disorders are driven by empirical advances in neuroscience and behavioral research rather than by theories alone. There is now good evidence that both biological factors and psychosocial experiences influence the development and continuation of disorders. Contributing experiences may occur at home, at work, or in the community, and a stressor or risk factor may have a small or profound effect, depending on individual differences. The following review of motivational interviewing (MI), motivational enhancement therapy (MET), personal reflective summary (PRS), and cognitive behavioral therapy (CBT) provides context for the treatment sessions in this guide.

Motivational Interviewing and Motivational Enhancement Therapy

MI is an effective, evidence-based method for helping patients with a variety of health and behavioral concerns. Motivational approaches, as developed by William Miller and Stephen Rollnick, seek to foster the

---

A Practitioner's Guide to Cannabis, First Edition. Win Turner and Joseph Hyde.
© 2023 John Wiley & Sons, Inc. Published 2023 by John Wiley & Sons, Inc.

54 | *Orientation to Clinical Interventions Addressing Cannabis Use Disorder*

intrinsic drive people have for healing, positive change, and self-development [145]. Since Miller and Rollnick's original work was published in 1983, more than 25,000 articles citing MI and 200 randomized clinical trials of MI have appeared in print. MI's efficacy has been substantiated by several MI training research projects [146].

Integrating motivational enhancement and cognitive behavioral skills building to elicit change—how it works:

- Motivation enhancement is achieved by building rapport through reflective discussions, helping patients understand the pros and cons of use, and helping to establish collaborative goals based on the patient's needs.
- Motivational enhancement strategies assess and increase the patient's readiness, willingness, and ability to change.
- The clinician's first and primary task is to understand how to engage and collaborate with the patient to build internal motivation.
- In cognitive behavioral therapy, cannabis use (and other behavioral health issues) is viewed as an intrapersonal and interpersonal issue, a recurring and habitual disorder that can be successfully treated.
- Through treatment, the patient learns to become aware of situations and emotions and how to avoid, cope, and adopt healthy replacement actions to achieve wellness.

MET is a structured intervention approach that uses MI techniques. MET interventions typically involve both a specific feedback and/or reflective discussion following screening and/or assessment and goal-setting interactions (planning). The descriptions of MET sessions in this guide include scripts illustrating the effective use of MI techniques.

Brief MI Interaction for Cannabis Misuse

A well-researched, potent, and common brief intervention model often delivered to engage and motivate cannabis users is called the Brief Negotiated Interview [147]. The BNI is structured on the four phases of motivational enhancement interventions (a) engage, (b) focus, (c) evoke, and (d) plan [148]. The BNI is commonly delivered within healthcare settings to activate patients where the specific goal or target of the intervention is based on the severity of risk that is, raising awareness for low risk, engaging in brief treatment (BT) for moderate risk and severe risk, and/or accepting a referral to longer treatment as needed. The endorsed responses from an effective screening tool (the Cannabis Intervention Screener) create the topics of personal consequence (i.e., possible reasons for change) and help to focus provider feedback discussions. Thus, using screening tools combined with motivational interviewing (MI) can providers in their interactions with cannabis users to develop more discrepancies, change talk, and activate patient motivation to reduce risk.

Cognitive Behavioral Therapy

Models of CBT are the most extensively evaluated interventions for the treatment of both mental health, alcohol, cannabis use disorders and co-occurring disorders. Multiple meta-analyses [149] have repeatedly demonstrated efficacy in the treatment of addictions and mental health disorders such as depression, traumatic stress, and anxiety. CBT is primarily based on the original work of Marlatt and Gordon (1985), and from this have grown models for recurrence of use prevention for cannabis use disorders and applications addressing other issues. These interventions for recurrence of use prevention have targeted cognitive, behavioral, affective, and situational triggers for cannabis use and provided clearly defined skills trainings in support of abstinence and recovery. CBT manuals have been developed since 1985 and adapted for use in a variety of clinical settings, with CBT interventions tested to examine their utility in real-world settings and their cost-effectiveness [150, 151].

All people develop habits to address life's complexities more efficiently and effectively. CBT clinicians view mental health coping strategies including cannabis use, in part, as a negative and repeated habit reinforced by the neuropsychological effects of the behaviors. The role of the clinician is to elevate the seemingly repeated ineffective and unhealthy coping strategies such as behaviors like self-harm, avoidance, negative looping thoughts, and/or substance-linked habits into conscious awareness. Awareness is created through a functional analysis discussion that reviews the relationships between the negative coping reactions for example, cannabis use and internal and external factors. The clinician's integration and proficient use of MI skills to create a therapeutic alliance founded on nonjudgmental trust is a critical element in utilizing CBT, especially functional analysis, to realize and change negative habitual patterns like cannabis use. By providing the "therapeutic environment" for honest dialogue, the triggers, feelings, thoughts, and underlying belief systems that help drive repeated patterns are more readily brought into cognitive awareness. The clinician must be adept at using MI to promote readiness and evoke awareness and equally adept at teaching and coaching to help patients develop new skills.

The value of skills training in the treatment of cannabis use and mental disorders has been described in previous writings on CBT [152]. Determining the targeted skills to be addressed requires some form of assessment (functional analysis is loosely defined as situational and personal awareness, knowledge is power, the ABCs of CBT, etc.). For each issue defined as a priority, the clinician works in partnership with the patient to assess readiness to address the issue, identify mastering the necessary skills as priorities, and help the patient develop reasonable expectations as to the intended outcomes.

Skills deficits are significant factors to be addressed as these challenges often lead to or perpetuate use of cannabis and drugs as a maladaptive coping strategy. To the extent the individual does not develop healthier coping skills, the risk for recurrence of use remains high if the deficits are not addressed. Similarly, certain kinds of skills deficits are associated with anxiety and depression (addressed in Integrated Combined Motivational Enhancement & Cognitive Behavior Treatment sessions). Managing these affective states is important in recovery and to the overall well-being of the patient.

With the use of MI/MET and CBT approach, the clinician selects skills sessions from a menu of possible choices based on information that emerged during the earlier motivation enhancement sessions. The sequence of the sessions corresponds to those in many researched, combined MET and CBT intervention manuals [153]. The purpose of the sequence of sessions is to immediately offer patients simple methods for increasing awareness and developing coping strategies.

Even though a sequence is offered, the clinician and patient should collaboratively decide which topics or skills to focus on, based on the patient's particular needs and presentation. For example, one patient

Cognitive Behavioral Therapy | 57

may describe struggling with depression or other difficult emotions and might benefit from the sessions that focus on emotions. Another patient may present with a history of difficulty expressing thoughts and feelings constructively and might be helped by assertiveness skills. Mindfulness and meditation may be helpful for the large majority of patients who are referred for brief treatment as these strategies have broad applications for treating difficulties with mood, substances, and anxiety.

Intrapersonal Skills Training

Intrapersonal skills training begins with building personal awareness (mindfulness), identifying and managing thoughts and urges to use substances, managing powerful emotions such as fear or anger, and addressing negative and self-defeating thoughts such as those associated with low self-esteem, low sense of self-efficacy, catastrophic expectations, and feelings of helplessness and hopelessness. On the positive and strengths-based side of treatment, skills training helps patients learn how to become calmer, problem-solve situations, internally assess thoughts and feelings, and successfully manage and navigate what can be powerful and uncomfortable emotional states. Other skills that have proven useful and effective include relaxation training, skills for positive use of unstructured time, mastering healthy physical and mental activities, decision making, and planning for the unexpected.

Interpersonal Skills

Interpersonal skills target management of situations where other people are an important factor or are actually part of the problem. Developing refusal skills in social situations is important for substance using patients because most will be confronted with the opportunity to use substances and will be faced with a choice. Learning how to say no convincingly and in a manner that works for the patient in their world and context is an important skill to develop.

Developing appropriate boundary management and assertiveness skills is important in multiple domains of a person's life. Failing to develop these skills often leads a person to feel unsafe, imposed upon, and resentful, and can serve as a trigger for mental health symptoms of trauma, anxiety, depression, and/or cannabis use. Addressing potentially contentious situations is important. It is challenging to be the

Orientation to Clinical Interventions Addressing Cannabis Use Disorder

recipient or the bearer of criticism; both can provoke feelings of frustration or anger.

CBT Introduction

As a framework for treatment, this section provides detailed guidance to clinicians for delivering any or all of the included sessions. Each session is organized according to the following headings:

- Introduction to the session
- The patient's experience: what the patient learns (intended outcome)
- Clinician preparation for the session
- Session outline, steps
- Protocol with scripts (and sidebar tips; some appear in the appendices)
- Handouts (appearing in corresponding sections at end of guide)

> We recommend that Sessions 1 and 2 are completed first and in order. These two sessions provide you (and your patient) valuable insights for setting priorities and for individualizing care. However, beyond that, we encourage you to sequence sessions based upon your patient's need. For instance, early in treatment some patients might benefit from mindfulness training and from working with self-limiting thoughts.

Sessions 1–7 are viewed as core and should be completed by all patients. Session 1 addresses engagement and motivation for change. Session 2 initiates the process of functional analysis to help the patient build situational awareness of internal and interpersonal factors affecting cannabis use and is used to individualize treatment strategies. Sessions 3, 4, 5, 6, and 7 are universally beneficial, and necessary skill-training sessions supporting substance use recovery as well as other concerns. The clinician and patient may decide to complete more sessions based on identified needs. While there is flexibility in the model, the clinician should not assume the patient has the sole responsibility for deciding the number of sessions. Rather, the clinician should guide the course and plan for treatment with considerable input from the patient. The clinician

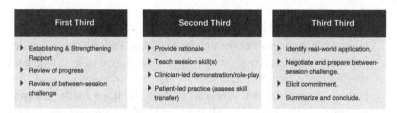

Figure 1 Sample Therapy Sessions according to the Law of Thirds.

must balance patient motivation and needs with clinician judgment when deciding on a reasonable duration of treatment for each patient.

The Structure of a Session Delivery: "Law of Thirds"

CBT is a structured treatment grounded in the "law of thirds." Studies in psychotherapy have determined that most successful therapy sessions occur in three phases. This came to be known informally as the law of thirds or the 20/20/20 rule [154]. As figure 1 illustrates the law of thirds describes the first third of the therapy session as engaging, building, or reestablishing rapport and reviewing progress since the last contact and between-session practice activities. The second third is the core of that session's activity and addresses a particular skill to be introduced and practiced during the session. The final third summarizes what took place during the session and the clinician and patient identify a real-life practice opportunity and make a mutual commitment to practice the new skill in the coming week outside of the session.

The First Third
The key goal of the First Third of the session is to connect and engage. Therefore, using the MI spirit is especially useful within this part of the session. There are three key activities delivered in the First Third of the session.

1) **Establishing and Strengthening Rapport.** The clinician works to develop or strengthen rapport by using the MI spirit (compassion, acceptance, autonomy, and evocation) and core MI skills (open-ended questions, affirmations, reflections, summaries) while engaging the patient in non-problem focused rapport building (i.e., exploring areas of their life not directly related to treatment).

60 | *Orientation to Clinical Interventions Addressing Cannabis Use Disorder*

2) **Review Progress.** This is the clinician's opportunity to identify and explore any changes in the patient's cannabis use, mental health, and related experiences since the previous session. The clinician asks the patient about what has gone well what has not gone so well, changes they've made since the last session, and any other element of the patient's experience that is related to their identified challenges and treatment goals. Using the MI core skills of open-ended questions, affirmations, reflections, and summaries allows the clinician to learn more about the patient's thoughts and feelings around what they think is going well or not so well, and why. In addition, progress review serves as a feedback loop for the clinician to learn how the treatment to date is or is not working and the reasons for the treatment response (or lack thereof). Some clinicians may find it beneficial to structure their review of progress using a tool that suggests key domains relevant to most patients to review an ongoing basis over the course of treatment. An optional Review of Progress handout is provided at the end of this chapter. The domains assessed include physical activity, sleep, diet, pleasurable activities, mastery activities, work/ school, cannabis use, and mood states.

3) **Review Between-Session Challenge.** In addition to reviewing progress over the course of treatment, it is critical in the combined MET & CBT framework to directly review the progress of between-session challenges. Between-session challenges provide patients the opportunity to apply the awareness and skills they are learning in the sessions, so they gain more confidence and practice applying the skills on their own "in the real world." By reviewing the patient's application of newly learned skills, the clinician is able to reinforce the patient's efforts, explore how skill application worked or did not work, and support the patient in identifying how to best continue working toward that skill on an ongoing basis. Some patients will benefit from re-training of the skill to maximize its utility for them. It is imperative the clinician ensure the patient knows the importance of the between-session challenges and that they will be expected to report on the application of new skills in every session. When a between-session challenge has not been completed, the clinician explores with the patient the barriers that led to that outcome. Common barriers that may need to be addressed include lack of motivation or perceived relevance of the skill, uncertainty about how to apply a newly learned skill, and

external challenges outside of the patient's control (e.g., sudden crisis situation that takes priority, medical illness, etc.). The clinician continues to use the core MI skills and other MI tools (e.g., decisional balance) to explore motivation around skills application. Revisiting the rationale for the skill and its relevance to the patient is a strategy that can increase their willingness and perceived importance of completing the between-session challenge. General troubleshooting can also be helpful to identifying solutions to other barriers. By focusing attention on the review of between-session challenges, the clinician reinforces the expectancy of patient skills practice outside of session. Where appropriate, the clinician can use a portion of the session to support the patient applying any missed between-session challenges in session. For example, if a patient previously committed to making an assertive request to a colleague, the patient and clinician could practice a similar scenario to provide the patient an opportunity to practice and explore the outcome of their use of assertive communication.

The Second Third

The key goal of the Second Third of the session is for the clinician to transfer a new skill to the patient. Thus the Second Third represents the core of that session's activity, where teaching and skill building occur. There are four key activities that occur during the Second Third of the session.

1) **Provide Session Rationale.** Combined MI and CBT (ICBT) sessions are designed to support the patient in learning and applying new coping skills. Just as patients may experience fluctuations in motivation for treatment, they may also feel ambivalent about or have misconceptions about a particular skill or set of skills. Thus, prior to delivering any intervention activity, the clinician should explain the rationale for using it to the patient. Delivering a personalized session rationale helps the patient understand the activity and the potential benefit for them, thereby facilitating their increased engagement in session and commitment to skill learning and application. The rationale is not just a review of the planned session activity but an individualized discussion of how and why the session activity is important for their own clinical progress and recovery; why is it relevant for them. A sample rationale is presented within each of the ICBT session chapters in this guide.

62 | *Orientation to Clinical Interventions Addressing Cannabis Use Disorder*

2) **Teach Session Skill(s).** To effectively teach coping skills, the clinician shares relevant information to enhance the patient's understanding of the skill and engages in a collaborative step-by-step application of the skill. The clinician does not simply talk "at" the patient, but rather engages them in discussion along the way, eliciting their baseline knowledge, resolving misconceptions, and addressing questions or concerns.

3) **Clinician-Led Demonstration/Skills Practice.** To reinforce the teaching of new skills, the clinician models skill application in session through demonstration. Clinician demonstration most commonly occurs through clinician coaching the patient through skill application (i.e., walking the patient through the application of the skill using the patient's experiences as content while going through the step-by-step teaching of the skill) and/or engaging in a role play scenario where the clinician acts out the skill.

4) **Patient-Led Practice.** Observing the patient delivering or applying a skill is essential to assessing whether skills transfer has occurred. Following clinician modeling of the skill, the patient practices skill implementation in session. Patient practice helps to build confidence in their use of the skill while allowing the clinician opportunity to reinforce skill application and provide feedback.

The Third Third

The key goal of the Third Third of the session is for the patient to prepare for transferring the skills they are learning in the ICBT sessions into their everyday life. The clinician uses their core MI skills and strategies to help patients make a connection between what they have learned in session and their daily life. There are four main activities that occur during the Third Third of the session.

1) **Identify Real-World Application.** The clinician works with the patient to connect newly learned skills to meaningful opportunities in their life. Patients will be more likely to practice and ultimately adopt skills if they perceive them to be relevant. The clinician helps the patient to identify real-life situations in which they can apply a coping skill.

2) **Negotiate and Prepare Between-Session Challenge.** The clinician elicits from the patient how and where in their life they can

apply awareness raising and other coping skills they are learning in session in their daily life. The negotiation of a challenge is a patient-centered, collaborative process, not an assignment given from the clinician to the patient. The more active the patient is in thoughtfully identifying real-world opportunities for skill application, the more relevant its implementation will be, thereby increasing buy-in and the likelihood of follow-through. Between-session challenges need to be specific. That is, it should be clear to both patient and clinician what they will do, when they will do it, and how often it will be done. To prepare the patient for the between-session challenge, the clinician walks through the application of the newly learned skill and supports the patient for how they will think through, approach, or deliver the skill in the identified scenario. This form of mental rehearsal sets the patient up for greater success in completion of the activity. Generally, it is recommended that patients complete at least two practice applications of newly learned skills in order for them to derive the intended benefit from the skill.

3) **Elicit Commitment.** After the patient has identified an area for real-world skill application, the clinician elicits commitment for engaging in skills practice. As needed, commitment can be directly assessed using the MI ruler and other MI skills used to strengthen patient commitment. The clinician also supports the patient in establishing a plan for success by having them write down their plan and think through any strategies they will use to set themselves up for success and overcome possible obstacles.

4) **Summarize and Conclude.** The clinician presents a session summary of what has been covered during the session and elicits the patient's feedback. While summaries are intended to be brief and follow the general timeline of the session, they serve the important function of reinforcing relevant themes, setting the stage for what comes next, and setting the stage for the patient to provide targeted feedback. The clinician directly asks the patient about how the session went for them, what was particularly helpful or less helpful, and other areas in which the patient would like to provide feedback.

Delivering clinical sessions consistent with the Law of Thirds requires some accommodation in approach for many clinicians. However, with practice, this soon becomes second nature.

Session 1. Eliciting the Life Movie

Introduction and Session Goals

This session focuses on building rapport and building motivation for change through the Eliciting the Life Movie conversation. Eliciting the Life Movie is an important part of ICBT. The Life Movie is a motivational interviewing, semi-structured discussion designed to explore the following domains of the patient's life in relation to their primary reasons for seeking treatment including history and severity, benefits of use, problems caused by use, reasons for considering change, and current motivation to change. The Life Movie is an opportunity to explore themes from the initial assessment in greater depth to increase the patient's insight, motivation, and readiness to enact changes.

Prior to the first session, the clinician uses the patient's assessment and screening information to further understand the patient's current cannabis use and other domains of their life. In reviewing the assessment information, the clinician begins to develop an understanding of the patient's cannabis use, how it has affected their life, and potential areas to explore to further build rapport and build motivation for change. Then, the clinician and patient discuss the core areas of the Life Movie during the initial treatment session as a way to begin the conversation about where the patient stands in relation to alcohol, cannabis, and/or other substance use, and what they would like to accomplish. The clinician identifies the patient's overall risk level related to cannabis use to share with the patient during the first session.

See the Session 1 handouts at the end of the guide, which provide the necessary framework to facilitate and deliver competent Life Movie discussions. The handouts include Treatment Information sheet as well as a clinician's reference sheet to help guide the Life Movie discussion.

With the approach described here, the patient experiences a nonjudgmental conversation with a skilled health person providing support, empathy, and a desire to collaborate on a journey toward wellness. The patient develops an awareness of substance-related health risks and begins to question their readiness to address the risks now. The patient commits to following through on any number of "readiness" tasks prior to the next meeting.

Clinician Preparation

Session 1. Eliciting the Life Movie	
Materials • ICBT Treatment Information Sheet • Eliciting the Life Movie Clinician Reference • Change Plan and Quit Agreement • Optional: Learning New Coping Strategies	**Session Length** 45–60 minutes **Delivery Method** MET-focused individual therapy

Strategies
- Follow OARS: Open-ended questions, Affirmations, Reflections, Summary.
- Make use of EDARS: Express Empathy, Develop Discrepancy, Awareness of Ambivalence, Roll with sustained talk/discord, Support self-efficacy.
- Identify stage of change.
- Engage in the four phases of MI: Engage, Focus, Evoke, and Plan.
- Discuss and offer feedback to help emphasize personal reasons for change.
- MI readiness ruler and decisional balance.
- Develop a "real-life practice challenge" and generate commitment.

Goals for This Session
- Build the alliance between the patient and clinician.
- Orient the patient to what might be expected in treatment sessions, the demands on time to attend, and the time needed for practice between sessions.
- Build on the data gathered during the assessment session by engaging the patient in the Life Movie conversation.
- Explore the domains of the Life Movie, eliciting the patient's core values, and enhancing the patient's motivation for change by:
- Discussing the patient's cannabis use and associations with problems in the Life Movie domains;
- Facilitating the patient's candid reflection on the consequences of cannabis use;
- Exploring the patient's attitudes about change, including ambivalent attitudes;
- Eliciting, acknowledging, and reinforcing the patient's expressions of motivation to change; and
- Affirming any patient expressions of readiness to develop a "change plan," and identifying change strategies.

Session 1 Outline and Overview

First Third

1) Establish Rapport:
   - Welcome the patient.
   - Share the session agenda. Invite items from the patient.
   - Engage in non-problem focused rapport building, exploring areas of the patient's life not directly related to treatment.
2) Review of Progress:
   - Ask the patient for their feelings and thoughts about the assessment session.
   - Engage the patient in a brief review of their progress related to their cannabis use, mental health, and related experiences since the previous session.
     - Did the patient make an effort to stop? Cut down?
     - Did the patient experience any high-risk or tempting situations?
   - Reinforce expressions of motivation.
3) Using the Treatment Information Sheet, discuss treatment expectations.

Second Third

4) Provide a rationale for the Eliciting Life Movie discussion.
   - Ask the patient if they understand the reasons why the activity will be helpful in their treatment.
5) Explore each domain of the life movie, conveying the MI spirit and using MI strategies. Elicit and reflect any problems related to cannabis use and any positive reasons for change including living by core values.
   - Reinforce confidence in efforts to reduce use and/or quit.
6) Summarize the Eliciting Life Movie discussion emphasizing "ambivalence" and readiness.
   - Elicit and reinforce the patient's readiness to change.

Third Third

7) Negotiate Between-Session Challenge
   For the patient ready to make change—
   - Assist the patient in preparing for change.
   - Ask and elicit a commitment from the patient to complete the "Change Plan" before the next session.

Session 1 Outline and Overview | **67**

- If appropriate, discuss and help the patient develop a specific reduction target, "sampling sobriety period," or a stop date (if the patient has not already stopped using).
- Review previous successful experiences at quitting to identify useful strategies.

If time and if appropriate, discuss the following:

- What the patient will do with the current supply of alcohol, cannabis, and/or other substances and paraphernalia.
- How the patient will disclose plans to family and friends.
- How the patient will address problems in maintaining abstinence.
- In the next session, communicate that you will explore what may be effective strategies, skills, and supports for the patient to reach their personal goals.

If the patient is not ready to make changes, ask to have an open discussion about use. The goal is to explore and build awareness regarding the patient's experience of cannabis use. An effective and nonconfrontational approach is to ask the patient to discuss an episode or episodes in the recent past where the patient has used substances. The clinician's role is to be open and reflective and to clarify the pros and cons of the patient's use. The discussion also starts to build situational awareness of factors associated with continued use. What might the patient do with a current supply of cannabis or other substances and paraphernalia? Will the patient disclose risky use to family and friends? How will the patient address problems in maintaining risky use?

For the patient not ready to change—

- Using the MI approach of looking forward, explore what might need to be happening for them to experience concern about their use or motivation to change.
- Explore what they might be willing to examine now; what might be some initial goals for them.
- Discuss the Learning New Coping Strategies (Session 1 handout).
- Assign an appropriate between-session challenge—often it can be selecting something new from the "Learning New Coping Strategies" for them to try.
- Discuss with the patient the rationale and need to adopt or continue doing substance-free pleasurable activities.

8) Summarize and conclude the session.

68 | *Orientation to Clinical Interventions Addressing Cannabis Use Disorder*

Session 1 Protocol with Scripts

Establish Rapport

The clinician welcomes the patient and provides an overview of the first session, in which the clinician further builds rapport and explores domains of the patient's life with the goal of exploring the potential relationship between these domains, the patient's personal goals, and their cannabis use. The clinician invites the patient to provide additional agenda items for the session.

As part of building rapport, the clinician should ask the patient about non-problem areas of the patient's life. For example, the clinician may offer:

> **Clinician (C):** Thank you for coming in today. I realize that you are here to explore your goals around your cannabis use. Before we get to that though, I would love to learn a little more about you. What do you feel it might be important for me to know about you—for example, your interests or ways you spend your time?

Review of Progress

Next, the clinician may ask the patient to express their thoughts regarding the assessment process and any major changes that have occurred since the assessment session. Possible responses from the patient might be—

- Abstinence since entering treatment
- A reduction in cannabis use
- Mood
- Seeking additional treatment or attendance at a mutual-help program
- Conversations about their use with others

The clinician responds empathically, uses opportunities to support the patient's self-efficacy for change, and reinforces expressions of motivation. See two examples below.

> **Clinician (C):** I know the last time you were here, you completed our assessment. I'm wondering how things have been since then.
> **Shirley (S):** After answering all those questions about my using, I am more aware of it than ever! Nothing has changed yet, but I'm thinking about it. My husband has been very supportive.

> **C:** And his support means a lot to you.
> **S:** You bet! He's someone I can count on.
> **C:** That's good to hear. Let's be sure to talk about specific requests you might make of him for support in the future.
> **C:** You arrived a little late for your appointment. Is this a good time for you, or would a different time work better?
> **Doug (D):** No; this is fine. There was a lot of traffic.
> **C:** How are things?
> **D:** Worse. My wife and my son are on my back; they're treating me as if I'm a leper.
> **C:** That sounds like an uncomfortable situation for you.
> **D:** Yeah. I feel like everyone is against me.
> **C:** How has this affected your using?
> **D:** At times I find myself using just to prove that it's not a problem for me!
> **C:** It's more of a problem for them.
> **D:** That's right. I don't think either one really understands me.
> **C:** You'd like them to understand you; that might remove some reasons for getting high.
> **D:** Yeah. At least I wouldn't be trying to get back at them.

Review of Treatment Information Handout

The clinician presents the patient with the Treatment Information Handout. The clinician and the patient review the handout together with the clinician inviting questions and/or input from the patient.

Introduce Eliciting Life Movie and Provide Rationale

The clinician shares the rationale for the Eliciting Life Movie by expressing a desire to learn more about the patient in addition to the assessment with the goal of being able to better collaborate together. The clinician also fosters patient collaboration by asking permission to engage in the activity.

> **Clinician (C):** "I would really like to understand more about you, your everyday life and important aspects of your background including family, other relationships, your work and other passions. This better prepares us to collaborate in ways that make sense for you. How does this sound to you as a place for us to start our work together, so you feel we understand you better and that we are on the same page?"

> **Shirley (S):** Sure but didn't I just answer all those questions in the assessment?
>
> **C:** Yes, you did and those were very helpful. However, those assessment questions tell me when you started using cannabis and how often you smoke and other details about your use. That information is important as it helps me begin to get a picture of your cannabis use and other areas of your life. The discussion I want us to have to day actually builds on that by exploring areas of your life we may not yet have asked about as well as by exploring connections between different areas of your life and your smoking. This conversation is different from the assessment because it helps me to better understand how you think and feel about your life and it also helps you to see how different parts of your life may be related to your smoking.
>
> **S:** OK. That makes sense. I just didn't want to feel like I was telling you everything all over again.
>
> **C:** I get that and I don't want you to feel that way either. Can I ask you—if you do start to feel that way, can you please let me know? I don't think you will but just in case, it is really important that you feel you can give me that feedback.

Engage in Eliciting Life Move Discussion

The clinician progresses through the Eliciting Life Movie handout, covering all of the more relevant domains. The session activity should feel like a conversation that builds or seeks elaboration beyond the initial assessment results. The goals of the activity are not only to build rapport and collaboration, to acknowledge and reflect patient core values and to develop discrepancies between the patient's goals and values and their current behaviors around cannabis use in order to build motivation for change. The clinician should not feel they need to ask every question in the handout but rather, focus on areas that seem more relevant to the patient's life and circumstances and that build on what is known already from the assessment.

Within the Life Movie, as different domains are discussed, it is important for the clinician to help explore connections between those domains and the patient's cannabis use. For example, one area of the patient's cannabis use could include what the patient likes about using or how it

Session 1 Protocol with Scripts | 71

is helpful in navigating one or more of the domains. The clinician listens reflectively to the patient's responses to questions in the Life Movie domains, inserting additional open-ended questions or reflections in an effort to help elucidate connections between the domain and the patient's cannabis use. The goal in making these connections is to acknowledge the importance of the perceived benefits and expressions of potential readiness for change. This is an opportunity to use MI techniques; for example, expressing empathy, identifying discrepancy, eliciting self-motivational statements, rolling with sustain talk/discord, and supporting self-efficacy.

The clinician may also affirm with the patient's active and thoughtful engagement in this process (rolling with resistance)—their willingness to explore these domains and their potential relationship to cannabis use. In keeping with the MI/MET approach, the clinician uses open-ended rather than closed-ended questions. For example, "Did you say you used in unsafe situations?" is a closed-ended question that invites a mere yes or no answer and possible disagreement with the PRS item. Saying instead, "Tell me about using in unsafe situations" invites elaboration and discussion.

Below is an example of what an exchange might look like within the family domain.

Clinician (C): I know you shared that you currently live with your husband and two daughters. I'd like to ask you a bit about your family growing up. What were things in your family like for you growing up?

Shirley (S): They were ok I guess. My mom was a single parent. She worked pretty hard between her job and raising my brother and me. We saw my dad occasionally. I think we had a pretty good childhood.

C: So your mom was there to provide for you and your brother and make sure you were cared for.

S: She was. She really was. I don't think it was always easy but she clearly put us first. I just think it was hard because she worked full time and then, when she got home, she had us to take care. Plus, as a mom, I realized how much she may have felt she missed out on because she was working so much.

C: Being a mom yourself has helped you gain perspective of what it was like for your mom raising you. How do you feel all of this has shaped your own views or beliefs about being a parent?

> **S:** I want to be the best parent I can be for my kids. I want to be able to have the energy to be there for them. I don't want to miss anything.
> **C:** Being there for your kids—really there—present for each day is a core value for you. You really want to be fully engaged with them.
> **S:** Yes, I do and I that is part of why I want to stop smoking. It makes me so tired at the end of the night. I just need a better way to handle stress and worry.

At the end of the Life Movie, the clinician should summarize the key themes voiced by the patient. The summary should be focused on themes that reinforce and help build motivation and a commitment toward change. Ideally, within the summary, the clinician will be able to include the following:

- Problems caused by cannabis use
- Reasons for quitting
- Risk factors for recurrence of use: The clinician points out possible risky situations the patient identified as risk factors for recurrence of use. The clinician explains that risk factors are warning signs that require the patient's attention and indicate a susceptibility to problems associated with cannabis use.

After summarizing the Life Movie discussion for the patient, the clinician asks the patient for reactions and responds to them with empathy.

Summarize the Eliciting Life Movie Discussion
The clinician summarizes the highlights from the Life Movie:

> **Clinician (C):** Let's review and summarize what we've talked about so far. How does that sound to you?
> **Shirley (S):** I'm ready!
> **C:** You stated your evening smoking and drinking are the only way you've found to really relax and reduce stress. But you also acknowledged that the amount of regular drinking and smoking has caused several problems including missing work, difficulty sleeping, and feeling bad about your use. Is there anything else you want to add?
> **S:** No; those are the main problems.

Session 1 Protocol with Scripts | **73**

> **C:** You mentioned one of the main reasons for quitting are because one of the things you value most is your relationship with your kids. You want to be a mom who is really present and engaged with her kids.
>
> **S:** Being the best parent I can be is really important.
>
> **C:** Being a good parent is important to you, and your using gets in the way. You get tired and feel like you just don't have the energy to be fully with them at night.
>
> **S:** It's my biggest reason for wanting to stop.
>
> **C:** When you talk about being a parent and your kids, you get enthusiastic and you light up, but when you talk about your using, you get discouraged and seem a bit down.
>
> **S:** I never noticed that before, but you're right.
>
> **C:** You also stated that high-risk situations for you would include being with others who smoke and seeing them enjoy it. Anything else?
>
> **S:** Not really, but that is a major concern for me as I try to quit. So many people in my life use cannabis or other substances.
>
> **C:** You've already identified how difficult it may be, but you've also identified some very strong reasons for changing your using habits.
>
> **S:** I know it'll be difficult, but I think it's worth it.
>
> **C:** Despite the obstacles, you're ready to take on this challenge.
>
> **S:** I really am.

Elicit and Reinforce the Patient's Readiness to Change

When the patient expresses motivation to change, the clinician acknowledges these expressions, seeks elaboration, and offers reinforcement:

> **Clinician (C):** You said your using has caused problems, including feeling that you have lower energy. Could you tell me about that?
>
> **Pat (P):** I find I mean to do things, but they never get done. It seems that I'm tired all the time. I can't help thinking it's related to my using.
>
> **C:** Related to your using?
>
> **P:** I don't think it affected me when I was young. But now, well, I'm not getting any younger!
>
> **C:** You think using is affecting you more as you get older. You feel less productive.

> **P:** I think that's related to the lower energy. I don't finish my work at my job, and I'm not as creative. And, like we talked about, I am so tired at home that I don't feel I'm there for my kids in the way I want to be.
> **C:** And you think that if you quit using, you will increase your productivity and most importantly, your energy at night, when you are with your family.
> **P:** Yeah.
> **C:** That's important to you. You'd like to regain your energy and time with your children as well as your creativity and productivity at work.
> **P:** I really would like that.

Negotiate Between-Session Challenge
Assist the Patient in Preparing for Change

The clinician assists the patient in preparing to reduce, and if ready, stop using cannabis or other substances by discussing several key issues. At the same time, the clinician needs to be prepared to promote contemplating change regardless of the patient's current stage of change. The goal is to support the patient to identify healthy change and begin to move toward what that would look like for them. The clinician provides the rationale for goal setting by explaining that most successful change processes, including this treatment, begin with a roadmap of where the "driver" (the patient) wants to go and what they would like to accomplish in a specific time period. This helps the patient choose options for achieving the goals. Writing down goals for change also helps measure progress once started. The idea is to plan a journey with the best potential for success within a specific period of time. The journey may change as the process unfolds, but it is critical to identify the goal, the reasons for wanting to achieve it, and specific directions for success—called the "action steps."

Elicit from the patient a commitment to complete the Change Plan on their own as the between-session challenge. The Change Plan would be discussed at the beginning of the next session.

> **Clinician (C):** The "Life Movie" conversation is designed to help you think about what changes in your life you might be willing to make to achieve your goals and have a healthier life overall. For many, the

Session 1 Protocol with Scripts | **75**

> Change Plan focuses on their cannabis use. That said, the Change Plan can apply to identifying any kind of change you want to make for your emotional and physical health. I would like to give you a Change Plan as your between-session challenge. It can be helpful for you to take time to think about these different aspects of making these changes—your specific goals, why they are important, and the specific steps you want to take to achieve them. If you are focusing on cannabis use, it can be helpful to think about times when you haven't used in the past or when you have cut down or quit. In general, it can also be helpful to think about other behaviors you have made changes and what helped you to make those changes. If you get stuck, do not worry. Just do the best that you can. If you feel comfortable, you could talk to a support person about any part of the Change Plan. The goal would be for you to think through each of the questions or prompts and write out your responses. I would ask you to bring the Change Plan to our next session. We will start our next session by checking in on what you came up with. How does that sound to you?

If the patient has not stopped using, the clinician might ask if the patient is willing to select a day to begin the process by reducing use by a specific amount, thus "sampling sobriety" or quitting. The clinician helps the patient consider several alternative stop dates. Topics to consider include what the patient will do with their substance supply and paraphernalia, how the patient will disclose the plan to family and friends (both supporters and those who might sabotage the patient's efforts), and how the patient will address challenges to maintaining abstinence (e.g., sleep difficulties, boredom, anxiety, restlessness) in the first week.

In addition to the Change Plan, another between-session challenge involves engaging in healthy coping strategies. The clinician summarizes the patient's readiness by briefly reviewing the main reasons for and against changing use. Then, regardless of the patient's stage of change, the clinician provides the rationale for adopting or continuing substance-free pleasurable activities and completing the challenge to utilize at least one of the coping strategies from the Learning New Coping Strategies worksheet.

> **Clinician (C):** Regardless of how ready you are to change your use, it is important for you to remain healthy and happy. One of the most proven approaches to feeling good is doing pleasurable activities. These pleasurable activities increase chemicals in the body that make us all feel good and can also help us remain calm through daily stressors like a decision to cut back or not use substances. We have a worksheet I can give you that defines some of the types of activities that can be beneficial. Before I do that though, what activities can you think of that you would enjoy doing and would help release stress?
>
> **Mary (M):** I used to be in a walking group with my friends. I haven't gone in a long time but I really liked it when I kept up with it. I just find it's easier to smoke when I get home from work.
>
> **C:** I get that, but if you continue to try other rewarding or pleasurable activities, they also become easier to do without the negative side effects and possible legal hassles. So, if it's ok with you, I'm going to ask you to commit to doing one or two pleasurable activities in the next week while not using. If it is hard to think of ones you want to do on your own, you could pick from this worksheet (Learning New Coping Strategies handout) and commit to doing them while not using.
>
> **M:** Ok.

The clinician elicits a commitment from the patient that is specific in that it identifies which activities and when the patient is going to do them, including the day of the week and possibly the time of day. The more specific, the better.

Summarize and Conclude the Session

The clinician reviews the session, asks the patient for feedback, responds empathically to their comments, troubleshoots any difficulties, and reminds the patient to review the handouts over the next week.

Note to Clinician: There is much material to successfully address in this session. If in your judgment, the patient is still processing this information and appears undecided or ambivalent, continue the discussion in a second or even third session to address the motivational concerns. To move forward before your patient is ready invites greater resistance to change and a higher likelihood of prematurely leaving services. See the sample language provided.

Below are several high-risk situations that confront people who use and suggestions for coping without using.

Specific Suggestions for Addressing Common High-Risk Situations
Tension Relief and Negative Emotions (e.g., depression, anxiety, nervousness, irritability). Develop relaxation techniques, exercises; write down your feelings or talk to a friend or clinician; do something enjoyable that requires little effort; figure out what you're feeling and whether you can do anything about it.
Anger, Frustration, and Interpersonal Conflict. Try to handle the situation directly rather than hiding your feelings; if appropriate, be assertive; get some release by squeezing a rubber ball, pounding a pillow, or doing some physical activity; write down your feelings or tell them to someone; take deep breaths.
Fatigue and Low Energy. Do muscle relaxations; take a brisk walk; do something enjoyable; eat properly and get enough sleep.
Insomnia. Don't fight being unable to sleep. Get up and do something constructive or relaxing. Read a book, watch television, or do muscle relaxations until you feel sleepy. Remember that no one dies from losing a night's sleep.
Timeout. Read, do a crossword puzzle, prepare a healthy snack, take up a hobby, knit or do other needlework (things you can carry with you for easy access).
Self-Image. Try a new image: get a new haircut or buy new clothes.
Social Pressure. Be aware when others are using. Remember your commitment not to use. Be assertive and request that people not offer you cannabis or substances. If appropriate, ask that they not use around you for a while. If necessary, be prepared to leave the situation, especially when you've recently quit.
Cravings and Urges. The only way to interrupt cravings is to break the chain of responding to them. That is, don't give in. Eventually they will decrease. Do something to distract yourself; use the techniques suggested; breathe deeply; call a friend; go for a walk; move around; time the urge. You'll find that it will disappear like a wave breaking.

The handout related to a change plan is optional and offered to patients ready to think about immediate ways of changing. This will be reviewed with the patient during Session 2.

Session 1. Eliciting Life Movie and Change Plan Handouts

Treatment Information Sheet

I just want to take a few minutes to discuss what you can expect from us and what we expect from you. Over the coming weeks we will be meeting together (individually or as part of a group) and developing goals that are important to you and that seem reasonable for you to achieve in this amount of time. You can set the pace of our work together and let me know if, at any point, I am moving too quickly or slowly. I have some ideas for how we can work together on the goals that you have identified already and hope to share these ideas and help you develop effective skills or build upon abilities you already have but may not recognize or be using to your best advantage. Following are some general guidelines:

- **Regular meetings.** Its most helpful if we can meet on a regular basis, such as weekly. If you need to cancel or are running late, I would appreciate your letting me know with as much advance notice as possible.
- **Commitment to treatment.** Change is difficult for everyone. I ask that you make every effort to participate fully in the treatment by coming to sessions, sharing your thoughts and feelings and frustrations, and staying the course, even if you feel at times our work is not helping as quickly as you would like.
- **Therapy process.** I will do my best to help you feel comfortable, and my hope is that we can work as a collaborative team. Therapy can be uncomfortable at times because different thoughts and feelings may come up. This doesn't mean that treatment isn't working. However, if at any point you find yourself upset with something that has happened, or something I have said or done, I encourage you to bring this up and let me know so that we can continue with a positive connection.
- **Cannabis use.** I ask that you refrain from using cannabis or substances on days or at times when we will be meeting together. I think our discussions together can be most productive and helpful to you if you are not under the influence of any substances.
- **Structure of meetings and practice exercises.** We will meet together for about an hour each time. I will usually want to hear about how things have been going the previous week and anything you want to share about events in your life. Then we will spend some time on a particular topic area or skill that will be helpful to you in accomplishing your goals. I may ask you to do some writing or thinking about

what we have discussed between sessions. It is up to you whether you do this and the goal is not to make you feel pressured or burdened. You will never be graded or judged on what you write. The purpose is to keep the material alive between the times we meet and encourage you to practice or apply some of the new ideas and skills in your real life, as opposed to merely discussing them. If I ask you to write or practice something that you are not comfortable with, please let me know so we can come up with an exercise that is more suitable to you.

- **Questions** you may have regarding treatment, what is involved, my background and role.
- **I look forward to working together with you.**

Eliciting the Life Movie: MI Conversation

Goal

Using motivational interviewing strategies focusing primarily on open-ended questions and reflections, the goal of this conversation is to get a deeper understanding of the person's life. Use open-ended questions and complex and compassionate reflections to promote an initial understanding of the person's values, beliefs, and priorities.

Provide rationale for the life movie

"I would really like to understand more about you, your everyday life & important aspects of your background including family, other relationships, your work and other passions. This better prepares us to collaborate in ways that make sense for you"

Ask permission

"How does this sound to you as a place for us to start our work together, so you feel I understand you better and that we are on the same page?"

General questions to start off with

"What was your last week like?"
"What do you feel has gone well for you recently?"
"What has been troubling for you?
"Has there been anything you'd like to change?"

Areas of Life Movie Exploration

- Family of origin
  Tell me about what it was like for you growing up in your family?
  What are the ways in which your family has influenced your cannabis or drug use?
  What are the ways you feel your early experiences with your family affect you now?
  What are some values you developed growing up that are important to you now?
- Today's significant others
  Tell me about the people in your life that you are closest to.
  What is your relationship with your spouse/partner/significant other like?
  How does your significant other feel about your cannabis and/or drug use?

Orientation to Clinical Interventions Addressing Cannabis Use Disorder

- Work (or school)

    What do you love about your work/school?

    What are the ways work/school causes stress or challenges for you?

    How has your cannabis and/or drug use affected your work/school?

    Ideally, what would you like to be doing for your career?

- Health (physical and mental)

    How do you feel physically? Emotionally?

    What are the ways you try to take care of yourself?

    What are the challenges you are experiencing in your health?

- Life activities that bring personal satisfaction

    What do you enjoy doing? What brings you happiness or joy?

    What is it like for you when you can do these activities more often?

    What gets in the way of being able to pursue these activities regularly?

- Spirituality

    How would you describe your spirituality? By spirituality, we do not necessarily mean a religion but rather what helps ground you, what feeds your spirit and your soul. It could even be a belief or value system that grounds you and helps to give you a sense of purpose and direction in life. What are the ways in which spirituality has been helpful to you in your life?

The conversation does not need to be complicated. Be present and curious. We have offered some questions within each domain that can serve as a starting point. However, do not feel you have to ask these questions if there are others that feel more natural and relevant to your conversation. Use your MI skills to explore deeper into feelings, values, and beliefs.

Clinicians Note: Some of our patients have had very difficult histories and in these early sessions with you, your patient may be only so ready just so far in these disclosures. That is understood and normal. You can respectfully "flag" content for future explorations.

> **Clinician**: "From what you are saying, it sounds like there is a lot going on there. Perhaps at a future time we can revisit that.

Clinician Note: Remember, use deeper/compassionate reflections, affirmations and summaries to better understand patient values, beliefs, areas of internal conflict, drivers of use behavior, etc.

In your final summary, link the key themes, especially values, you hear from your patient to help develop discrepancy and build motivation for change. Through the Life Movie discussion both the patient and you gain a richer understanding of the person's life, some of the drivers for use, and the impact that cannabis use has had. The life movie conversation can add depth and context to these areas that may not have been explored during the clinical intake.

A Change Plan—Optional

It is important to be thinking about the changes you would like to make in your life now. Regarding cannabis use, you may be ready to become abstinent or perhaps you want to decrease your use or even consider changing when or how you use. You likely are thinking about other changes in addition to cannabis use as well. The change plan should be expressed verbally at a minimum but can also be in writing. Ideally, making changes and sticking to commitments works best when you actually write out your goals. Responses to the following questions will create a simple but powerful plan for change.

Change Plan

Person's Name _____

The changes I want to make are—(specifics)

_____

_____

_____

2. The most important reasons I want to make these changes are—

a) _____

b) _____

c) _____

3. The steps I plan to make in changing are—

a) _____

b) _____

c) _____

Learning New Coping Strategies (Handout)

Developing Alternatives ...

You can do many things to stop using. Some may work better than others. Some help you resist the urge to use or avoid tempting situations or satisfy your needs in more constructive ways than using. Expect to try several new strategies and add any that may be helpful for you. Think about what worked when you gave up (e.g., drinking, smoking, using substances) before or when you made other changes in your life. Be kind to yourself as you begin this change process—you're doing something to take care of yourself, and you deserve all the comfort and self-acceptance you can get! Remind yourself that learning and changing inevitably mean giving up old ways and that, in time, you will feel more comfortable. Remember the changes your body and mind went through when you learned to drive, got to know a new person, started a new job, or learned a new skill. Chances are you felt awkward, uncomfortable, silly, dumb, nervous, frustrated, impatient, or anxious, in addition to hopeful, excited, and challenged. What helped you then? How long did it take you to feel relaxed? Did you learn all at once, or were improvement and progress gradual?

First Actions

- Avoid or escape from situations that make you want to use; sometimes this is the easiest and most effective way to resist temptation, especially at the beginning.
- Delay decisions to give in to urges; for example, you could make a decision to wait 15 minutes. Take several deep breaths. Focus on the fresh air entering your lungs, cleansing and nourishing your body. Let out tension with each exhalation.
- Change your physical position. Stand up and stretch, walk around the room, or step outside.
- Carry things to put in your mouth: toothpicks, gum, mints, plastic straws, low-calorie snacks.
- Carry objects to fiddle with: a rubber ball to squeeze, a small puzzle, a pebble, worry beads.
- Have a distracting activity available: a phone call, a crossword puzzle, magazine, book, a postcard to write.

New Activities

- Exercise or take a brisk daily walk. Get your body used to moving; use stairs instead of elevators; park farther away from your destination; walk instead of drive.
- Practice relaxation or meditation techniques regularly (we will have opportunity to learn and practice these techniques later in our work together).
- Take up a hobby or pick up an old hobby you used to enjoy.
- Drink less coffee; switch to decaf; drink herbal teas.
- Engage in an enjoyable activity that is not related to work several times a week.
- Change routines associated with using, at least temporarily; for example, don't turn on the TV when you get home from work; don't spend time with friends who smoke.

New Thoughts

- **Self-talk.** Give yourself a pep talk; remind yourself of your reasons for quitting; remind yourself of the consequences of using; challenge any wavering in your commitment to quit.
- **Imagery and visualization.** Visualize yourself as a nonsmoker, happy, healthy, and in control; imagine your lungs getting pink and healthy; or focus on negative imagery and imagine yourself with cancer, emphysema, unable to breathe, needing constant care. Visualize yourself in a jail made of cannabis or substances, symbolizing the way it controls your life.
- **Thought-stopping.** Tell yourself loudly to STOP; get up and do something else.
- **Distraction.** Focus on something different: the task at hand, a daydream, a fantasy, counting

Social Interactions and Environment

- Remove paraphernalia (pipes, papers, bongs, ashtrays, matches, lighters, etc.) from your home and car.
- Go to places where it's difficult to get high, such as a library, theater, swimming pool, sauna, steam bath, restaurant, and public gatherings (not rock concerts).

Learning New Coping Strategies (Handout) | 87

- Spend time with friends who don't smoke. Enlist support from family and friends. Announce that you've quit; ask people not to offer you cannabis or other substances, to praise you for stopping, to provide emotional support, and not to smoke around you.
- Learn to be appropriately assertive; learn to handle frustration or anger directly instead of by using.

Specific Suggestions for Some Common High-Risk Situations

Below are several high-risk situations that people who use confront, along with suggestions for coping without using.

- **Tension Relief and Negative Emotions** (e.g., depression, anxiety, nervousness, irritability): Develop relaxation techniques, exercise, write down your feelings or talk to a friend or counselor, do something enjoyable that requires little effort, figure out what you're feeling, and whether you can do anything about it.
- **Anger, Frustration, and Interpersonal Conflict:** Try to handle the situation directly rather than hiding your feelings; if appropriate, be assertive; get some release by squeezing a rubber ball, pounding a pillow, or doing some physical activity; write down your feelings or tell them to someone; take deep breaths.
- **Fatigue and Low Energy:** Do muscle relaxations; take a brisk walk; do something enjoyable; eat properly and get enough sleep.
- **Insomnia:** Don't fight being unable to sleep. Get up and do something constructive or relaxing. Read a book, watch TV, or do muscle relaxations until you feel sleepy. Remember that no one dies from losing a night's sleep.
- **Time-Out:** Read, do a crossword puzzle, prepare a healthy snack, take up a hobby, knit or do other needlework (things you can carry with you for easy access).
- **Self-Image:** Try a new image: get a new haircut or buy new clothes.
- **Social Pressure:** Be aware when others are using. Remember your commitment not to use. Be assertive and request that people not offer you cannabis or substances. If appropriate, ask that they not use around you for a while. If necessary, be prepared to leave the situation, especially when you've recently quit.
- **Cravings and Urges:** The only way to interrupt cravings is to break the chain of responding to them. That is, don't give in. Eventually they

will decrease. Do something to distract yourself; use the techniques listed under Thoughts; breathe deeply; call a friend; go for a walk; move around; time the urge, and you'll find that it will disappear like a wave breaking.

This handout is optional and offered to patients ready to think about immediate ways of changing. This will be reviewed with patients during the next session.

Session 2. Enhancing Awareness

Introduction and Session Goals

This session focuses on further building rapport, building situational awareness, setting priorities based on what is important to you and defining the goals and activities of the upcoming therapeutic journey. The clinician continues to use motivational strategies to increase change talk and reduce sustain talk and introduces the process of functional analysis to help the patient build situational awareness of internal and interpersonal factors affecting cannabis use. Clinicians may refer to the eliciting change talk strategies presented in Section 1 and reinforce any successful efforts at initiating change.

As the clinician expresses genuine interest in the patient's well-being since the last meeting, the patient experiences how a therapeutic relationship can provide the necessary support and guidance to push past obstacles and begin to make steps toward change. Through use of, and continued practice, the Cannabis Use Awareness record is a potent strategy, and is a set of patient skills for bringing unconscious thoughts, feelings, and belief into conscious awareness and enables the patient to make conscious decisions about behavior change. This awareness raising process also better enables both patient and clinician to prioritize and individualize treatment sessions. As a result of this exploration, the patient can gain a deeper understanding of their cannabis use, including internal and situational factors associated with use. The patient can receive support, guidance, and assistance in creating a personalized plan for change.

This experience can result in a rich conversation that may span more than one session. Patients often experience strong affect as they explore. Frequently, the clinician instructs the patient to continue completing the Awareness Record handout as a between-session challenge over several weeks and possibly months.

📋 *Clinician Note*: The Awareness Record is a universal strategy throughout all CBT. It can as easily apply to anxiety, depression, or anger management.

Orientation to Clinical Interventions Addressing Cannabis Use Disorder

Clinician Preparation

MET Session 2. Enhancing Situational Awareness	
Materials • Review of Progress • Learning New Coping Strategies and the Change Plan (see Session 1) • Blank copy of the Cannabis/Cannabis use Awareness Record • Plan to Feel Good (optional)	**Session Length** 1 hour **Delivery Method** MET-focused individual therapy with case conference elements
Strategies • OARS (Open-ended questions, Affirmations, Reflections, Summary). • EDARS (Express Empathy, Develop Discrepancy, Awareness of Ambivalence, Roll with sustained talk/discord, Support self-efficacy); identify stage of change. • Discuss and offer feedback to help emphasize personal reasons for change. • Develop "real-life practice challenge" and generate commitment.	
Goals for This Session • If not completed in a previous session, review the patient's Change Plan. • Support the patient to enhance awareness around the internal and situational factors associated with their use, mood, and other behaviors. • Explore how a supporter may help the patient achieve and maintain change.	

Session 2 Outline and Overview

First Third

1) Strengthen Rapport:
   - Welcome the patient, and if present, the support person.
   - Share the session agenda; invite items from the patient.
   - Engage in non-problem focused rapport building, exploring areas of the patient's life not directly related to treatment.
2) Review of Progress:
   - Engage the patient in a brief review of their progress related to their cannabis use, mental health, and related experiences since the previous session. Use the Review of Progress handout as a guide.
     - Did the patient make an effort to stop? Cut down?
     - Did the patient experience any high-risk or tempting situations?
     - If the patient engaged in cannabis use, explore their use event(s) using the *Cannabis/Cannabis use Awareness Record* to assess internal and external triggers, cravings, and consequences.
3) Review of Between-Session Challenge:
   - Review any between-session challenges from the previous session.
     - Did the patient complete the Change Plan? If so, review the Change Plan as a Personalized Reflective Discussion.
     - Did the patient use any strategies from the *Learning New Coping Strategies* handout? Were the strategies successful?

Second Third

4) Provide Rationale:
   - Provide a personalized rationale for the session activity
   - Ask the patient if they understand the reasons why the activity or skill will help build recovery strength.
5) Teach Session Skill:
   - Share relevant information to help the patient understand the skill and provide them the step-by-step approach of how to implement the skill.
     - Describe the components of the Cannabis/Cannabis use Awareness Record to the patient.
6) Clinician-Led Demonstration/Role-Play:
   - Demonstrate the skill by leading the patient in a role-play of the skill to model the way it is done. Be clear and ensure the patient understands the lesson.

92 | *Orientation to Clinical Interventions Addressing Cannabis Use Disorder*

- Have the patient identify one incident of use or craving to use in recent history.
- Walk the patient step-by-step through the Cannabis/Cannabis use Awareness Record using the identified event. Use open-ended questions, reflections, and summaries to gain a deeper understanding of the patient's experiences within each of the components on the awareness record. Respond to any questions the patient has regarding skill application.

7) Patient-Led Practice (Assess Skills Transfer):
- Have the patient lead a role-play or engage in real-play of the skill. If role-playing, encourage the patient to use real-life examples.
  - Have the patient walk through each component of the Cannabis/ Cannabis use Awareness Record, step-by-step and aloud, for two recent incidents of use or craving to use. Ideally, one of these incidents will reflect a situation in which the patient was triggered but did not use.
  - Use open-ended questions, reflections, and summaries as patient completes the activity to elicit a deeper understanding of the patient's experiences.

Third Third

8) Identify Real-World Application:
- Help the patient to identify real-life situations in which they can apply the skill.

9) Negotiate and Prepare Between-Session Challenge:
- Elicits from the patient how and where in their life they can apply awareness raising and other coping skills they learned in session in their daily life.
- The patient is encouraged to continue practicing awareness raising by complete the *Cannabis/Cannabis use Awareness Record.*
- Ensure that the challenge is specific and support the patient by rehearing their application of the new skill—What will they do? When will they do it? How often will it be done (i.e., at least two times)?

10) Elicit Commitment:
- Elicit commitment for completion of the between-session challenge at least two times before the next session.
- Use MI strategies as needed to strengthen commitment.

11) Summarize and Conclude:
- Present a session summary of what has been covered during the session and elicit the patient's feedback.
  - What did the patient learn through the awareness raising activity?
  - Use the information generated in completing the *Cannabis/ Cannabis use Awareness Record* to discuss relevant skills and associated treatment sessions.
  - Explore supporter involvement.
- Conclude the session.

Session 2 Protocol with Scripts

Strengthen Rapport

The clinician welcomes the patient and provides an overview of the second session, in which the clinician further develops and reinforces the patient's change process and helps the patient to enhance their awareness around cannabis use. The clinician invites the patient to provide additional agenda items for the session.

Review of Progress: Examining the Patient's Recent Experiences

The clinician uses the Review of Progress handout to support a brief review of the patient's progress in key domains since the last session, including cannabis use, mental health symptoms, and related wellness areas.

The clinician asks the patient to describe their recent experiences with cannabis or other substances:

- Did the patient stop use since the previous session?
- Did the patient make an effort to stop?
- Was the patient confronted with any high-risk or tempting situations?
- What strategies did the patient use? Did the patient try any of the strategies in Learning New Coping Strategies? Were they successful?
- Were there any instances when the patient effectively handled a "hot" situation (i.e., very high risk)?

As the patient talks, the clinician's objective is to elicit information and to use that information to provide reflections, express empathy, identify discrepancies, elicit self-motivational statements, and roll with sustain talk/discord. See the sample language provided.

> **Shirley (S):** Well, I've almost completely stopped using since our last session.
>
> **Clinician (C):** You seem very pleased with yourself! How did you do that?
>
> **S:** Right after the last session I kept thinking about how with smoking cannabis has kept me from doing the things I want to do. I really want to be a teacher, and I realized that as long as I kept smoking, I would always feel bad. So I went home and smoked one last time, then flushed all the remainder of my stash down the toilet. During the last week, I've wanted to smoke several times, but I didn't.

> **C:** What did you do when you felt like smoking?
> **S:** Well, I talked to my husband. I read about that in the handout you gave me last week.

Review of Between-Session Challenge: Assessing the Patient's Progress and Readiness to Proceed

The clinician asks the patient how they feel about the previous session and responds to concerns, addressing any comments or questions about the Change Plan or Learning New Coping Strategies activities. If the patient has completed the Change Plan, they are asked to read it and discuss the choices. The clinician reviews the Change Plan as a Personalized Reflective Discussion. Specifically, the clinician reaffirms the patient's written statements, provides feedback and discusses adjustments (e.g., is the patient setting unrealistically high standards that may set them up for failure? has the patient identified salient reasons for wanting to make changes in cannabis or other cannabis use?), evokes the personal meaning of the change plan elements to the patient, enhances motivation and resolves ambivalence about change, and reinforces the patient's commitment to their goals. The clinician photocopies the agreement as a record of the patient's goals.

The clinician must be vigilant about maintaining the patient's level of motivation for change and engagement in treatment. If the Change Plan was not completed, the clinician elicits the patient's reasons for not engaging in the change process at home to assess, for example, ambivalence, other obstacles, or both. Strong ambivalence may be manifested in nonverbal behavior (e.g., level of comfort, reluctance to establish treatment goals). If the reason appears to be ambivalence, the clinician uses MI strategies described in Section 1, asking open-ended questions, reflecting, etc. Specific MI strategies depend on the nature of the sustain talk and the assessed stage of change (i.e., precontemplation or contemplation). If the patient still is uncertain or unaware of any need to change, the clinician can focus the discussion on reflections, normalizing uncertainty, reviewing health risks again, asking future-oriented questions, or imagining extreme questions (e.g., "What would it take or what would have to happen for you to want to make a change?").

If there is awareness of a need to change, the clinician can use the Decisional Balance form (Session 8 handout) and reemphasize the benefits and risks. This technique can help the patient develop further discrepancy and swing the balance toward change. If the lack of follow-through was the result of more simple obstacles such as being too busy or forgetting, the clinician can brainstorm solutions and have the patient choose and commit to the choice. (One method for problem solving—I-SOLVE—will be presented in Session 6.) Forgetfulness is a common challenge for persons in treatment. A strategy that can help a patient remember the between-session practice is to encourage use of a smart-phone calendar, typing in the assigned challenge using the alarm function. Regardless of why the assigned challenge was not completed, the clinician should reinforce the need to complete the practice work to achieve goals.

Provide Rationale

The clinician shares the rationale for the awareness raising activity by describing how and why building personal awareness is essential in the change process. The clinician also personalizes the rationale by sharing how personal awareness skills will support the patient's own recovery process.

Clinician (C): I want to explain how we think about cannabis use. When someone has used cannabis or other drugs over time, we think of it as a negative habit, similar to other habits like biting your nails or eating junk food. We try to help the person figure out what has been keeping the habit going. This way, if someone wants to stop the habit and knows what is keeping it going, they can use this information to help stop it. Does thinking of it as a habit make sense to you?

Shirley (S): Completely! It's like to just start smoking without even thinking about it the second I walk into the door after work.

C: Yes, and after a while of smoking in similar situations, just being in those situations can make that person feel like smoking. We call that a trigger. It could be anything about the situation like the time of day, whom you're with, or even something like a type of music. You have mentioned some things that sound like triggers for you. What do you think some of your triggers are?

S: Well definitely the time of day. In fact, I even start thinking about smoking as I'm pulling out of the school parking lot and heading home from the day. On the weekends, I smoke a lot with my close group of friends. So just getting together in the evening to hang out is a pretty strong trigger for me.

C: For you, some of the external aspects of a situation are strong triggers. Another type of trigger can be how someone is feeling. Some people say that they feel more like using cannabis or other drugs when they are feeling badly—like feeling bored, nervous, or angry. They say that using is a way of trying to cope with the bad feelings. Some people especially feel like using cannabis or other drugs when they are happy or excited. Does this part of it—someone using to affect how they feel—make sense to you?

S: You know, I think that my desire to smoke after work is probably in large part due to having such stressful work days. There is very little down time in my job.

C: Stress is a very common trigger. I wonder whether you sometimes find yourself having certain thoughts or ideas about your use as these can also lead to urges to use. These might be thoughts like, "My friends will think I'm boring if I don't smoke," or "I deserve this after the day I've had."

S: I often feel like my thoughts are my own worst enemy, and I really do believe that I deserve some type of reward for all the hard work of the day."

C: Based on all the triggers you just identified, this shows how cannabis use doesn't just suddenly happen. Usually there are things going on around a person or in the way someone is thinking or feeling that affect whether or not they make a choice to use. Knowing what affects your own use gives you more power to decide whether or not to use. And looking at both the pros and cons of what happens after you use also helps you understand why you use and helps you make decisions about what you want to do in the future.

Figuring out the factors that lead to your own cannabis use, like the time of day, being around friends, work stress, and your own thoughts, gives you more power to decide what to do next, and to break the habit, if you want to. That's the main thing that we are trying to do in this treatment—to give you a lot of different ways to take back control instead of being under the control of the habit.

98 | *Orientation to Clinical Interventions Addressing Cannabis Use Disorder*

Teach Session Skill

Introduce the patient to the Cannabis/Cannabis use Awareness Record. Provide them a blank copy and retain one for yourself. Describe the awareness record by walking the patient through each column in the awareness record and explaining each component in depth, checking in to assess the patient's understanding along the way.

The components of the Cannabis/Cannabis use Awareness Record include:

- **Trigger.** Triggers here refer to external and situational characteristics that stimulate a craving for use and make it more likely that a patient will engage in cannabis use. Identifying external triggers involves pinpointing the many external stimuli that may be present in a given situation.
- **Thoughts, Feelings, and Beliefs.** These internal experiences often serve as triggers for use. The way people respond to external events are largely shaped by the thoughts people have about those events, the feelings that are generated, and the belief systems that are activated.
- **Intensity of Craving.** The experience of a craving of urge takes different forms for different people. It is helpful to understand patient's craving experience and the intensity of the craving. To capture the intensity of a craving, cravings are rated on an intensity scale from 0 (not at all intense) to 10 (extremely intense).
- **Behavior.** Behavior refers to the action(s) taken in response to urges and cravings which are triggered by external events and internal thoughts, feelings, and beliefs. Behavioral responses often serve to decrease or lessen the intensity of the craving and can range from healthy and helpful behaviors to unhealthy and less helpful behaviors.
- **Positive Results.** Whether a person's behavior results in use or not use, there are potentially both positive and negative outcomes. Here we explore the good things that came out of the behavioral choice.
- **Negative Results.** In addition to exploring positive outcomes, we explore the not as good things that resulted from the behavior response.

Clinician-Led Demonstration/Role Play

The clinician demonstrates the awareness raising activity by walking the patient through a detailed exploration of one incident of use or craving to use in recent history. The patient identifies the situation and the clinician uses core MI skills (open-ended questions, reflection, and summaries) to gain a deeper understanding of the patient's experiences. It is important to probe enough within each component of the awareness record to gain a comprehensive, thorough understanding of the incident. The clinician will most often need to ask multiple follow-up questions within each element to dive deeper into the details of the patient's experience. The clinician checks in with the patient as to their experience in completing the awareness raising activity and addresses any questions regarding how to complete the activity.

Patient-Led Practice (Assess Skills Transfer)

The patient then takes the lead at walking the clinician through each component of the awareness record for up to two recent incidents in which the patient did use and was triggered but did not use. The purpose for focusing on an event in which the patient did not use is to bring understanding to the factors that led to the choice to not use in a given situation. During the patient's application of the awareness raising activity, the clinician affirms the patient's skill application and offers follow-up questions to encourage the patient to explore the incident more thoroughly.

Identify Real-World Application

The clinician helps the patient to think through opportunities for how they might continue strengthening their awareness around cannabis use through additional awareness raising practice throughout the week. These might be situations in which the patient might benefit from "slowing down" their automatic behavioral response to use when having cravings. Relatedly, the patient may consider using the awareness raising activity before a potentially triggering event to prepare for how they may experience the trigger and plan for health choices. The patient may also consider reflecting back on incidents in which they did use to bring clarity to the multiple factors that led to their behavioral response and the outcomes of that response.

Negotiate and Prepare Between-Session Challenge

The exploration of real-world skill application is a natural transition into negotiation of a between-session challenge. The clinician encourages the patient to continue reviewing the materials handed out at this session and last week's session. The clinician asks the patient where, when, and how they can apply awareness raising in their daily life, working to generate a

100 | *Orientation to Clinical Interventions Addressing Cannabis Use Disorder*

specific plan for continued practice of the awareness record and completing one of the newly developed specific steps in the Change Plan. If the patient is uncertain which one to choose, discuss options and indicate that one good initial choice would be the step the patient is most ready to complete. For any identified between-session challenges, the clinician works with the patient to ensure that they know what they will do, when they will do it, and how often it will be done, mentally rehearsing its application in their daily life. Most patients benefit from writing down this plan somewhere accessible to them, to also serve as an ongoing reminder.

Elicit Commitment
The clinician explores the patient's commitment for completing the between-session challenge and uses MI strategies as needed to assess and strengthen commitment. The clinician also asks the patient to think through any potential obstacles to their skills practice and works with them to identify solutions and activate resources as needed to support their skill application.

Summarize and Conclude the Session
The clinician reviews the session, asks the patient for feedback, responds empathically to their comments, and troubleshoots any difficulties. Specifically, the clinician will want to explore the patient's response and perceived utility of learning the awareness raising activity. Through completing the Cannabis/Cannabis use Awareness Record with several different incidents, the clinician begins to identify cannabis use patterns and common challenges the patient experiences that increase their likelihood of using. The clinician engages the patient in their identification of use patterns and associated areas of difficulty (e.g., boredom, not asserting oneself, lack of coping skills to manage strong emotions).

With this information, the clinician and patient should also discuss the likely scenarios for future treatment sessions. At this point, the clinician reminds the patient they will be meeting for 4–10 more sessions (in most cases) and that they have some flexibility as to what they can do for those meetings. The clinician should suggest the kinds of skill topics they might cover based on what they've learned about the patient's use experiences thus far, and seek input from the patient about how to spend the remaining sessions. Explain that the sessions focused on skills are meant to provide the patient with new tools for being able to make the important changes they have begun. See the sample language.

Session 2 Protocol with Scripts | **101**

> **Clinician**: I appreciate being able to get to know you over these few weeks and admire your courage in undertaking the important goals you have started to work on regarding your use of cocaine. We will be meeting for 6 to 10 more weeks, and what I'd like to do is help you learn some new skills that are meant to help you with keeping your resolve. One of these sessions focuses on learning a skill called mindfulness, which can be very helpful for people trying to make a change the way you are. I also want to help you with the problem you described where you said it's sometimes difficult to say no when your friends offer you cannabis or invite you to a party. There are some other tools I want to share with you that I think will be useful. How do these ideas sound to you? Any questions so far?

Session 2. Enhancing Situational Awareness Handouts

Review of Progress and Between-Session Challenges

Directions: Use the table below to support weekly progress review in key domains relevant to the patient's cannabis use and overall well-being. This table can also be used to review the between-sssion challenges.

Domain	Sun	Mon	Tues	Wed	Thu	Fri	Sat
Physical activity							
Sleep							
Diet							
Pleasure/Replacement activities							
Mastery activities							
Work/School							
Mood states							
Tobacco/Nicotine							
Cannabis							
Marijuana							
Other drugs							
Between-session challenge							

Alcohol/Cannabis use Awareness Record

As a way to increase awareness about your patterns of use, use this form to identify the kinds of situations, thoughts, feelings, and consequences that are associated with your cannabis/cannabis use.

Clinician Note: *The awareness record can be applied all manner of concerns such as mood, anxiety, anger etc.*

Describe Incident

Trigger	Thoughts, Feelings, and Beliefs	Intensity of Craving	Behavior	Positive Results	Negative Results
(What sets me up to be more likely to use cannabis or drugs?)	(What was I thinking? What was I feeling? What did I tell myself?)	Low– high, 1–10	(What did I do then?)	(What good things happened?)	(What bad things happened?)

Date and Time:_____

Alcohol/Cannabis use Awareness Record Example

As a way to increase awareness about your patterns of use, use this form to identify the kinds of situations, thoughts, feelings, and consequences that are associated with your cannabis/cannabis use. Below is an example of how the form might be used.

Describe Incident: Spent evening with my friend smoking weed and drinking beer.

Trigger	Thoughts, Feelings, and Beliefs	Intensity of Craving	Behavior	Positive Results	Negative Results
(What sets me up to be more likely to use cannabis or drugs?)	(What was I thinking? What was I feeling? What did I tell myself?)	Low– high, 1–10	(What did I do then?)	(What good things happened?)	(What bad things happened?)
Friend called and invited me to get high with him. Nothing else to do.	"I want to reward myself." "I'm bored." "Felt good about going 15 days without using, so felt OK about getting high today."		Went out with friend and used.	Had fun. Felt good to get high, having gone 15 days without.	Broke the 15-day abstinence (although wasn't too worried about this). Didn't get as much done. Didn't feel as healthy.

Orientation to Clinical Interventions Addressing Cannabis Use Disorder

Planning to Feel Good (Optional)

I am doing this right now.	I used to do this and I want to try again.	I have never done this and I want to try.

Session 3. Learning Assertiveness

Introduction and Session Goals

During Session 3, the clinician first provides a rationale by explaining the critical need for effective communication in general to get needs met and more specifically in trying to change substance using behaviors. The clinician then discusses the different communication styles illustrating effective and less effective communication. Through a series of engaging interactive discussions and role plays the clinician helps the patient identify their own style of communication and the communication style of family and friends. The clinician then assists the patient with practicing ways to be assertive in a variety of everyday situations and in challenging situations they are facing while moving toward recovery. The clinician helps the client realize the difference between their expression of a definite more assertive "no" and one where the client feels less definite and uncertain. The patient learns about effective and ineffective communication and develops increased awareness of their own communication and those of their social network. Patients become familiar with expressing their needs assertively in a variety of real-life situations and practices in and out of sessions. Patients commit to practicing assertiveness and assertive refusal in the upcoming weeks.

Clinician Preparation

CBT Session 3. Learning Assertiveness	
Materials	**Total Time**
• Review of Progress	1 hour
• Communication Styles Handout	**Delivery Method**
• Between-Session Challenge: Assertiveness	CBT-focused individual or group therapy

Strategies
- OARS (Open-ended questions, Affirmations, Reflections, Summary)
- EDARS (Express Empathy, Develop Discrepancy, Awareness of Ambivalence, Roll with Sustained Talk/discord, Support self-efficacy); identify stage of change
- Demonstrate skill, role-play and give feedback
- Handouts utilized to focus the session helping to transfer knowledge and skill
- Develop "real-life practice challenge" and generate commitment

Goals for This Session

Enhance the patient's understanding of different styles of communication and teach ways to express one's views and feelings. The following communication styles are discussed:
1. Passive
2. Passive-Aggressive
3. Aggressive
4. Assertive
- Role-play scenarios of relevance to the patient and practice these different communication styles.
- Identify a current situation or relationship that could benefit from the patient's communicating in a more assertive way; practice.

Source: Monti, Abrams, Kadden, & Cooney, 1989

Session 3 Outline and Overview

First Third

1) Strengthen Rapport:
   - Welcome the patient, and if present, the support person.
   - Share the session agenda; invite items from the patient.
   - Engage in non-problem focused rapport building, exploring areas of the patient's life not directly related to treatment.
2) Review of Progress:
   - Engage the patient in a brief review of their progress related to their cannabis use, mental health, and related experiences since the previous session. Use the Review of Progress handout as a guide.
     - Did the patient make an effort to stop? Cut down?
     - Did the patient experience any high-risk or tempting situations?
     - If the patient engaged in cannabis use, explore their use event(s) using the *Cannabis/Cannabis use Awareness Record* to assess internal and external triggers, cravings, and consequences.
3) Review of Between-Session-Challenge:
   - Review any between-session challenges from the previous session.
     - Did the patient complete the Situational Awareness Record? If so, review the Record: triggers, beliefs, cravings, behaviors, pros and cons.
     - Discuss the different situations recorded and see if patterns emerge to the reactions—note any signs of particular internal or external triggers that can be addressed through better communication to self or others.
     - Did the patient use any strategies from the session one *Learning New Coping Strategies* handout? Were the strategies successful?

Second Third

4) Provide Rationale:
   - Provide a rationale for assertive communication in general and assertive refusal skill. Ask the patient if they understand the reasons why the activity or skill will help build recovery strength.
5) Teach Session Skill:
   - Share relevant information to help the patient understand the skill and provide them the step-by-step approach of how to implement the skill.

110 | *Orientation to Clinical Interventions Addressing Cannabis Use Disorder*

- Engage and elicit patient communication styles:
  - Make an offer to the patient to reveal the patient's communication style.
  - Example: Offer the patient a food you know they dislike or even despise or ask them to lend you $20. The objective is to make a request that you know the patient can refuse or say "no" to without internal conflict or guilt.
  - How do they express their refusal?
  - Take note to discuss after communication styles lesson.
- Define aggressive, passive, passive-aggressive, and assertive communication.

6) Discuss benefits of assertiveness:
  - Increases likelihood person will achieve goal or objective.
  - Increases chance the person will feel more satisfied with a situation.

7) Clinician-Led Demonstration/Role-Play:
  - Model different styles of communication.
  - Identify scenarios exemplifying these styles.
  - Develop role-play exercise of relevance for patient.
  - Practice assertiveness in the context of role-play. Identify obstacles and barriers.

Third Third

8) Identify Real-World Application:
  - Help the patient to identify real-life situations in which they can apply the skill.

9) Elicit Commitment:
  - Negotiate and Prepare Between-Session Challenge: Review the patient's communication style and the skill of assertiveness.
  - Hand out Between-Session Challenge: Assertiveness, and ask the patient to commit to a weekly between-session real challenge using assertive communication in several upcoming situations.
  - Discuss the real-life "assertive" situation details—when, with whom, where.
  - If time allows, practice the between-session challenge to help client prepare.

Session 3 Protocol with Scripts

Strengthen Rapport
The clinician welcomes the patient and provides an overview of the third session, where the clinician further strengthens recovery skills through understanding and learning most effective types of communication. The clinician invites the patient to provide additional agenda items for the session.

Review of Progress: Examining the Patient's Recent Experiences
Review the current status regarding alcohol or cannabis use and the goals of change or abstinence. The clinician uses the *Review of Progress* handout to support a brief review of the patient's progress in key domains since the last session, including cannabis use, mental health symptoms, and related wellness areas.

The clinician asks the patient to describe their recent experiences with cannabis or other substances:

- Did the patient stop use since the previous session?
- Did the patient make an effort to stop?
- Was the patient confronted with any high-risk or tempting situations?
- What strategies did the patient use? Did the patient try any to see what triggers were most inviting to use and if so did they try any of the strategies in the handout on Learning New Coping Strategies? Were they successful?
- Were there any instances when the patient effectively handled a "hot" situation (i.e., very high risk)?

Again, and throughout the model when the patient talks, the clinician's objective is to elicit information and to use that information to provide reflections, express empathy, identify discrepancies, elicit self-motivational statements, and roll with sustain talk/discord.

Review of Between-Session Challenge: Assessing the Patient's Progress and Readiness to Proceed
Inquire about any between-session practice challenge. Did the patient find recording situations in the awareness record helpful? If appropriate, praise the patient's efforts accomplishing the between-session challenge

Orientation to Clinical Interventions Addressing Cannabis Use Disorder

and maintaining changes or abstinence. If the patient did not complete the situational awareness record—ask them what happened—and why they did not complete the challenge. If they state that they did not understand the challenge—it is fine to go ahead and do it with them but emphasize their taking the lead in the activity. Holding patients accountable in a clear manner but one that is not off putting is essential to potent CBT. Thus, the clinician again reaffirms that between-session challenges are an expectation of work in treatment and explains the reason for the between session again. Elicit a confirmation of patient if their understanding. Then have the patient do the challenge with you now to demonstrate the importance.

Provide Rationale. Introduce the current topic involving styles of communication.

> **clinician (c):** Have you ever been in a situation where you wanted to tell someone how you felt but weren't able to for some reason? Can you explain to me what made it difficult? Did not saying anything help or hurt the situation or your feelings in general?

What about having a time where you felt really upset or angry but waited to tell the person so that when you finally spoke up you ended up saying a lot of negative things that you later regretted? Many of us can identify with both of these kinds of situations.

Provide the Rationale

Provide the rationale for the benefit to use assertive communication to get needs met and the need for assertive refusal skills to strengthen the path toward recovery. Sample language follows:

> **Clinician (C):** Communication is much more complex than it seems, so we all struggle with miscommunication. This is because in any conversation there is a speaker and a listener, and both verbal and nonverbal expressions are used to determine the meaning. The listener has a filter already in place to influence and interpret what is seen and heard. Therefore, to be clear and have our needs met, we all must rely on practiced and effective communication strategies.

There is an extra burden to use effective communication when trying to change any behavior, especially cannabis use behaviors. The repetitive nature of negative habits increases the likelihood there will be an increase in situations to use along with associated thoughts and feelings. Sample language follows:

> **Clinician (C):** As one's use increases, there's a funneling effect or narrowing of your own thoughts and coping strategies. Your nonuse coping thoughts like your circle of non-using friends gets smaller, while your circle of using friends gets bigger. This increases recurrence of use risk.
>
> When was the last time you celebrated without using? When was the last time you handled a negative situation, feeling, or thought without using?

Affirm any instances of nonuse and support these as assertive/refusal communication skills that are critical to maintaining recovery; for example:

> **Clinician (C):** Given the increased risk of using thoughts, behaviors, and social pressure, the best initial step is to avoid situations involving cannabis and/or other drug use. This is not always possible, and so it's important you feel comfortable refusing cannabis and other drugs when offered them in social situations. You also need to be able to tell yourself it's okay not to use and to cope or celebrate in other ways. Knowing good strategies and practicing those strategies will help your ability to refuse cannabis and other drugs.

Teach Session Skill
Begin the in-session practice of assertive communication with real situations to evoke natural skill level for being direct with refusal.

> **Clinician (C):** "Can you tell me a food you dislike and would not eat?"

Pressure the patient to eat the disliked food and see how they respond. Use any strategy necessary to try to get the patient to accept it, such as you made

114 | *Orientation to Clinical Interventions Addressing Cannabis Use Disorder*

it just for them and in a way it would not taste like that food, etc. Discuss the patient's response and how clear they were about refusing the food.

Incorporate the patient's communication style from the discussion above. Ask about the patient's understanding of the term assertiveness or assertive communication. Discuss whether and when the patient has been successfully assertive.

Teach Communication Styles

Define different styles of communication. The clinician identifies types of communication and asks the patient to define their understanding of them. Next the clinician provides definitions of each style and compares them to the patient's definitions, not to evaluate, but to ensure accurate understanding. The clinician clarifies any areas of misconception according to the definitions below.

Passive communication: With this style, a person is often unable to or fearful of expressing themselves directly. The individual tends to acquiesce or go along with what another person wants. The person may not feel entitled to their opinions or believes the other person will not listen or care. An example: Someone is asked to attend an event for work that is inconvenient, and rather than asking to be excused or to reschedule, the person agrees immediately. With this form of communication, the individual does not express their needs and wants in a clear way.

Passive-aggressive communication: With passive-aggressive communication or behavior, someone may appear to agree or go along with a plan of action but engages in other behavior that conveys true feelings. For example, a woman asks her husband to attend a family gathering. He is not enthusiastic about family events and has somewhat difficult relationships with some of his wife's family members. He would much prefer to stay home and watch a tennis match on television. Instead of telling his wife his feelings, he agrees to go to the family party and arranges to meet her there after he completes some errands. He ends up being "held up" with some of his chores and arrives at the party two hours late. This would be considered passive aggressive because on the surface he seemed willing to go along with his wife's wishes, but by arriving late he conveyed his real preference indirectly. Passive-aggressive communication can be difficult to identify because often people are not aware of their behaviors. See the example provided.

> Yes, that sounds just great. I want to go the party, but I really have a few things I must do beforehand so why don't I meet you there? It starts at 3, right? Oh, 2. Okay, see you then.

Aggressive communication: When someone behaves or communicates in an aggressive manner, the person tends to ignore the rights or feelings of others. That person prioritizes their own experiences and needs above those of others. The person may communicate through loud tones, yelling, threats, and intimidation. They may be insensitive to how a message is conveyed to others. This individual may not be willing to hear how someone else feels or wants in a particular situation. A fairly benign example: A group of friends go out to dinner and begin talking about their children. One member of the group proceeds to comment and give unsolicited advice to each of the parents about all the mistakes they are making and how they are damaging their children through their behavior. See another example below.

> I hope you understand that you are working for me. I am in charge. You'd better be willing to stay late or come in early if I tell you to, and I don't want to see any mistakes, or you won't be seeing a paycheck too much longer. Is that clear enough?

Assertive communication: With assertive communication, a person expresses thoughts, feelings, or needs directly and clearly but is respectful and sensitive to the rights and feelings of others. This person does not yell or intimidate, but they also do not sugarcoat a message to the point of meaninglessness. An example appears below.

> When you tell me I'm stupid or will never accomplish anything important, that makes me feel hurt. In the future, I ask that you communicate in a more constructive and supportive way, or I'll have to consider how to continue in this relationship.

Assertive people decide what they want, plan a constructive way to involve others, and then act on the plan. It can be very effective to state one's feelings or opinions and request the changes one would like from others without

116 | *Orientation to Clinical Interventions Addressing Cannabis Use Disorder*

being threatening, demanding, or negative. In sum, assertiveness means recognizing one's right to decide what to do in a given situation rather than giving in to others. Assertiveness recognizes the following rights:

- To inform others of your opinion
- To inform others of your feelings in a way that is not hurtful
- To ask others to change their behavior that affects you
- To accept or reject what others say to you or request from you

Next, the clinician discusses the patient's understanding of the terms discussed and asks for examples that could be shared of each style. The examples could be situations the patient has experienced, heard about, or imagined. The clinician also asks the patient to identify how they speak to themself (self-talk). For example: "Given that most of us are critical when we make mistakes, it is also important to realize the style of communication we use for self-talk and how practicing assertiveness with ourselves will likely lead to a better feeling inside and perhaps an increased desire to change."

Explain the benefits of assertiveness. The clinician explains the benefits of assertiveness; for example, as below.

> Assertiveness is the most effective way to let others know what's going on or what effect their behavior has. By expressing themselves, assertive people resolve uncomfortable feelings that otherwise build up. Because being assertive often results in correcting a source of stress and tension, it can lead to feeling more in control of life. Assertive people do not feel like victims of circumstances. However, their goals can't be met in all situations; it isn't possible to control how another person will respond. Nevertheless, behaving assertively has two benefits: it increases the chances goals will be met, and it makes people feel better about their role in the situation.

Introduce Skill Guidelines: The clinician explains that the guidelines in the Assertiveness handout can help the patient become assertive.

> **Take a moment to think before you speak.** What did the other person do or say? Try not to assume the other person's intentions. Don't assume that they know your mind. Plan the most effective way to

make statements. Be specific and direct. Address the problem without bringing in other issues. Be positive. Don't put others down; blaming others makes them defensive and less likely to hear your message.

Pay attention to your body language: eye contact, posture, gestures, facial expression, and tone of voice. Make sure your words and your expression communicate the same message. To get your point across, speak firmly and be aware of your appearance.

Be willing to compromise. Let others know you're willing to work things out. No one has to leave the situation feeling as if they have lost everything. Try to find a way for everyone to win. Give others your full attention when they reply, try to understand their views, and seek clarification. If you disagree, have a discussion. Don't dominate or submit to others. Strive for equality in the relationship. If you feel you're not being heard, restate your assertion. Persistence and consistency are necessary parts of assertiveness. Changing the way you respond requires effort. The first step is to become aware of habitual responses and make an effort to change.

The most difficult situations in which to respond assertively are those that may end with negative consequences. Examine the thoughts that prevent you from acting assertively with others and yourself ("My boss will fire me if I can't work overtime because I have my counseling session.") This examination uses many skills discussed in other sessions:

- **Determine the thought or fear.** What am I afraid will happen? What's the worst that could happen?
- **Assess the probabilities.** How likely is the negative consequence?
- **Evaluate the catastrophe.** What would happen if the worst occurred? Would it really be so terrible?
- **Identify the rules.** What assumptions and beliefs govern feelings?

Clinician-Led Demonstration/Role Play

The clinician and patient role-play a situation in which the clinician plays a person refusing the offer of substances from a friend; the patient plays the person offering the substance or cannabis. The clinician models passive, aggressive, passive-aggressive, and assertive responses. After each response, the clinician asks the patient to identify the behavior and determine the success of that approach.

Patient-Led Practice (Assess Skills Transfer)

Guide the patient to lead a role-play exercise with a relevant and current situation. After discussing and reviewing the different styles of communication, the clinician asks the patient to identify a current problem or situation where there is difficulty communicating needs in an effective manner. The situation might be one involving alcohol or cannabis use, such as being able to resist or refuse offers to use at a party, or from a long-time smoking buddy. It could also involve the patient expressing feelings in an important relationship. If the patient has difficulty generating a role-play scenario, the clinician can suggest some general topics or relationships, or a specific idea based on knowledge about the patient where assertive communication could be of benefit. The clinician gives the patient the Assertiveness: Between-Session Challenge handout and asks the patient to try at home.

Identify Real-World Application

Summarize the assertive communication session. Then, get a specific commitment for completion of the between-session work and prepare for the next session. The summary is an opportunity to reinforce the patient's personal awareness and assertiveness refusal skill learning to increase a sense of self-efficacy. The preparation statement could sound like the following:

Clinician (C): "Today we covered a lot of information about your use, what sets you up to use, and communication skills that are helpful in working toward your recovery goals. You most frequently reported your triggers are likely to be [___] and that knowing these triggers ahead of time and avoiding certain places and people has helped increase successful experiences without use." (Summarize the types of triggers: the time of day, the situation, the feelings and thoughts—positive and/or negative). "But as you've stated, you can't avoid all people, places, or situations all the time, and trying to do is also stressful. As today's lesson has demonstrated, it's possible to practice assertive refusal skills that allow you to be clear on how to get your needs met, and to refuse in ways others will understand.

"For example: Today you practiced refusal skills in several situations with others and in self-talk to help you gain confidence in saying no and not feel guilty or confused during risky times or events in the upcoming weeks.

> "I wonder if you can tell me how you would use the assertive refusal skills in the next weeks to help you meet your goals?"

Negotiate and Prepare Between-Session Challenge

Hand out the between-session challenge Assertiveness worksheet. Ask the patient to use assertive communication for self-talk and with others when confronted by a trigger to use (negative thought, feeling, celebration, or social pressure situation).

> "During the next week, I would like you to practice using the Knowledge Is Power worksheet and your assertive refusal skills, similar to how we did today.
> "How does that sound to you?"

If the patient says it will be hard, try to help remove any obstacles.

Elicit Commitment

If the patient agrees, say, "I am asking you to commit to filling out the sheet and using your refusal skills in two situations between sessions." Elicit: "Please identify a specific day, time, and place when you will complete the worksheet. Is there anything I can do to help you complete the real-life practice at the times you committed to?"

Provide a brief summary of the next session topic and how the lessons will help the patient strengthen recovery. The clinician might say: "In our next session together, we will focus on [___], working with your thoughts and learning a method to change them to enhance how you feel and what you do."

Summarize and Conclude the Session

Review and summarize session activities and key points. Prepare the patient for the next session by introducing the topic and explaining how it will be helpful on the path toward wellness.

Session 3. Learning Assertiveness Handouts

Review of Progress and Between-Session Challenges

Directions: Use the table here to support weekly progress review in key domains relevant to the patient's cannabis use and overall well-being. This table can also be used to review the between-session challenges.

Domain	Sun	Mon	Tues	Wed	Thu	Fri	Sat
Physical activity							
Sleep							
Diet							
Pleasure/ Replacement activities							
Mastery activities							
Work/School							
Mood states							
Tobacco/Nicotine							
Alcohol							
Marijuana							
Other drugs							
Between-session challenge							

Communication Styles

Passive-Aggressive	Aggressive
With passive-aggressive communication or behavior, someone may appear to agree or go along with a plan of action but engage in other behavior that conveys their true feelings. Passive-aggressive communication can be difficult to identify because often people are not aware they are doing it.	When someone behaves or communicates in an aggressive manner, they tend to ignore the rights or feelings of another person. They prioritize their own experience and needs over and above others involved. They may communicate through loud tones, yelling, threatening, and/or intimidating. They may be insensitive to how their message is coming across to others. They also may not be willing to hear how someone else feels or what they want in a particular situation.
Example: A woman asks her husband to attend a family gathering. He is not enthusiastic about family events and has somewhat conflicted relationships with some of his wife's family members. He would prefer to stay home and watch a tennis match on television. Instead of telling his wife his feelings, he agrees to go to the family party and arranges to meet her there after he completes some errands. He ends up being "held up" with some of his chores and arrives at the party two hours late. This would be considered "passive-aggressive" because on the surface he seemed willing to go along with his wife's wishes, but by arriving late he conveyed indirectly his preference to be elsewhere.	**Example:** A group of friends goes out to dinner and begins talking about their children. One member of the group comments and gives unsolicited advice to the parents about all the mistakes they are making and how their behavior is damaging their children.

Passive	Assertive Communication
This style occurs when someone feels unable to or fearful of expressing themselves or their feelings directly. They tend to acquiesce, or go along with, what the other person wants. They may not feel entitled to their opinions or believe the other person will not listen or care. **Example:** Someone is asked to attend an event for work that is really inconvenient, but rather than asking to be excused or reschedule the person agrees immediately. With this form of communication an individual does not express their needs and wants in a clear way.	With assertive communication, a person expresses their thoughts, feelings, or needs directly and clearly, but is respectful and sensitive to the rights and feelings of others. They do not yell or intimidate, but they also do not sugarcoat their message to the point of meaninglessness. *Benefits of being assertive—* • Most effective way to let others know what is going on or what effect their behavior has • Resolve uncomfortable feelings that otherwise build up • Can lead to feeling more in control of life • Increases the chances that goals will be met • Makes people feel better about their role in the situation

Between-Session Challenge Assertiveness

Assertiveness
Remember the following points in practicing assertiveness—

- Take a moment to think before you speak.
- Be specific and direct in what you say.
- Pay attention to your body language (use direct eye contact; face the person you are addressing).
- Be willing to compromise.
- Restate your assertion if you feel that you are not being heard.

Practice Exercise
The following exercises will help you become aware of your style of handling various social situations. The four common response styles are **passive, aggressive, passive–aggressive, and assertive**.

Pick **two** different social situations. Write brief descriptions of them and of your responses to them. Then decide which of the four common response styles best describes each response.

Situation 1 (describe)—

_____

_____

Your response—

_____

_____

Circle response style: passive aggressive passive–aggressive assertive
If your response was not assertive, think of an assertive response and write it down here:

_____

_____

Situation 2 (describe)—

_____

_____

Your response—

_____

_____

Circle response style*: **passive aggressive passive–aggressive assertive***
If your response was not assertive, think of an assertive response and write it down here:

_____

_____

Source: *Monti, Abrams, Kadden, & Cooney, 1989.*

Session 4. Supporting Recovery through Enhanced Social Supports

Introduction and Session Goals

Effective therapy starts with building rapport and trust and enhancing the therapeutic alliance developed in earlier sessions. The therapeutic alliance is essential to honest appraisal and recall of situations, triggers, and consequences of use. A main goal of all ICBT skill sessions is activating the patient in and out of treatment; so sessions are not just discussions, but a chance to introduce and practice skills, where the client takes the lead.

In Sessions 4 and 5, the clinician and patient address two essential areas of recovery: (a) social supports and (b) healthy replacement activities. Both of these aspects of the patient's life are a necessity to finding a life worth living without using substances. The clinician teaches the patient about the quality and scope of their social network (using the social atom diagram). Session 4 includes skills introduced in Session 3. Clinicians discuss and ask the patient how they might use their assertive communication skills from the previous session to engage social supports in a clear fashion that helps to build connections. The patient will have an opportunity to better understand and resolve reluctance in reaching out for support. The patient will identify those who could be there are allies and develop and activate a plan for building a more vibrant network of support.

A main goal for this first part of the session is not only discussing social supports but actually role playing the social interaction and eliciting a commitment to asking for support from an identified person. finding alternative rewards and pleasures in life.

📝 **Note to Clinicians:** Yes, there are some individuals who recover from a use disorder without social support. However, research demonstrates that social support is strongly associated with recovery (Atkins & Hawdon, 2007; Humphreys et al., 2011). In fact, social support is understood as so crucial that most evidence-based treatment maintains a significant focus on social support (Miller, Forchimes & Zweben, 2011).

In the Session 5 on healthy replacement activities, the clinician provides insights into the rationales that underlie most cannabis use/smoking habits; which are often maintained because they increase feelings of pleasure and/or they take away pain. Such experiences result from chemical changes in the brain after smoking or using drugs. One of the primary neurochemicals involved is dopamine. Dopamine and other reward sensation chemicals such as serotonin can also be produced by activities that are healthy and pleasurable. These are called replacement activities.

One of the best ways to increase dopamine is through physically new and challenging activities that require making effort and practicing skills. In Session 5, the patient brainstorms both activities that give immediate pleasure (effortless) and those that require mastery (effortful) experiences and commits to engaging in both types in the next weeks.

Orientation to Clinical Interventions Addressing Cannabis Use Disorder

Enhancing Social Support

Session 4. Supporting Recovery Through Enhanced Social Supports	
Materials • Review of Progress • Social Atom Diagram Handout • Social Support • Between-Session Challenge: Plan for Seeking Support Handout	**Total Time** 1 hour **Delivery Method** CBT-focused individual or group therapy

Strategies
- OARS (Open-ended questions, Affirmations, Reflections, Summary)
- EDARS (Express Empathy, Develop Discrepancy, Awareness of Ambivalence, Roll with Sustained talk/discord, Support self-efficacy); identify stage of change
- Demonstrate skill, role-play and give feedback
- Handouts utilized to focus the session helping to transfer knowledge and skill
- Develop "real-life practice challenge" and generate commitment

Goals for Session 4
- Enhance the patient's understanding of their social network as it pertains to connections that strengthen recovery.
- Discuss, elicit, and role-play how a helpful supportive relationship in the patient's life can become aware of their role as a recovery support.
- Identify a current situation or relationship that could benefit from the patient's communicating in a more assertive way; about needing help and also offering help.

Session 4 Outline and Overview for Enhancing Social Support

First Third

1) Strengthen Rapport:
   Welcome patient and build rapport:
   - Share the session agenda; invite items from the patient.
   - Engage in non-problem focused rapport building, exploring areas of the patient's life not directly related to treatment.
   - Use this as an opportunity to continue to explore patient's passions, interests, social connection and strengths.
2) Review of Progress:
   - Engage the patient in a brief review of their progress related to their cannabis use, mental health, and related experiences since the previous session. Use the *Review of Progress* handout as a guide.
     - Where is the patient in their readiness to fully commit to abstinence?
     - Did the patient make an effort to stop? Cut down?
     - Did the patient experience any high-risk or tempting situations?
     - If the patient engaged in cannabis use, explore their use event(s) using the *Alcohol/Cannabis use Awareness Record* to assess internal and external triggers, cravings, and consequences.
3) Review of Between-Session Challenge:
   - Did patient make an effort to stop? Cut down? Maintain abstinence?
   - Did the patient experience any high-risk or tempting situations?
   - Did the patient use the communication assertiveness strategies from the previous sessions?
   - Were the strategies successful?
   - Did the patient complete the between-session challenge? How did it go?
   - If the patient did not complete the between-session challenge, explore what got in the way, practice it if time allows, and potentially problem solve in anticipation of this week's challenge.

130 | *Orientation to Clinical Interventions Addressing Cannabis Use Disorder*

Second Third

4) Provide Rationale:
   - Explain the rationale for building the patient's social support networks (see *Social Support* handout and Social Atom handout).
   - Use the Social Atom to get a quick snapshot who are the persons in your patient's life today.
   - Ask the patient about the qualities of people that the patient has and would like to have in their social network. Elicit types of support the patient is currently receiving or has received in the past: Who provided it? What did it look like? In what ways was it helpful? Unhelpful? What type of support does the patient feel is needed most? Why?
5) Discuss the different types of social support:
   - Continue reviewing the different types of support from the *Social Support* handout.
   - Elicit examples from the patient for each type.
   - Ask the patient to consider supports not used in the past but which they might be willing to consider. Reference Social Atom handout.
6) Develop a plan for enhancing social support:
   - Continue reviewing the different types of support from the *Social Support* handout.
   - Elicit examples from the patient for each type.
   - Ask the patient to consider supports they have not used in the past but might be willing to consider.
   - Have patient activate seeking support in session (if possible). Examples could be sending a text message, email of making a phone call in session.

Third Third

7) Identify Real-World Application
   - Have the patient complete the *Plan for Seeking Support* handout.
8) Review tips on how to ask for support and address potential obstacles:
   - Continue reviewing the tips on how to ask for support from the *Social Support* handout (hint: draw from the assertiveness guidelines from previous session).

Session 4 Outline and Overview for Enhancing Social Support | **131**

- Discuss any potential barriers to getting the support identified in the patient's plans and engage the patient in group problem solving.
9) Negotiate between-session challenge and elicit commitment:
  - Elicit commitment from patient to seek out one support identified in the plan during the next week.
  - Have patient define specifically when they will seek out the support and how.

Session 4 Protocol with Scripts

Strengthen Rapport

The clinician welcomes the patient and provides an overview of the fourth session, where the clinician further strengthens recovery capitol through understanding and learning about the patient's relationships including the quality, the depth and type. The clinician and patient also explore the patient's healthy action based coping strategies. Both mastery and immediate pleasure replacement activities are discussed and activated. The clinician invites the patient to provide additional agenda items for the session.

Review of Progress: Examining the Patient's Recent Experiences

Review the current status regarding alcohol or cannabis use and the goals of change or abstinence. The clinician uses the Review of Progress handout to support a brief review of the patient's progress in key domains since the last session, including cannabis use, mental health symptoms, and related wellness areas.

The clinician asks the patient to describe their recent experiences with cannabis or other substances:

- Did the patient stop use since the previous session?
- Did the patient make an effort to stop?
- Was the patient confronted with any high-risk or tempting situations?
- What strategies did the patient use? Did the patient try any to see what triggers were most inviting to use and if so did they try any of the communication strategies from the last session or any other coping strategies? Were they successful?
- Were there any instances when the patient effectively handled a "hot" situation (i.e., very high risk)?

Again, and throughout the model, when the patient talks, the clinician's objective is to elicit information and to use that information to provide reflections, express empathy, identify discrepancies, elicit self-motivational statements, and roll with sustain talk/discord.

Review of Between-Session Challenge: Assessing the Patient's Progress and Readiness to Proceed

Inquire about any between-session practice challenge. Did the patient find being assertive with themself or others helpful? If appropriate,

Session 4 Protocol with Scripts | **133**

praise the patient's efforts accomplishing the between-session challenge and maintaining changes or abstinence. If the patient did not complete the challenge—ask them what happened—and why they did not complete the challenge. Holding patients accountable in a clear manner but one that is not off putting is essential to potent CBT. Again, remind the patient that the between-session challenges are an expectation of work in treatment and explain the reason for the between-session challenge again and then have the patient do the challenge with you now to demonstrate the importance.

Provide a Rationale

Introduce the concept of enhanced social supports and how vital that is to creating a stimulating and fulfilling lifestyle. Share with the patient that often when reducing cannabis use, there is a sense of absence or loss as old habits, people and places may create risks for continued use. Social support is a very powerful and beneficial force in the recovery process and in living well. The benefits of social support are many:

- a sense of belongingness and inclusion,
- a sense of safety and security,
- reduced stress, decreased isolation, and loneliness,
- an enhanced sense of meaning and purpose,
- hope and optimism about the future,
- the opportunity to escape the narrow world of cannabis use
- social support can counteract shame, isolation, and secrecy

> **Clinician (C):** Most of our patients talk about the importance of examining and rebuilding social supports. Let's face it. We are social creatures and social connection is part of our well-being.
>
> **Patient (John = J):** That's true, but a lot of my friends and family smoke or do drugs. So what do I do?
>
> **C:** An excellent question! So let us start with getting a better picture of who actually is in your world and can they be an ally for your making changes. Let us first use the social atom tool to understand who all are in your world today.
>
> Clinician and Patient complete the social atom together.
>
> **C:** So, when you think about social support that would work for you, what do you want in that relationship?

> **J:** I want someone who will respect my privacy, someone who I can hang out with, someone who doesn't judge me if I use and someone who don't want to give me grief if I don't want to use.
>
> **C:** This is good. You are clear about what's important for you in a person who could be a support. Let's take a look again at the social atom and see who might have those characteristics you value.
>
> Clinician and Patient review the social atom together and identify one or more persons who could be social supports.
>
> **C:** Can you imagine for a minute that I am this person. How would you reach out to that person and what would you say?
>
> Clinician and Patient role play the conversation. The clinician may first model the behavior and next the patient demonstrates the behavior. The clinician may need to use MI skills to process uncomfortable feelings of the patient connected to help seeking.
>
> **C:** Is there something you might do right now in session that gets this started?

Patient-Led Practice (Assess Skills Transfer)

> **Patient:** I'd feel too weird calling in the middle of the day, but I could send a text message about catching up tonight or over the weekend. And then when we talk, I can say what's going on and ask.
>
> *Clinician has Patient send text message (Activation in session).*
>
> *Clinician and Patient complete the Plan for Seeking Social support and discuss any potential challenges to the plan.*

Identify Real-World Application

Clinician and Patient negotiate between-session practice:

Elicit commitment from patient to seek out one support identified in the plan during the next week.

Negotiate and Prepare Between-Session Challenge

Have patient define specifically when they will seek out the support and how.

Session 4 Protocol with Scripts | **135**

Note: Mastery and immediate pleasure activities can be the focus of the seeking support from relationships in the social network. Again, since a main goal of the social support session is to activate supportive relationships, this can be accomplished by directly seeking support to do a mastery activity together—and then the patient's challenge commitment integrates parts of this and the next the session.

Session 5. Supporting Recovery through Healthy Replacement Activities

Introduction and Session 5 Goal
The goal of the replacement activities is to help activate patient's experiences through a focused conversation in how they obtain feelings of joy and pleasure in life. The patient talks about past and present ways of feeling good, and what it would take for them to reengage old activities or consider trying new ones. The patient also experiences having a supportive coach helping to exchange their daily routines for ones that can become new, perhaps healthier habits. The patient expresses optimism and commitment for trying to replace use by engaging in immediate pleasurable activities and longer term, skills-based activities.

Healthy Replacement Activities Rationale
Participating in healthy replacement activities is vital to creating an enjoyable and fulfilling lifestyle. Often when reducing cannabis use, patients feel a sense of absence, boredom, or loss owing to the physiological and psychological effects of no longer using, or using less. Some of the best ways to increase feeling good is through physically new and challenging activities that require making effort and practicing skills. In this session, we will brainstorm activities that give immediate pleasure and those that require mastery experiences and to make commitment to engaging in both types in the next weeks.

Clinician Preparation

Session 5. Supporting Recovery Through Healthy Replacement Activities	
Materials • Engaging in Replacement Activities (handout) • Increasing Pleasant Activities (handout)	**Total Time** 45–60 minutes **Delivery Method** Skill-focused individual or group therapy

Strategies
- OARS (Open-ended questions, Affirmations, Reflections, Summary), support self-efficacy, identify stage of change
- MI Eliciting Change Talk (Looking Back, Looking Forward, Pros and Cons, Decisional Balance Use)
- Brainstorm
- Develop "real-life practice challenge" (prescription for fun)
- Follow CBT skills session reminders

Session 5 Outline and Overview for Enhancing Healthy Replacement Activities

📋 **Note:** If the session on replacement activities is done on its own and not coupled with the social supports, deliver all elements in a CBT session including the first third of the session: Engage and Build Rapport, Review Progress, and Review Between-Session Challenge. In the following text, we assume that the social support and replacement activities are being delivered in one session; so some of the full CBT elements are truncated but the goal of patient activation for the skills involved is met.

Second Third

- Rationale: Introduce increasing pleasant activities:
  - Explain the rationale that often people use cannabis and/or other drugs because of the pleasure they get from the experience or because they alleviate boredom.
  - Over time, it can be hard to have fun or enjoy oneself without using.
  - Related to this is the idea that drugs operate on specific reward centers in the brain.
  - Those reward centers are also affected by other, exciting, nonsubstance-related activities such as running or playing basketball.
  - Discuss the two different types of activities including the differences between mastery and pleasure and why having mastery activities is important.
  - Finding sober activities that are rewarding, challenging, and stimulating can help increase long-term abstinence.
- Explore the patient's interests and passions regarding sober activities:
  - Have the patient complete the top part of the Increasing Pleasant Activities handout by placing a "P" next to activities they select which are pleasurable and an "M" next to activities they select which incorporate a sense of mastery.
  - Brainstorm additional activities if needed.

Third Third

- Identify real-world application.
- Elicit commitment from the patient to engage in one activity two times between sessions:
  - Patient completes bottom portion of Increasing Pleasant Activities handout.
  - Explore with the patient what could get in the way or pose a barrier to engaging in the chosen activities.
  - Problem-solve to resolve any challenges to completing the task.

Session 5 Protocol with Scripts

Provide Rationale

Introduce the concept of participating in healthy replacement activities and how vital that is to creating a stimulating and fulfilling lifestyle. Share with the patient that often when reducing cannabis use, there is a tremendous sense of absence or loss owing to the physiological and psychological effects of no longer using, or using less.

> **Clinician:** Most of our patients tell us loud and clear that their cannabis use produced a sense of immediate pleasure and/or reward both biologically and psychologically—feelings that they depend on to get through the daily boredom or stress of life.
>
> **Patient:** That's right! Using helps me spice up life when I need to, and at other times it chills me out so I don't feel so anxious.
>
> **Clinician:** So it does different things for you and, either way, it is mind altering and you have come to rely on that experience. To replace the sense of loss as you reduce your use, most people find they need activities that include two important aspects of their life: pleasure and mastery. Pleasure activities bring us the immediate rewards that we all need to feel good; for example, watching a movie, reading a book, listening to music, and eating a nice meal. Mastery activities, because of the challenge they present, remain novel over time, lead to a long-term sense of accomplishment, and ultimately can produce feelings of passion for life (similar to passions for cannabis use). Mastery activities are challenging and demand creativity and effort in either or both the use of physical and mental skill.
>
> **Patient:** That makes sense because we'd even get bored of using the same thing in the same amount every day. Besides, I always switch it up and smoke weed sometimes and drink booze on other days, or do both. It helps to give me different kinds of experiences.

Clinician Led Brainstorm to Identify Real-World Application

Clinician: Given the need for both pleasure and mastery activities, what can you do every day or week to engage in one type or the other so you feel passion in your life? Let's take a minute to brainstorm some

Session 5 Protocol with Scripts | **141**

possibilities, check off some listed ones, and discuss the choices in this handout on replacement activities.

Offer the client the handout called Increasing Pleasant Activities Handout.

Clinician: The handout lists a combination of Mastery activities (Ms) and Immediate Pleasures (Ps)—you'll notice some could be both dependent on how you commit to doing them.

Patient: How many of each should I choose?

Clinician: best to try to choose 3 to 5 of the different activity types that way you will have options should one or a few not work out.

Patient: Ok I'll do the immediate ones and some are not listed—drinking tea, listening to music, calling a friend and taking a brief walk outside all let me calm down and feel ok.

Clinician: Awesome list of pleasurable activities. What about the MASTERY (Ms) effort activities that you find rewarding, enjoyable, and stimulating?

(If needed, prompt the patient with examples: **playing a musical instrument, writing, singing, and playing a sport (golf, walking, distance running, skiing, etc.**).

Patient: There are many I used do a lot—dance, cook, and play the guitar. Dancing seems the most fun for next week as it lifts my mood and I don't need to do it alone all the time.

Negotiate and Prepare Between-Session Commitment

Once the patient has listed three or more choices for each type of activity on the sheet, the clinician elicits a commitment for the upcoming week.

Clinician: Now on the Engaging Replacement Activities Handout, please write the choice in the appropriate space provided. Remember, all lifelong and stimulating habits take time to generate feelings of comfort. Even activities we think will be simple or enjoyable at first can become tedious or off-putting owing to the effort needed to begin and learn the basic skills (i.e., "the devil is in the details"). Mastery activities can take more initial effort to pursue, but once you acquire some success, the activities can become habit and enjoyable.

> **Patient:** That makes sense and I remember when I first started dancing it was actually embarrassing and I never thought I would get good at it. But, I realized I could do it over time and it got more fun as I could make the dance go with the music better and be in sync with my partner.

Cultivating the quality of persistence can be important in the development of new skills and activities, solving a problem, or meeting a challenge. The ability to sustain effort in the face of difficulty or adversity is an important lifelong skill that is worth pursuing. Delay of gratification is important to being able to put off immediate rewards or benefits for the purpose of having something more valuable and lasting over the long term (e.g., sacrificing the immediate pleasure of an ice cream sundae in favor of the larger goals of health and weight management).

Elicit Commitment

> **Clinician:** The handout titled 'Engaging in Replacement Activities' is what you'll use to now write down your identified Ms and IPs and commit to one for next week.
>
> Take a couple of minutes to write down your ideas and then we can go over it together and determine when, where, and with whom you will do your Mastery. It is harder to predict when you will do your immediate pleasure because you may have a craving at any time during the week but still it is good for you to commit to using the IPs when you are triggered.
>
> **Patient:** Great I now have a few ways of coping with triggers and cravings—and I think since I committed to dance I will ask Bob—my main support person in my social network to join me in dancing.

Summarize and Conclude Session

The clinician makes sure that the challenges are clear for both parts of the session if it is done combined and the client has specified how they will use the skill, where, when and with whom.

If the session skills on social supports and replacement activities are done in two sessions the sessions end with the challenge for the recovery skill discussed.

Session 5. Supporting Recovery Through Healthy Replacement Activities Handouts

Review of Progress and Between-Session Challenges

Directions: Use the table here to support weekly progress review in key domains relevant to the patient's cannabis use and overall well-being. This table can also be used to review the between-session challenges.

Domain	Sun	Mon	Tues	Wed	Thu	Fri	Sat
Physical activity							
Sleep							
Diet							
Pleasure/ Replacement activities							
Mastery activities							
Work/School							
Mood states							
Tobacco/ Nicotine							
Alcohol							
Marijuana							
Other Drugs							
Between-session challenge							

Social Support

Why is social support important?

We all need support at different times in our lives. Having people in our lives to support us can help us reach our goals and deal successfully with any challenges that come our way. When trying to quit cannabis and/or drug use, you may experience the following:

- Continuing to interact with family and friends that use cannabis or drugs.
- Missing out on social interactions that involve cannabis or drug use.
- Feeling anxious about socializing without cannabis or drug use.
- Facing a diminished social network of people who do not engage in cannabis or drug use.

Having a network of people who understand and support your efforts to change can be extremely helpful.

What types of support is out there?

- Self-help groups
- Professional help
- Spiritual or religious affiliations
- Personal relationships
- Coworkers
- Community service agencies

How to ask for support

- Be specific about what type of support you need.
- Show appreciation for the person's support if it was helpful.
- Give feedback to the person if they are giving support that was not helpful.
- Find a way to support the other person.

My Social Atom

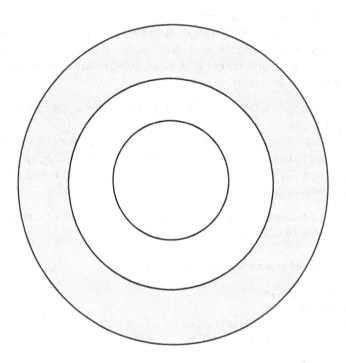

Instructions: The social atom is a direct way to better understand your social world. In the center include yourself and those closest to you. In the next ring include associates and others with whom you have somewhat regular contact. In the third ring include those with whom you have occasional contact. Outside the circles include those with whom you have lost contact.

Plan for Seeking Support

Support	How this support will help	Plan for getting this support
Support	How this support will help	Plan for getting this support
Support	How this support will help	Plan for getting this support

148 | *Orientation to Clinical Interventions Addressing Cannabis Use Disorder*

Increasing Pleasant Activities

Following is a list of both effortful Mastery and effortless immediate pleasure activities that people find pleasurable. Please check those that seem appealing to you, either because you know you like them, or you imagine you would like them if you tried. *Please put an M = Mastery or a P = immediate pleasure on any item checked.* Also check any items that you're not sure about but might be willing to consider if you had some support or encouragement to try it out. There are no grades on this exercise. Check as many as you wish. If there are things that are not listed that you want to include, please add them. Thanks.

❑ Reading a book	❑ Going to the movies	❑ Going out to a meal
❑ Exercising	❑ Listening to music	❑ Writing or journaling
❑ Dancing	❑ Singing	❑ Computer/Internet
❑ Photography	❑ Drawing	❑ Writing/calling friend
❑ Making jewelry	❑ Baking/cooking	❑ Shopping
❑ Painting	❑ Swimming	❑ Boating
❑ Ice skating	❑ Knitting/crocheting	❑ Taking a bath
❑ Gardening/lawn	❑ Fixing things	❑ Refinishing furniture
❑ Going to live theater	❑ Library	❑ Visiting park, garden
❑ Skydiving	❑ Running	❑ Organizing
❑ Party/social event	❑ Hiking	❑ Fishing
❑ Skiing	❑ Playing competitive sports	❑ Yard Sales
❑ Spending time with friends/family		

Other activities:

_____

_____

Commitment

I will do the following activity,_____
number of times in the next week. I will do the activity on_____
(list specific dates) at _____(list specific times).

Engaging in Replacement Activities

Why?

- When we reduce immediate pleasure/reward, it is important to replace it.
- Both immediate PLEASURE type activities and more skill-based MASTERY activities are needed.
- They produce the same brain chemicals.
- They tap into life passions and keep us feeling better.

What types of immediate pleasure activities do you like to do?

_____

_____

_____

Which are you willing to commit to doing this week?

_____

What types of skill-based MASTERY activities would you like to do?

_____

_____

_____

Which are you willing to commit to doing this week?

_____

_____

_____

150 | *Orientation to Clinical Interventions Addressing Cannabis Use Disorder*

Session 6. Problem Solving

Introduction and Session Goals

Session 6 reviews the types of experiences and problems that cause stress for the patient and offers an easy-to-remember and effective method for how to choose the best possible solutions to most types of problems. The clinician explains that most recurrence of use may be attributed to either interpersonal (the self in relation to others) or intrapersonal (within the self) stress, which often leads to unpleasant feelings such as anger, fear, shame, sadness, or guilt. The clinician explains that people successful at handling problems realize they cannot avoid all problems, but they can learn strategies to overcome them. They can develop ways of coping more skillfully and efficiently with predictable stresses that arise in the course of daily life and the larger, more life-altering and disruptive types of stressful events.

As the clinician introduces and progresses through the session, the patient hears that they are not alone with troubles but shares them in common with most others as part of life's struggle. The patient also hears that the problems do not lie within oneself as flaws or deficits, but rather they reflect universal experiences that can be addressed practically and successfully in the context of supportive relationships (such as counseling). The patient also learns to approach problems or challenges in creative ways, recognizing there are multiple paths that can lead to health and healing. Using the I-SOLVE acronym (explained in the following paragraphs) helps clinicians transfer a six-step model to patients. Providing formal training in solving problems may accelerate the development of higher order coping strategies that go beyond situation-specific skills. This training helps the patient act as their own clinician when no longer engaged in a formal treatment situation. The problem-solving approach used in this guide is adapted from D'Zurilla & Goldfried (1971); see also CSAT (1999).

Clinician Preparation

CBT Session 6. Problem Solving	
Materials • Review of Progress • Problem-solving (I-SOLVE) handout for between-session challenge • Large paper, poster board, or dry-erase board to diagram problem-solving steps	**Total Time** 1 hour **Delivery Method** Skill-focused individual or group therapy
Strategies • OARS (Open-ended questions, Affirmations, Reflections, Summary) • Support self-efficacy • Demonstrate skill, role-play including transfer of skill—having patient go through an example on their own with you present • Follow CBT skills sessions	
Goals for This Session • Introduce a strategy for solving problems. • Apply the problem-solving approach to alcohol or other cannabis use and related problems. • Prepare for termination of treatment if applicable.	

Source: Kadden, Litt, & Cooney, 1994

Session 6 Outline and Overview

First Third

1) Strengthen Rapport:
   - Welcome the patient, and if present, the support person.
   - Share the session agenda; invite items from the patient.
   - Engage in non-problem focused rapport building, exploring areas of the patient's life not directly related to treatment.
2) Review of Progress:
   - Engage the patient in a brief review of their progress related to their cannabis use, mental health, and related experiences since the previous session. Use the *Review of Progress* handout as a guide.
     - How is the patient doing with changing their cannabis use? What is going well? What are they struggling with?
     - If the patient engaged in cannabis use, explore their use event(s) using the *Alcohol/Cannabis use Awareness Record* to assess internal and external triggers, cravings, and consequences.
3) Review of Between-Session Challenge:
   - Review any between-session challenges from the previous session.
   - Did the patient engage in pleasant activities? How did it go? If not, what got in the way?
   - Did the patient seek support? Explore their experience of doing so.

Second Third

4) Provide Rationale:
   - Discuss the importance of recognizing problems as opportunities to learn.
   - Explain the rationale that everyone has problems (the rich, the famous, the not-so-famous), and provide relevant examples.
   - Provide the rationale that we often cannot control much of what happens in life, so we say problems are not the problem; rather, how we react to problems is important. Problems can be seen as opportunities rather than roadblocks.
   - For patients, problem situations result in alcohol or cannabis use when people feel they have no effective coping responses to handle them or their range of abilities is narrow or constricted. However, these same situations can be managed by practicing effective problem-solving skills, so the choices diminish the negative consequences of the situations and even sometimes create opportunities.

Session 6 Outline and Overview | **153**

5) Teach Session Skill:
- Provide examples of problem-solving practice and how it is effective.
- Explain how firemen practice setting fires to be prepared for the real fire, similar to other emergency workers who develop response routines so the incidents do not become overwhelming when they occur. This is similar to learning to do CPR or the Heimlich maneuver, gaining needed skills to respond to problem situations.

Brainstorm problems and describe problem-solving skills:

- Recognize the problem.
- Identify or elaborate on the problem.
- Consider various approaches.
- Select the most promising approach.
- Evaluate effectiveness.

6) Clinician-Led Demonstration/Role-Play:
- Practice problem solving skills by identifying a problem and applying the problem-solving steps to solving the identified problem.
- Once it is clear the patient understands the problem-solving process, collaborate with them to identify another problem they can try to solve. When the problem is identified, ask them to go through the problem-solving steps, out loud, so that they demonstrate to you, the clinician, that they can utilizes these steps on their own.
- Role-play solutions to one of the problems and evaluate effectiveness.

7) Patient-Led Practice (Assess Skills Transfer)
- Have the patient engage in a real-play of the skill.
- Have the patient identify another problem and engage in the problem-solving steps, the I-SOLVE model, on their own.
- Be there for questions or if the patient feels stuck. Ideally, the patient is able to move through the steps to identify solutions to the problem on their own and you are there to play a more supportive, affirming role.

Third Third

8) Identify Real-World Application:
- Help the patient to identify a real-life problem in which they can apply the skill.

154 | *Orientation to Clinical Interventions Addressing Cannabis Use Disorder*

9) Negotiate and Prepare Between-Session Challenge:
   - Elicit from the patient when and where in their life they can use the problem-solving steps to address the identified problem.
   - Ensure that the challenge is specific and support the patient by rehearsing their application of the new skill—What will they do? When will they do it?
   - Encourage the patient to continue using the Alcohol/Cannabis use Awareness Record when they are triggered to use, to continue engaging in pleasant activities, and to continue to build support.
10) Elicit Commitment:
   - Elicit commitment for completion of the between-session challenge for the identified problem before the next session.
   - Use MI strategies as needed to strengthen commitment.
11) Summarize and Conclude:
   - Present a session summary of what has been covered during the session and elicit the patient's feedback.
     - What did the patient learn through the problem-solving activity?
   - Conclude the session.

Session 6 Protocol with Scripts

Strengthen Rapport

The clinician welcomes the patient and provides an overview of the fifth session, in which the clinician further supports the patient to build coping skills by normalizing the experience of facing problems and enhancing their ability to resolve problems independently using a step-by-step system that has been shown to be helpful to others. The clinician invites the patient to provide additional agenda items for the session.

Review of Progress: Examining the Patient's Recent Experiences

The clinician uses the Review of Progress handout to support a brief review of the patient's progress in key domains since the last session, including cannabis use, mental health symptoms, and related wellness areas.

The clinician asks the patient to describe their recent experiences with cannabis or other substances:

- How are their efforts to quit or cut down going?
- Was the patient confronted with any high-risk or tempting situations?
- What strategies did the patient use? Did the patient try any of the strategies in Learning New Coping Strategies? Were they successful?
- Were there any instances when the patient effectively handled a "hot" situation (i.e., very high risk)?

As the patient talks, the clinician's objective is to elicit information and to use that information to provide reflections, express empathy, identify discrepancies, elicit self-motivational statements, and roll with sustain talk/discord.

Review of Between-Session Challenge: Assessing the Patient's Progress and Readiness to Proceed

The clinician asks the patient how they feel about the previous session and responds to concerns, addressing any comments or questions about the patient's experience of seeking support and engaging in pleasant, healthy activities.

What type of support did they seek and from who? How did it go when they asked? Were they able to get the support they needed? What was it like for them to ask and then to receive support?

Orientation to Clinical Interventions Addressing Cannabis Use Disorder

Note: If the patient expresses discomfort or even guilt at asking for support, it is important for the clinician to explore with them their experience of providing support to others in the past. How did they feel when they were asked to offer their help? Often, the patients will indicate that they had a positive experience in being able to support someone else. The clinician reflects this back to the patient and asks if they people whom they ask for support from might feel the same way.

Provide Rationale

The clinician explains the rationale for learning an approach to solving difficult problems using examples from real life and how they affect every type of person, including the rich, famous, poor, and brilliant. The clinician might use examples of people in the media, in the community, on news programs, etc. The clinician also explains that all people have problems, and the problems come in all forms, such as emergencies, illness, and loss of employment. However, even a seemingly positive event, such as a party, can be a problem for someone trying to avoid using.

> **Clinician:** As you know, life throws all of us problems; they are part of the fabric of life for everyone. We like to say, problems are not the problem, it is what you do with them that matters. Every person, no matter how rich, poor, brilliant, or famous can have problems, and the problems can come in as many forms as the types of people. Some problems are emergencies caused by health issues, the stress of job demands, and money issues. Even a party can be a problem for someone trying not to use.
>
> **Patient:** So you mean that what I experience is not unusual, but that it bothers me more than people who experience the same types of things. How does knowing that help me not to feel bad and use?
>
> **Clinician:** Situations become problems when people think they have no effective coping responses to handle them. Individuals can be flooded by emotions when faced with a problem and may be unable to manage the problem constructively. People who use cannabis or other substances may encounter the following types of problems:
> - Situations where alcohol or cannabis use occurred
> - Situations that arise after cannabis use has been stopped (e.g., social pressure to use, cravings, slips)

> • Difficulties developing new activities that help maintain abstinence (e.g., new recreational habits)

Give examples of firemen and emergency responders who learn to more easily overcome adversities by practicing possible responses. The clinician will use this session to help the patient practice a problem-solving model to deal with situations that normally would trigger them to use.

The clinician describes steps to solve problems and situations where the approach is helpful. See the sample language provided.

> Effective problem solving requires recognizing when you're confronted with a problem and resisting the temptation to respond impulsively or to do nothing. Coming up with an effective solution requires that you assess the situation to decide the best course of action. Sometimes the problem involves wanting to use cannabis or substances, such as at a party. At other times, the problem may be the urge to find a quick and easy solution. The pressure may build up and trigger using. Effective problem-solving strategies must be part of your abstinence program because the occurrence of problems can set the stage for a slip or longer periods of recurrence of use.

Teach Session Skill

Elicit information from the patient and review some of the problems mentioned in past sessions. Then describe the effective problem-solving approach called I-SOLVE.

I-SOLVE

I—Identify the problem.
S—State the problem.
O—Consider options.
L—Look at the consequences of the choices.
V—Vote on the most promising approach.
E—Evaluate effectiveness.

The clinician describes the steps in I-SOLVE, provides examples, and encourages questions and feedback from the patient as to how this fits with their situation.

158 | *Orientation to Clinical Interventions Addressing Cannabis Use Disorder*

Okay, so we are going to go through the steps of problem solving using a tool called I-SOLVE. I will describe each and give an example. Please ask questions or make any comments as we go along, okay?

The first step is to **identify** the problem. What clues indicate there may be a problem? You may get clues from your body (e.g., indigestion, craving), your thoughts and feelings (e.g., feelings of anxiety, depression, loneliness, fear), your behavior (e.g., have you been able to keep up with plans and commitments you make to others or yourself?), the way you respond to others (e.g., feeling irritable, impatient, having less interest in things, feeling withdrawn from people who might be supportive of you), and the way others respond to you (e.g., they appear to avoid you, seem frustrated or critical of you).

The second step is to **state** or elaborate the problem. What is the problem? Having recognized that something is wrong, you identify the problem by gathering as much information as you can. Break the problem down into smaller parts; you may find it easier to manage several parts than to confront the entire problem all at once. State the problem beginning with an "I" statement. For example, if you must complete a large project at work, it can be helpful to break it up into smaller, more manageable parts and perhaps consult with colleagues on aspects that are particularly challenging for you. "I have a project due at work and will need someone with advanced computer skills to help me finish it on time."

The third step is to consider **options** in addressing the problem. Develop several solutions; the first one that comes to mind may not be the best. Use the following methods to find a good solution.

Brainstorm. Generate ideas without judging or stopping to evaluate how good or bad they are. Write down all the ideas that come to mind, even ones that seem unrealistic. Later you will review and make decisions about which you will actually try out. More is better. Don't evaluate these ideas at this stage.

Consider strategies that require action or behavior change on your part (e.g., changing your routines related to social activity) and also strategies that involve your changing how you think about a situation. For example, when the problem involves negative

Session 6 Protocol with Scripts | 159

emotional reactions to uncontrollable events, change how you view this situation and your role in it (cognitive coping). Some problems require both behavioral and cognitive coping.

Once you have generated a list of ideas for coping with the problem, the fourth step is to **look** at the long and short term, including positive and negative consequences of choosing those options. Consider the resources you'll need for each solution. Here it is helpful to list the options and then write either +,—, or 0 = neutral next to each choice, depending on your thoughts about the outcome.

The fifth step is to **vote** for the most promising approach. Rank the possibilities by their consequences and desirability. The solution with the most positive and fewest negative consequences is the one to try first.

Finally, the sixth step is to **evaluate** effectiveness. How did it work out? Evaluate the strengths and weaknesses of your plan. What difficulties did you encounter? Are you obtaining the expected results? Can you do something to make the approach more effective? Use the same clues as before (e.g., from your body, thoughts, feelings, other people) to decide whether your solution is effective. If you give the plan a fair chance and it doesn't solve the problem, move to your second choice and follow the same procedure.

The clinician should try to address only a problem with a solution that is within the control of the patient. The model will not work if the answer to the problem relies on someone else's control. The following is an example of someone else's problems: *I need to make it so my family stops complaining, I need them to learn to speak in a different tone* ...versus: *I need to figure out a way of expressing myself so my family quits complaining about my tone of voice.*

If the patient chooses a problem where the solution is not in their control, the clinician collaborates with the patient to clarify the difference between the self's and another's ability to influence change (use examples). Then, together the patient and clinician reselect or redefine the problem to one where there is primary influence over the outcome, thus emphasizing self-efficacy.

The clinician wants to ensure the brainstorming of options feels fun and the spirit is creative. At this point in the I-SOLVE discussion, it does not matter if the solutions are realistic as long as the patient understands

160 | *Orientation to Clinical Interventions Addressing Cannabis Use Disorder*

the problems can be better solved when the solutions are in their control. The clinician can gently guide the patient toward a realistic solution they have the skills and will to carry out successfully (e.g., planning to create an enormous quilt when one has never picked up a needle and thread may be a setup for failure).

When leading a patient in brainstorming, it is usually best to elicit at least five solutions to assess which option might be best. This facilitates a choice should the option chosen and evaluated turn out not to be helpful and highlights problem solving as a learning opportunity rather than a stagnant process. Problem solving can be revised to adapt to evolving awareness in a manner similar to the recovery process, which is characterized by a variety of external and internal triggers. Each situation affords another chance to problem solve and test which option leads to the healthiest outcomes.

Clinician-Led Demonstration/Role Play

The clinician encourages the patient to work through the problem-recognition stage: identifying problems, describing them, and writing solutions on paper. The clinician asks the patient to weigh alternatives, select the most promising one, and describe both advantages and disadvantages for every alternative. Finally, the patient prioritizes the alternatives. The clinician and patient role-play and evaluate the effectiveness of the most promising solutions. See the sample language provided.

> **Clinician (C):** Your upcoming 4th of July picnic will put you in a difficult situation because you'll be around old friends and family members with whom you used to get high. What is the problem as you see it?
>
> **Steve (S):** Well, I have really enjoyed these parties in the past, even though they tend to be a blur because I've been so stoned. But it will be difficult to be there and not smoke with people. They will be offering me stuff for hours and I'm worried I'll just get worn down. Then I'll be mad at myself for not sticking to my guns.
>
> **C:** You anticipate it being difficult to stick to your plans when you are around people you have used with in the past.
>
> **S:** Yeah, I also don't want to let them down. I know that sounds kind of weird.

> **C:** It doesn't sound weird at all. It also sounds like there's a tension between staying focused on your goals and plans and worrying about disappointing people you care about by not being "part of" things as usual.
> **S:** Yes, I guess that's just how I feel.
> **C:** Have you thought about any ideas for how you might deal with this situation? Maybe we could come up with some possibilities and then see which ones might work better than others.
> **S:** Okay.
> **C:** Great.

The patient now uses the I-SOLVE model in the session to state the problem in a brief "I" statement, generate options, examine long-term and short-term consequences, vote, and then commit to trying the option chosen and evaluating the results of that choice.

Patient-Led Practice (Assess Skills Transfer)
The patient then takes the lead at walking the clinician through each component of the I-SOLVE model for a second problem thee patient identifies. The purpose for focusing on a second problem in which the patient uses the I-SOLVE model is to allow the patient to demonstrate their ability using the model more autonomously, unless the patient specifically asks for help. During the patient's application of the I-SOLVE model, the clinician affirms the patient's skill application and offers follow-up questions to encourage the patient to explore the incident more thoroughly.

Identify Real-World Application
The clinician asks the patient to commit to applying the I-SOLVE model to another problem before the next session. They commit to check in next session on the outcome of the solutions identified and applied.

Negotiate and Prepare Between-Session Challenge
The exploration of real-world skill application is a natural transition into negotiation of a between-session challenge. The clinician encourages the patient to continue reviewing the materials handed out at this session and previous sessions including the Alcohol/Cannabis use Awareness

Orientation to Clinical Interventions Addressing Cannabis Use Disorder

Record, Assertive Communication, Increasing Pleasant Activities, and asking or support. The clinician asks the patient where and when the patient can commit to working through the I-SOLVE model for a problem in their life. For any identified between-session challenges, the clinician works with the patient to ensure that they know what they will do, when they will do it, and how often it will be done, mentally rehearing its application in their daily life. Most patients benefit from writing down this plan somewhere accessible to them, to also serve as an ongoing reminder.

Elicit Commitment
The clinician explores the patient's commitment for completing the between-session challenge and uses MI strategies, as needed, to assess and strengthen commitment. The clinician also asks the patient to think through any potential obstacles to their skills practice and works with them to identify solutions and to activate resources, as needed, to support their skill application.

Summarize and Conclude the Session
The clinician reviews the content of the session, solicits feedback from the patient, responds empathically to their comments, and troubleshoots any difficulties. The clinician asks that the patient report back on their efforts to complete the between-session exercise at the next session. If the patient seems disinclined to complete the exercise in writing, ask them to think about a problem and go through the steps mentally and report back during the next session. The clinician might remind the patient that treatment will be ending soon and solicit the patient's feelings about ending treatment and the best way to spend the remaining sessions.

Session 6. Problem Solving Handouts

Review of Progress and Between-Session Challenges

Directions: Use the table below to support weekly progress review in key domains relevant to the patient's cannabis use and overall well-being. This table can also be used to review the between-session challenges.

Domain	Sun	Mon	Tues	Wed	Thu	Fri	Sat
Physical activity							
Sleep							
Diet							
Pleasure/ Replacement activities							
Mastery activities							
Work/School							
Mood states							
Tobacco/Nicotine							
Alcohol							
Marijuana							
Other Drugs							
Between-session challenge							

Problem Solving

Here is a brief list of the steps in the problem-solving process:

I = Identify. Is there a problem? Recognize that a problem exists. We get clues from our bodies, our thoughts and feelings, our behaviors, our responses to other people, and the ways that other people respond to us.

S = State. What is the problem? Identify the problem. Describe the problem as accurately as you can, using an "I" statement where the outcome is in your control. Break it into manageable parts.

O = Options. What can I do? Consider various approaches to solving the problem. Brainstorm to think of as many solutions as you can. Consider acting to change the situation; consider changing the way you think about the situation.

L = Look. What will happen if ... ? Select the most promising approach. Consider all the positive and negative aspects of each approach.

V = Vote. Select the one most likely to solve the problem.

E = Evaluate. How did it work? Assess the effectiveness of the selected approach. After you have given the approach a fair trial, determine whether it worked. If it did not, consider what you can do to improve the plan, or give it up and try one of the other approaches.

Practice Exercise

Select a problem that does not have an obvious solution. Describe it accurately. Brainstorm a list of possible solutions. Evaluate the possibilities, and number them in order of your preference.

Identify the problem:

_____

_____

_____

List brainstorming solutions:

_____

_____

_____

166 | *Orientation to Clinical Interventions Addressing Cannabis Use Disorder*

Examine the (+, -, 0) long-term and short-term results.
Select the achievable option that has the most benefits.
Commit to using.
Evaluate outcome.
Source: Kadden, Litt, & Cooney, 1994.

Session 7. Handling Urges, Cravings, and Discomfort (urge Surfing)

Introduction and Session Goals

Session 7 focuses on helping the patient gain an overall understanding of urges, cravings, and triggers. Urge surfing is a mindfulness skill. After normalizing the occurrence of automatic thoughts or urges, the clinician helps the patient identify how and when they experience urges or automatic thoughts. The clinician and patient collaborate on developing a menu of coping or response strategies that are relevant to the patient's experiences and environment. The session concludes with the clinician encouraging the patient to track their urges and coping and response strategies during the week. The clinician suggests reviewing them with the patient at the next session.

The patient will leave the session with—

- A general understanding of the nature of cravings and urges.
- An increased understanding of their own urges and cravings.
- The ability to identify specific triggers or cues for cravings.
- An awareness of their preferred strategies for addressing cravings.

_168_ | _Orientation to Clinical Interventions Addressing Cannabis Use Disorder_

Clinician Preparation

Session 7. Handling Urges, Cravings, and Discomfort (Urge Surfing)	
Materials • _Review of Progress_ • _Coping with Cravings and Urges handout_ • Urge Surfing handout • _Daily Record of Urges To Use handout_	**Total Time** 1 hour **Delivery Method** CBT-focused individual therapy

Strategies

- OARS (Open-ended questions, Affirmations, Reflections, Summary)
- Support self-efficacy
- Demonstrate skill, role-play including transfer of skill—having patient go through an example on their own with you present
- Discuss value of journaling/logging the patient's urges
- Follow CBT skills sessions

Goals for This Session

- Enhance the patient's understanding about cravings and urges for cannabis or another drug.
- Identify specific triggers or cues for cravings (see Carroll, 1998).
- Review and practice specific skills for addressing cravings.
- Examine the patient's high-risk situations, triggers, and coping strategies.

Session 7 Outline and Overview

First Third

12) Strengthen Rapport:
    - Welcome the patient.
    - Share the session agenda; invite items from the patient.
    - Engage in non-problem focused rapport building, exploring areas of the patient's life not directly related to treatment.
13) Review of Progress:
    - Engage the patient in a brief review of their progress related to their cannabis use, mental health, and related experiences since the previous session. Use the *Review of Progress* handout as a guide.
        - How is the patient doing with changing their cannabis use? What is going well? What are they struggling with?
        - If the patient engaged in cannabis use, explore their use event(s) using the *Alcohol/Cannabis use Awareness Record* to assess internal and external triggers, cravings, and consequences.
14) Review of Between-Session Challenge:
    - Review any between-session challenges from the previous session.
        - Did the patient use the I-SOLVE problem-solving approach? How did it go? If not, what got in the way?

Second Third

15) Provide Rationale:
    - Elicit from the patient their experiences with cravings and current coping methods.
    - Provide reasons for focusing on cravings, including basic information about the nature of cravings:
        - Cravings and urges are a part of the repeated use of any substance. Understanding urges and developing skills to address them is essential to recovery.
        - Cravings may feel very uncomfortable but are a common experience.
        - Cravings are experienced most often early in abstinence but can occur weeks, months, and even years later.
        - It is important to recognize urges and develop realistic strategies to manage them than can be practiced almost anywhere, and anytime.

170 | *Orientation to Clinical Interventions Addressing Cannabis Use Disorder*

16) Teach Session Skill:
- Provide a framework for understanding urges or cravings. Provide the patient with a copy of the Coping with Cravings and Discomfort handout.
  a) Urges/cravings are a subset of the universal experience of longing or desire.
  b) The role of urges or cravings in cannabis use.
- Discuss the patient's experience with and recognition of an urge.
- Identify the patient's cues or triggers for cravings.
  - Give the patient examples of common cues:
    o Exposure to cannabis, substances, or paraphernalia
    o Seeing other people using substances
    o Contact with people, places, times of day, or situations associated with using
    o Particular emotions and physical feelings
  - Distinguish external or environmental triggers from internal states.
- Discuss strategies for coping with triggers.
  - Avoidance
  - Escape
  - Distraction
  - Embrace
17) Clinician-Led Demonstration/Role-Play:
- Practice one of the Embrace strategies (Urge Surfing) for coping with triggers by walking the patient through a brief demonstration of how to implement the Urge Surfing strategy.
  a) Focus on *how* the strategy is implemented (the steps involved)
  b) Focus on the *experience* of the activity by walking through each step while sharing out loud your experiences, as if you were engaging in the strategy in that moment.
- Once it is clear the patient understand the Urge Surfing technique, have them demonstrate the skill.
18) Patient-Led Practice (Assess Skills Transfer)
- Have the patient identify a recent urge or craving. With that experience in mind, the patient is encouraged to practice Urge Surfing using a similar talk aloud method. The clinician may need to support the patient by reading the instructions and prompts to them.

Third Third

19) Identify Real-World Application:
- Help the patient to identify real-life situations in which they can apply the skill.
- Work with the patient to make a list of cravings triggers and a cravings plan for responding to those triggers.

20) Negotiate and Prepare Between-Session Challenge:
- Elicit from the patient how and where in their life they can apply Urge Surfing and other strategies they learned for coping with cravings.
  - Introduce and encourage the patient to use the *Daily Record of Urges to Use* handout to track their urge experiences throughout the week.
- Ensure that the challenge is specific and support the patient by rehearsing their application of the new skill—What will they do? When will they do it? How often will it be done (i.e., at least two times)?

21) Elicit Commitment:
- Elicit commitment for completion of the between-session challenge at least two times before the next session.
- Use MI strategies as needed to strengthen commitment.

22) Summarize and Conclude:
- Present a session summary of what has been covered during the session and elicit the patient's feedback.
  - What did the patient learn through Urge Surfing activity and broader discussion of strategies for coping with urges and cravings?
- Conclude the session.

172 | *Orientation to Clinical Interventions Addressing Cannabis Use Disorder*

Session 7 Protocol with Scripts

Strengthening Rapport
The clinician welcomes the patient and provides an overview of the seventh session, in which the clinician supports the patient in developing awareness around their experiences with urges and cravings and learning strategies for coping with these experiences. The clinician invites the patient to provide additional agenda items for the session.

Review of Progress: Examining the Patient's Recent Experiences
The clinician uses the Review of Progress handout to support a brief review of the patient's progress in key domains since the last session, including cannabis use, mental health symptoms, and related wellness areas.

The clinician asks the patient to describe their recent experiences with cannabis or other substances:

- How are their efforts to quit or cut down going?
- Was the patient confronted with any high-risk or tempting situations?
- What strategies did the patient use? Were they successful?
- Were there any instances when the patient effectively handled a "hot" situation (i.e., very high risk)?

As the patient talks, the clinician's objective is to elicit information and to use that information to provide reflections, express empathy, identify discrepancies, elicit self-motivational statements, and roll with sustain talk/discord.

If the patient engaged in cannabis use, explore their use event(s) using the Alcohol/Cannabis use Awareness Record to assess internal and external triggers, cravings, and consequences.

Review of Between-Session Challenge
The clinician asks the patient how they feel about the previous session and responds to concerns, addressing any comments or questions about the patient's experience with implementing the I-SOLVE problem-solving model. The clinician elicits how the patient's implementation of the I-SOLVE technique went for them, exploring what went well and what went less well. If the patient did not complete the activity, the clinician engages the patient in a discussion about the barriers

that got in the way and how they might respond to similar barriers in the future.

Provide Rationale

The clinician asks about the patient's experiences with cravings and current coping methods. See the sample discussion provided.

Many people report they have strong urges to smoke or get high when they first stop using. In the beginning the urges can feel overwhelming and hard to manage.
Is this something you've experienced when you've tried to stop using?

Some important messages the clinician conveys about urges during this discussion are summarized below:

- Urges are common during recovery.
- Learning to identify urges is important for gaining control over them.
- Urges are predictable and have understandable triggers.
- Identifying triggers can help in the selection of effective coping strategies.
- Everyone can learn to manage their urges.
- Urges are like stray cats: If you don't feed them, they go somewhere else.

Eliciting the patient's view first is the most desirable approach. However, if the patient is not able to provide this information, the clinician should be more direct in approaching the discussion to cover the points listed above. In this discussion, it is important to try to understand the patient's experience with urges in the past, including their overall perception of the predictability of urges and confidence in managing them. Once the clinician has reviewed the points, it is helpful to summarize what has been learned about the patient's perception of urges. See the sample discussion provided.

Before we move on, let me see if I've heard you correctly so far. It sounds like you've experienced quite a few urges in the past when you've tried to stop using. There have been times when you were able to deal with them, but there have also been other times when you've given into them. Your urges are generally more frequent and intense in the first few months after you stop using, but when you've been able to hang in there you've noticed you have urges even sometimes when you are really committed to not using,

174 | *Orientation to Clinical Interventions Addressing Cannabis Use Disorder*

and you tend to feel discouraged and disappointed in yourself for having these urges. When this happens, you also feel less confident about your ability to stay sober.

Although part of you realizes that having urges is normal and to be expected, you worry about your ability to manage them some of the time and would like some help with that.

So, it may be helpful to talk more about how you experience urges to get a better handle on them. What are your thoughts?

Specify the rationale

Cravings and/or urges are a part of the repeated use of any substance. Understanding your urges and developing skills to address them is essential to recovery. One thing we know about cravings is that everyone experiences them differently, and in the recovery process, how one person experiences them will change over time.

The good news is that urges are like stray cats: If you don't feed them, they eventually go somewhere else. There are a number of strategies that can be used to manage urges. These fall into a few categories—escape, distraction, avoidance, and embracing. Learning to use one or all of these strategies will help you to diminish the craving/urge.

What I'd like us to focus on today is how we can work together to support you in recognizing urges and developing realistic strategies to recognize your triggers, reduce your exposure to them, and cope with urges.

Teach Session Skill
Provide a Framework for Understanding Urges or Cravings and Their Role in Cannabis Use
The clinician gives the patient Coping with Cravings and Urges handout and explains the importance of recognizing cravings. Provide your patient with a framework for understanding the role of cravings. Explain that when someone tries to quit using cannabis or another substance, they often have cravings or strong urges to use that could be triggers for recurrence of use. Normalize the experience of cravings, not just in the area of cannabis use. Cravings and desires for things are universal human experiences and can cause discomfort and suffering. Throughout life, people struggle with wanting things or the belief they would feel better and be happier if only they had [_____] (e.g., a new house, a better job, a more satisfying relationship). The craving or urge for cannabis or

Session 7 Protocol with Scripts | 175

substances is no different from this basic human experience. When one can recognize that craving, and the discomfort that comes from this unfulfilled experience is universal, the craving may become more manageable. It is also important to understand that giving in to the craving or urge does not usually solve the underlying problem of discontent and can reinforce it. The saying, "The only thing worse than not getting what you want is.... getting it" has relevance here. The patient can be helped to see craving as just another psychological state—like sadness, joy, or fear—that need not take on special importance.

Discuss the Patient's Experience with and Recognition of an Urge

The clinician shares a general overview of how cravings or urges are often experienced, then elicits from the patient their unique experiences.

> **Clinician (C):** Cravings often are experienced when a person first tries to quit, but they may occur weeks, months, even years later. Cravings may feel uncomfortable, but they are common experiences. An urge to smoke doesn't mean something's wrong. Many people learn to expect cravings on occasion and how to cope with them.
>
> Things that remind you of using cannabis or other substances can trigger urges or cravings. Physical symptoms include tightness in the stomach or feeling nervous throughout the body. Psychological symptoms include thoughts about how using cannabis or other substances feels, recollections of using, developing plans to get cannabis or other substances, or feeling that you need cannabis or other substances.
>
> Cravings and urges usually last only a few minutes or at most a few hours. Rather than increase until they become unbearable, they usually peak after a few minutes and then die down, like a wave. Urges become less frequent and less intense as you learn more methods for coping with them.

Discussing what the patient experiences when they have an urge may help the patient identify an urge early and respond before it becomes overwhelming. There are many different ways of experiencing an urge, only some of which are recognized by most patients (e.g., physical sensations). Recognizing all aspects of the experience of an urge will help the patient label the experience and prevent automatic responses (i.e.,

176 | *Orientation to Clinical Interventions Addressing Cannabis Use Disorder*

returning to cannabis or drug use). This should enhance the patient's ability to manage urges. The clinician may explore with the patient the various ways an urge may be experienced. This is important before moving on to coping strategies to ensure the patient can recognize it.

Some examples appear below:

- Physical sensations (e.g., sweating, heart racing, queasy stomach)
- Thoughts (e.g., "wouldn't it be nice to have a smoke," "I'd rather be with my friends getting high tonight")
- Positive expectancies (e.g., "I'd feel better if I did some cocaine")
- Emotions (e.g., anxiety, depression, irritability)
- Behaviors (e.g., pausing while passing the beer display in a store, going by an old neighborhood where the drug dealer hangs out)
- Experiencing hunger

Open-ended questions about the patient's experiences with urges can be used to explore the patient's awareness of the symptoms of an urge.

We've spent some time talking about your general experiences with urges. Before we move on to talking about coping with urges, I'd like to get a better sense of how you know when you're having an urge. Some urges may be very easy to recognize, but others are less obvious. I'm wondering how you know when you're having an urge.

What is the first thing you notice when you are having an urge? How do you know that an urge is coming on?

What is the most obvious sign that you are craving cannabis?

If somebody were with you when you were experiencing an urge, would they notice anything?

As the discussion progresses, the clinician may want to ask more directed questions for the areas the patient has not already identified.

Physical Sensations

I'm wondering if you can tell me a bit about the physical sensations you experience when you have an urge to smoke or use drugs.

Thoughts

What about your thoughts? What kinds of thoughts do you recall having when you wanted to use cannabis or drugs?

Positive expectancies

People say they imagine something positive will happen if they smoke or use drugs. For instance, they think it will help them unwind after a tough day, or they will have a better time with other people, or simply help them feel better. What types of positive expectations have you had when you had an urge to use?

Emotions

Many people find their mood changes just before they use ... they feel anxious or depressed. Other people report feeling excited. I'm wondering what types of mood changes you've noticed.

Behaviors

Do you find yourself becoming less tolerant or more irritable? Do you find yourself getting into more arguments or fights with people? Do you find yourself hanging around more in some of the old places, or with people that you used to smoke or get high with? Have you impulsively decided to leave treatment?

Identify Cues or Triggers for Cravings

At this point in the session, it might be helpful for the clinician to summarize what they have learned about the patient's experience of urges and transition to identifying triggers for having urges.

It sounds like you have a good sense of how you experience an urge, particularly when it comes to the physical sensations. You've noticed your heart starts racing and you feel a knot in your stomach.

The goal of the next discussion is to establish a link between triggers and urges. Triggers are generally situations associated with a patient's use of cannabis or drugs in the past. With this repeated association, the patient tends to have urges in these situations when stopping or making attempts to cut down. If a patient understands this connection, it may make the urges more predictable. If the patient feels urges are somewhat predictable, this should help the patient feel more in control and also make it easier to identify specific coping strategies that may address urges in response to specific triggers.

The clinician should follow this brief explanation and presentation of examples by asking the patient about their triggers for urges. Once again,

178 | *Orientation to Clinical Interventions Addressing Cannabis Use Disorder*

it is important for the clinician to begin by asking, in an open-ended format, about the patient's understanding of triggers. Triggers can be recorded on the *Coping with Cravings and Discomfort* handout as the patient identifies them. The *New Roads* worksheet referred to in Session 9 may provide valuable information about triggers that can be used to supplement this discussion. If information about various types of triggers is not elicited, the clinician may follow with more directive questioning and discuss some of the common triggers listed below.

Clinician:

It's important to learn how to recognize triggers so you can reduce your exposure to them. Common triggers include—
- *Exposure to cannabis, substances, or paraphernalia*
- *Seeing other people using substances*
- *Contact with people, places, times of day, and situations associated with using (such as people you used with, parties, bars, weekends)*
- *Particular emotions (such as frustration, fatigue, feeling stressed), even positive emotions (elation, excitement, feelings of accomplishment)*
- *Physical feelings (feeling sick, shaky, tense)*

Some triggers are more difficult to recognize. Self-monitoring can help begin to identify them. The easiest way to cope with cravings and urges is to minimize their likelihood of occurring. You can reduce your exposure to triggers by getting rid of cannabis or substances in your home, not going to parties or bars, and limiting contact with friends who use.

Using the common triggers described below, it may be helpful to guide the discussion about internal and external triggers for urges. Primarily, it is important to let the patient know urges can be external (things that happen outside the person) or internal states (such as thoughts, feelings, and ideas).

External situations

- Exposure to cannabis or drugs
- Smell, sight, and sounds of other people smoking or using drugs
- Particular times during the day when smoking or drug use tended to occur (e.g., getting off work, weekends, payday)

Session 7 Protocol with Scripts | **179**

- Stimuli previously associated with smoking or drug use (e.g., wine glasses, bar, crack pipe, medicine bottle, ATM machine)
- Stimuli previously associated with withdrawal (e.g., hospital, aspirin, morning)

Internal states

- Unpleasant emotions (e.g., frustration, depression, anger, feeling "stressed out")
- Pleasant emotions (e.g., elation, excitement)
- Physical feelings (e.g., sick, shaky, tense, in pain)
- Thoughts about smoking or drug use (e.g., "I'll feel better if I get high")
- Beliefs or ideas such as, "I will always be an addict"

Discuss Strategies for Coping with Triggers

Since it can be expected that the patient will experience triggers for use, the clinician presents several categories and examples of coping strategies that have been found to be helpful.

Many times cravings can't be avoided, and it becomes necessary to cope with them. The nice part of that is there are many strategies that can be helpful for coping with cravings/urges. I want to talk about some different ways people have learned to cope with urges and cravings and we can consider which might be a good fit for you. How does that sound?

The clinician teaches the client four key approaches for managing urges: avoidance, escape, distraction, and embrace.

Avoidance. Avoidance is a strategy that involves reducing exposure to high-risk situations that trigger urges. Avoidance appears especially important early in recovery.

Examples of avoidance strategies include—

- Get rid of cannabis or drugs at home.
- Avoid parties or bars where smoking or drug use occurs.
- Reduce contact with old friends who smoke or get high.
- Avoid circumstances that increase temptation (e.g., cash in pocket, unstructured free time, home alone).

Escape. Escape is a strategy that focuses on finding a safe way out of situations where an urge might occur. This may involve an unexpected situation (e.g., drug dealer shows up at the door) or a situation the patient

180 | *Orientation to Clinical Interventions Addressing Cannabis Use Disorder*

sees as unavoidable (e.g., wedding). The patient should have a plan for getting out of the situation as quickly as possible if strong urges occur.

The clinician should recommend that the patient consider the following when making their plan for escape:

- Have the means ready; be careful not to get stranded without the means for getting out of a situation if necessary (e.g., transportation).
- Plan what to say or do; know what to say to people if leaving a risky situation in a hurry.
- Feel good about your choice; using escape is a sign of strength and determination to stick with your goal; don't be dissuaded by pressure from people to do what you have typically done in the past.

Distraction. Distraction is a strategy involving a shift in attention away from thoughts about using cannabis or drugs. There are numerous distracting activities that can take a patient's mind off urges to use cannabis or drugs, such as going to a movie, calling someone, reading a book, or exercising. Urges tend to pass more quickly when a person becomes involved with an alternative activity. The clinician might offer guidance as follows:

Embrace or "sit with" the urge. Sometimes patients may need to face the urge and cope with it directly, and the following embrace strategies may help:

- *Talk it through* with someone who is supportive and nonjudgmental. Talking can provide you with support when you need it and can help you to get through the urge without using again. Remember the "larger picture," including why you are trying to make this important change. It is important to talk with someone who won't judge or criticize you for having these feelings or urges but will give you permission to express yourself.
- *Meditation or mindfulness* activities can help you stay present with your experience without the need to act or react; they can also increase awareness generally.
- *Wait it out*; urges are only temporary.
- *Take protection* when faced with a high-risk situation.
- Use a *reminder card*.
- *Urge surfing.* Delay the decision to use. Most urges to use can be likened to ocean waves—they build to a peak and then dissipate. For many patients, if they choose to wait 15 minutes, the wave will pass.

Try imagining you're a surfer riding the wave of craving until it subsides, or use another image that works for you.

- *Use imagery.* If you feel you are about to be overwhelmed by urges to use, imagine scenes that portray those urges as storms that end with calmness, mountains that can be climbed, or waves that can be ridden. Everyone can find an image to maintain control until the urge peaks and then dissipates.

You might envision yourself sitting at the edge of a riverbank and seeing the urge as a boat that is sailing in your direction. You can simply observe the boat from this "distance," note certain qualities or characteristics, but not feel compelled to get on the boat and ride. Just see it come and then pass you by. Images can be made vivid by using relaxation techniques and all the senses (e.g., seeing the thick green jungle, hearing the blade swishing through the leaves, smelling the tropical plants). Photographs of loved ones can also distract.

Additional cognitive, or thinking strategies, can also be helpful in managing urges or cravings.

Challenge and change your thoughts. When experiencing cravings, many remember only the good effects of using and forget the negative consequences. You may find it helpful to remind yourself of the benefits of not using and the negative consequences of using. Remind yourself you will not feel better by getting a little buzz, and that you will lose a lot by using. It is helpful to have these benefits and consequences listed on a small card to carry around.

Self-talk. People often engage in a running dialogue or commentary with themselves about the events that occur in their day and their actions. These thoughts can strongly influence the way you feel and act. What you tell yourself about your urges to use affects how you experience and handle them. Your self-talk can be used to strengthen or weaken your urges. Making self-statements is so automatic you may not notice it. For example, a self-statement that is automatic for you may be, "I am a skilled photographer," or, "I have no willpower." Hidden or automatic self-statements about urges can make them hard to handle. ("I want to get drunk now. I can't stand this. The urge is going to get stronger and stronger until I use. I won't be able to resist.") Other types of self-statements can make the urge easier to handle. ("Even though my mind is made up to stay clean, my body is taking

182 | *Orientation to Clinical Interventions Addressing Cannabis Use Disorder*

longer to learn this. This urge is uncomfortable, but in 15 minutes or so, I'll feel like myself again.")

There are two basic steps in using self-talk constructively:

1) Try to identify the things you are saying to yourself that make it more difficult to resist an urge. One way to tell whether you're on the right track is when you hit on a self-statement that increases your discomfort. For example, "I will never be able to withstand this urge." That discomfort-raising self-statement is a leading candidate for challenge.

2) Use self-talk constructively to challenge the statement. An effective challenge makes you feel better (less tense, anxious, and panicky), even though it may not make the feelings disappear entirely. The most effective challenges are ones tailored to specific self-statements. Listed below are some challenges that people find useful:

   a) **What is the evidence?** What is the evidence that if I don't smoke in the next 10 minutes, I'll die? Has anyone ever died from not smoking? What's the evidence that people recovering from an cannabis problem don't have the feelings I'm having? What is the evidence that I'll *never improve*?

   b) **What's so awful about that?** What's so awful about feeling bad? Of course I can survive it. Who said that abstinence would be easy? What's so terrible about experiencing an urge? I can get through it. I've gotten through other difficult feelings and experiences and can live to tell about them. These urges are not like being hungry or thirsty; they're more like a craving for a particular food or an urge to talk to a particular person—they'll pass.

   c) **I'm a human being and have a right to make mistakes.** Maybe I worry about not getting everything done that I hope to, or not being as patient as I should be. What's so bad about that? We all make mistakes, and in a situation that's complicated, there may not be a clear "right" or "perfect" way to handle things. Some of these strategies will be necessary or helpful only initially to distract yourself from persistent urges; in the long run, you'll have an easier time if you replace the thoughts with other activities. After a while, abstinence will feel more natural. The urges will diminish in intensity and will come less often. You will also know how to cope with them.

In the example below, the clinician and patient discuss craving triggers and self-talk strategies.

> **Clinician (C):** You identified one of your strongest triggers as seeing other people smoking, especially family members. Let's try to pinpoint exactly what's going on.
>
> **Shirley (S):** I feel that if I don't smoke with some family members, they might think I'm above them. They already make fun of me, calling me the college girl, and I want to fit in.
>
> **C:** You're sensitive to your family members and concerned they'll think you're trying to be better than they are by not smoking. What is the evidence this will happen?
>
> **S:** Well, I guess it's more a fear than a fact. I really do love them and know they love me. But I don't know how they would respond.
>
> **C:** What thoughts have you had about telling them?
>
> **S:** I almost told my uncle the other day when he lit up. But then I ended up smoking, and I just couldn't.
>
> **C:** You realize that once you get high, it's difficult to make changes.
>
> **S:** I've been thinking that I need to tell them when there's no chance that we would be smoking. But I dread it!
>
> **C:** What are some other ways you might let them know?

Clinician-Led Demonstration/Role-Play

The clinician gives the patient the *Urge Surfing* handout and orients them to the activity by summarizing the rationale) Much of this will have already been discussed in the session. The clinician then walks the patient through a brief demonstration of how to implement the Urge Surfing strategy. This is done by describing each step in the activity and modeling how the technique is applied. A useful strategy when modeling this technique is to share out loud your experiences, step by step, as if you were engaging in the strategy in that moment.

Patient-Led Practice (Assess Skills Transfer)

To prepare the patient to practice Urge Surfing, ask them to identify a recent situation in which they felt a strong craving or urge to use. Ask the patient to describe the trigger(s) and their experience of the craving/urge with enough detail to stimulate some degree of craving in that moment. Then, the clinician supports the patient in practicing Urge Surfing. The

Orientation to Clinical Interventions Addressing Cannabis Use Disorder

clinician walks the patient through the activity, step by step, reading the instructions and prompts aloud and checking in with the patient as needed throughout the activity. When the practice is complete, the clinician affirms the patient's skill application and offers follow-up questions to encourage the patient to explore their physical, emotional, and cognitive experiences throughout the Urge Surfing activity.

Identify Real-World Application

The clinician helps the patient to think through opportunities for how they might continue strengthening their skills in managing cravings and urges. These might be upcoming situations in which the patient anticipates encountering a craving trigger. Ideally, the patient would initiate practice of new skills for managing cravings when they are experiencing mild-to-moderate intensity cravings. This intensity level is heightened enough to provide the patient with an opportunity to practice skill application outside of a high-risk situation. As the patient's skills strengthen, they will become more adept at using these coping strategies and more prepared for managing high-intensity cravings. At the same time, the clinician also supports the patient in planning response strategies for high-intensity cravings or urges by identifying a combination of strategies that can be deployed if needed.

The clinician introduces the following exercises to support the patient in identifying potentially triggering situations and a plan for responding to those triggers. Using the *Coping with Cravings and Discomfort* handout, the clinician asks the patient to generate a list of any additional triggers they encounter in daily life. The patient is then asked to circle any triggers they can more easily avoid or reduce their exposure to, such as having cannabis or substances in the home. The clinician then supports the patient in generating a craving plan. The clinician asks the patient to select two or three of the general coping strategies discussed and think through how they will put them into practice when experiencing an urge. For example, if the patient seemed to gravitate toward distracting activities, ask them to identify which specific activities would be most helpful? Encourage the patient to consider: Which strategies are available? Which take preparation? If one does not work, what will they try next?

Negotiate and Prepare Between-Session Challenge

The exploration of real-world skill application is a natural transition into negotiation of a between-session challenge. The clinician encourages the patient to continue reviewing the materials handed out at this session and previous sessions. The clinician asks the patient where and when the patient can commit to using avoidance, escape, distraction, and embrace coping skills to manage urges and cravings. The patient is encouraged to continue practice of Urge Surfing along with other strategies as relevant to their identified triggers and craving plan.

For any identified between-session challenges, the clinician works with the patient to ensure that they know what they will do, when they will do it, and how often it will be done, mentally rehearsing its application in their daily life. Most patients benefit from writing down this plan somewhere accessible to them, to also serve as an ongoing reminder. For this session, the clinician also introduces and encourages the patient to use the *Daily Record of Urges to Use* handout to track their urge experiences and coping responses throughout the week.

Elicit Commitment

The clinician explores the patient's commitment for completing the between-session challenge (at least two times) and uses MI strategies as needed to assess and strengthen commitment. The clinician also asks the patient to think through any potential obstacles to their skills practice and works with them to identify solutions and activate resources as needed to support their skill application.

Summarize and Conclude the Session

The clinician reviews the content of the session, solicits feedback from the patient, responds empathically to their comments, and troubleshoots any difficulties. The clinician asks that the patient report back on their efforts to complete the between-session exercise at the next session. The clinician prepares the patient for the next session by introducing the topic and explaining how it will be helpful on the path toward wellness.

Session 7. Handling Urges, Cravings, and Discomfort Handouts

Coping with Cravings and Discomfort

About Urges and Cravings

- Urges are common in the recovery process. Do not regard them as signs of failure. Instead, use your urges to help you understand what triggers your cravings.
- Urges are like ocean waves. They get stronger only to a point; then they start to subside.
- You win every time you defeat an urge to use. Urges get stronger the next time if you give in and "feed" them. However, if you don't feed it, an urge eventually will weaken and die.

My Craving Triggers

Make a list of craving triggers. Circle the triggers you can more easily avoid or reduce your exposure to, such as removing cannabis or substances in your home.

23.	24.
25.	26.
27.	28.
29.	30.
31.	32.
33.	34.
35.	36.

My Craving Plan

Select two or three of the general strategies discussed and plan how to put them into practice if you experience an urge.

I will use these strategies if I experience an urge.

1) _____
2) _____
3) _____
4) _____
5) _____

Between-Session Challenge

For the next week, make a daily record of urges to use cannabis or substances, the intensity of those urges, and the coping behaviors you used.

Fill out the *Daily Record of Urges to Use* handout:

- Date
- Situation: Include anything about the situation and your thoughts or feelings that seemed to trigger the urge to use.
- Intensity of cravings: Rate your craving; **1 = none at all, 100 = worst ever.**
- Coping behaviors used: Note how you attempted to cope with the urge to use cannabis or substances. If it helps, note the effectiveness of your coping technique.

Daily Record of Urges to Use

Date	Situation (Include Thoughts and Feelings)	Intensity of Cravings (1–100)*	Coping Behaviors Used

*Intensity of cravings scale: 1 = none at all, 100 = worst ever

Orientation to Clinical Interventions Addressing Cannabis Use Disorder

Urge Surfing

Many people try to cope with their urges by gritting their teeth and toughing it out. Some urges, especially when you first return to your old using environment, are too strong to ignore. When this happens, it can be useful to stay with your urge to use until it passes. This technique is called urge surfing.

Urges are like ocean waves. They are small when they start, grow in size, and then break up and dissipate. You can imagine yourself as a surfer who will ride the wave, staying on top of it until it crests, breaks, and turns into less powerful, foamy surf. The basis of urge surfing is similar to that of many martial arts. In judo, one overpowers an opponent by first going with the force of the attack. By joining with the opponent's force, one can take control of it and redirect it to one's advantage. This type of technique of gaining control by first going with the opponent allows one to take control while expending a minimum of energy. Urge surfing is similar. You can join with an urge (rather than meet it with a strong opposing force) as a way of taking control of your urge to use. After you have read and become familiar with the instructions for urge surfing, you may find this a useful technique when you have a strong urge to use.

Urge surfing has three basic steps:

1) Take an inventory of how you experience the craving. Do this by sitting in a comfortable chair with your feet flat on the floor and your hands in a comfortable position. Take a few deep breaths and focus inward. Allow your attention to wander through your body. Notice where in your body you experience the craving and what the sensations are like. Notice each area where you experience the urge and tell yourself what you are experiencing. For example, "Let me see—my craving is in my mouth and nose and in my stomach."

2) Focus on one area where you are experiencing the urge. Notice the exact sensations in that area. For example, do you feel hot, cold, tingly, or numb? Are your muscles tense or relaxed? How large an area is involved? Notice the sensations and describe them to yourself. Notice the changes that occur in the sensation. "Well, my mouth feels dry and parched. There is tension in my lips and tongue. I keep swallowing. As I exhale, I can imagine the smell and taste of [____]."

3) Refocus on each part of your body that experiences the craving. Don't try to escape from or avoid the experience of craving. Accept its presence. Pay attention to and describe to yourself the changes that occur in the sensations. Notice how the urge comes and goes.

Many people notice that after a few minutes of urge surfing, the craving vanishes. The purpose of this exercise, however, is not to make the craving go away but to experience the craving in a new way. If you practice urge surfing, you will become familiar with your cravings and learn how to ride them out until they go away easily.

Session 8. Making Important Life Decisions

Introduction

There are many paths to recovery, and the path your client may take may differ from what science may suggest. The right path for your client is what works for that person.

So many people experiencing cannabis use, depression, or other life challenges live their lives by habit and circumstances. They often hope things will get better when circumstances change, not fully recognizing that we bring who we are wherever we go. And waiting for things to get better is often to consign ourselves to be the observer and not the architects of our own lives. Often this waiting for things to get better takes us away from what is most important to us: our values and beliefs of the person we want to be and the life we want to live.

One of the things we have learned from persons in long-term recovery is they strive to live and act each day grounded in their chosen values and acting with intention. This is the spiritual core often spoken of in the fellowships.

Our purpose in this session is to support our clients to become aware of and to own those values and to make decisions for living and acting in accord with that which they hold most important.

So what do we mean by values? "Values are freely chosen ways that we understand our place in the world. They are patterns of behavior that evolve over time based on our actions and the satisfaction we feel doing those things for their own sake. Acting in accord with our chosen values is intrinsically rewarding (SC Hayes et al. 2011).

Session 8 expands on previous motivational activities and is applicable to anyone making an important life choice. We can normalize ambivalence and the real, normal angst that is healthy in making a change that is in line with that which is most important in the life your patient wants to live. Yes, change is not without risk and so is staying the same. We support our patients to identify and embrace areas where decisions need to be made. In your previous work in Sessions 1, The Life Movie, and Session 2, the Awareness Record (functional analysis), the clinician and patient have a growing awareness of those values and in what way your patient is living and acting. The first part of this session is a reflective discussion where you, the clinician, clarify and bring to light (again) your person's chosen values and determine is your patient acting in alignment with or disconnected from those values. This conversation

Session 8. Making Important Life Decisions | **193**

about disconnection from valued living can be uncomfortable. (e.g., I feel like such a failure that I have not been here for my kids the way they need me). We facilitate agreement in those life areas where your patient seeks to make change.

When your patient is ready, you can provide them with a consistent decision-making method designed to provide clarity while increasing readiness and action. Handouts for this session include a values clarifying tool, readiness rulers, and the decisional balance. The primary discussion strategies include scaling (using readiness rulers), double-sided reflections, pros and cons of change (using a decisional balance sheet), looking ahead, looking back, clarification of values using compassionate reflections, and imagining extremes.

A supportive other person may be invited to join Session 8 to provide additional statements about the benefits of making a decision to stop using (or another important prosocial change) and if necessary an accurate recollection of "negative events associated with continued use." It is important for the clinician to monitor and prevent this from becoming a negative or overwhelming experience for the patient (e.g., the supporter is angry or frustrated with the patient over past use and threatens dire consequences).

Session 8 focuses on the following:

- Identifying key decisions that need to be made.
- Explore and clarify core values that could inform decision.
- Decisional balance to tip the scales in favor of change.
- Readiness rulers.
- Affirming the patient's ability to take action on a decision.
- Use of double-sided reflection to showcase where your patient is and where they want to be.
- Affirm that change can feel uncomfortable and so is staying the same.

The Patient's Experience

- The patient experiences a nonjudgmental conversation about ambivalence and decisions regarding continued use or other important life decision.
- The patient learns a process for making decisions intentionally with comprehension and clarity.
- The patient develops a thorough understanding of current reasons for staying the same and current reasons for making a different choice.

Clinician Preparation

MET Session 8. Making Important Life Decisions	
Materials • Values Clarifying Tool • Readiness Rulers (Pre and Post) • Decision-Making Guide	**Session Length** 45–60 minutes **Delivery Method** MET-focused individual therapy

Strategies
- OARS (Open-ended questions, Affirmations, Reflections, Summary)
- EDARS (Express Empathy, Develop Discrepancy, Awareness of Ambivalence, Roll with Sustained talk/discord, Support self-efficacy); identify stage of change
- MI Eliciting Change Talk, Current Motivation (Readiness Ruler), Elaboration, Looking Back, Looking Forward, Pros and Cons (Decisional Balance), Imagining Extremes
- Develop "real-life practice challenge" (sampling sobriety)

Goals for This Session
- Further explore the patient's attitudes and values.
- Elicit ambivalence and increase verbalized discrepancies in favor of change.
- Use MI to strengthen change talk strategies and tools to enable visual record of the patient's values and goals.
- Provide patient with clear set of strategies for making important life decisions.
- Elicit commitment from patient to take one action step to reinforce decision made during session.

Session 8 Outline and Overview

1) Engagement and assessment of the patient's readiness to proceed
   - Welcome the patient and continue to build rapport; address any obstacles to the therapeutic alliance.
   - Share the session agenda.
   - Ask whether any changes have occurred since the last meeting.
   - Discuss the decision to continue use, the benefits, and any consequences.
   - Review the between-session challenge(s).
   - Review the daily check-in and supporter plan completion.
2) Motivational strategy involving readiness for change?
   - Introduce important life decision of concern for patient (e.g., being the person that I want to be; achieving abstinence from substances; being a good father, mother, or parent; leaving or remaining in uniformed service; marriage or divorce; disclosure of sensitive information to an important other). Explore through compassionate reflections patient core values.
   - Introduce the readiness ruler.
   - Elicit the patient's readiness score.
   - Use double-sided reflection to bring into the conversation where your patient is and where they want to be. Reflect on alignment or disconnect with values.
   - Discuss real and potential future for patient without change and with change.

Clinician Note: When exploring with patients where there is a values disconnect, this is often accompanied by a strong affect of shame and guilt.

3) Introduce and teach decision-making steps
   - Discuss concept of decision making, normalizing ambivalence as part of the process.
   - Provide a rationale for focusing on decision making.
   - Introduce idea that certain steps can make the decision-making process less overwhelming and potentially clearer.
   - Emphasize that while these steps can be used for any decision, today's session focus will be on the decision as to whether to continue use of substances or _____.
   - Give patient Decision-Making Guide and review steps 1 through 5.

196 | *Orientation to Clinical Interventions Addressing Cannabis Use Disorder*

4) Complete steps 1 through 3 of the Decision-Making Guide for decision regarding use.
   - Elicit the decision topic from the patient and options the patient can choose.
   - Using Decision-Making Guide, explore pros and cons of each choice, including how the choice relates to patient's short- and long-term goals and the feelings each decision evokes.
   - Discuss the history of patient's life prior to use.
   - Discuss real and potential future for patient without change and with change.
   - Elicit the patient's top three statements in each category; end with the benefits of changing.
5) Using the readiness ruler in the Decision-Making Guide, ask the patient to rate their readiness.
6) Summarize the change talk discussions, emphasizing any change in readiness:
   - Illustrate any increased readiness or continued ambivalence.
7) Have patient complete step 5 of the Decision-Making Guide.
8) If appropriate, assign a between-session challenge, and elicit a specific commitment to complete the challenge:
   - If the patient is not ready to make changes but is willing to engage in continued exploration, suggest committing to accurately monitoring use to identify any possibility of change or reduction.
   - If/when the patient has decided to end treatment, affirm the patient's efforts to date and end in a positive fashion. It may be possible to ask the patient to think it over, talk about it with a significant other, and then call with a final decision in a day or two.
9) Conclude the session.

Session 8 Protocol

The clinician welcomes the patient, asks about the week in general, and proceeds to focus on use behaviors. The clinician uses rapport-building strategies to understand and nonjudgmentally reflect the patient's reasons and decision to continue using.

> **Clinician (C):** Thanks for sharing the highlights of your week with me. You paint the picture of how busy you are at work and how much you need to find quick, easy ways to relax when you get home.
>
> **Michael (M):** That's right. My time feels so limited and my energy is pretty low by the time I get home, and I just look forward to a couple of cold beers and a few hits off my pipe. Then I can settle into being with my wife and family for dinner, or whatever else is on the schedule.
>
> **C:** You've identified an efficient and nice way of taking care of yourself to ease the transition from work to home life.
>
> **M:** Right, and so when my doctor asked me to see you, I was a bit annoyed and wondered why, in the scope of all the possible problems, she figured I needed to address this first. Anyway, I'm still not convinced I need to change, even though the assessment and our first discussions make it clear that my regular and long-term use of cannabis and weed, combined with my lack of exercise, is contributing to my risks for heart trouble.
>
> **C:** That makes sense because your habit of relaxing works well, and why bother changing if there is no immediately obvious sign of damage to your health but rather a risk in the future.
>
> **M:** You said that perfectly. There's just not enough reason for me to change right now.

The clinician takes out the readiness ruler sheet and asks the patient to respond to the first ruler by marking the appropriate level of "readiness." The clinician explains this will also be looked at after talking today. (The delivery of the pre-readiness ruler can be adjusted in any way that is appropriate for the patient; it can be handed out in the second session as part of the between-session challenge and then discussed at the beginning of Session 3 as a way to get into the conversation about readiness.)

_198_ | _Orientation to Clinical Interventions Addressing Cannabis Use Disorder_

> **C:** All right, you sound pretty definite about your position here. And it can be helpful to actually state a number on where you stand now with regard to changing your use, a baseline marker (similar to a cholesterol test), so if for any reason you decide to make changes, we can see where you started. Here is a ruler and I'd like you to score where you believe you stand right now.
>
> **M:** That's easy. I'm like 10 percent on this. I know there are a few important health reasons to do something, but like I said, it's just not enough now.

The clinician takes out the Decision-Making Guide and readiness ruler sheet and introduces the idea of learning a decision-making process. The clinician could say something like:

> **C:** I get it. While you care about your health, being able to use is really important to you. Given that you're not really in a place to want to make a big change right now, would you be willing to talk with me just a little bit more today? I'd like to talk to you about a few strategies that can help you make and commit to important life decisions. Many individuals wrestle with making important life decisions: a soldier telling his commander that he has a cannabis problem; partners deciding whether to stay in or leave a relationship; stopping smoking or drug use are a few examples. Sometimes, when we feel overwhelmed or unsure of what direction to go, being able to go through a set of steps can slow things down, help us to think logically, and remind us of our goals and how our choices can affect our ability to reach our goals. While these steps can be used for any type of decision, I thought it might be helpful if we use them to go through your choices around your use. How does that sound to you?

The clinician reviews steps 1 through 5 generally on the Decision-Making Guide. After briefly teaching the patient about the five steps, the clinician then begins to engage the patient in a decision-making discussion about use using the five-step process. The clinician should have the Decision-Making Guide out to complete with the patient.

The clinician may use strategies to elicit change talk but clearly realize the patient is on the low end of desire and perceived reasons for needing

Session 8 Protocol | 199

to change. The clinician asks the patient to think back to a time when he did not regularly use to relax and to discuss the differences. The clinician probes for other strategies the patient used in the past to feel good after a busy day. Then the clinician asks the patient to look ahead, assuming there are no changes, to predict what life and health will feel like. The clinician reflects and illuminates the differences between the two descriptions: (a) when not using but doing other activities and (b) when use is continued into the future. The patient is asked to look at the Decision-Making Guide and asked to list the pros and cons.

- Accept all answers (do not argue with answers given by patient).
- Explore answers.
- Be sure to note both the benefits and costs of current behavior and change.
- Explore the costs/benefits with respect to patient's goals and values.
- Summarize the costs and benefits.

After the patient completes a few statements for each category, the clinician asks the patient to read them aloud, finishing with the benefits of changing use. The clinician summarizes the benefits and returns to the *Learning New Coping Strategies* handout describing a few potential replacements for the patient's stated benefits of use. Next, the clinician switches gears and asks the patient to imagine some possible extremes in a real future without change.

> **C:** What will it be like in a few years if you continue using and go back to your doctor for a cardiac wellness visit? What's the worst news you can imagine getting?
>
> **M:** I never really like to think about that. Like I said, I just live day to day and that kind of thought is above my pay grade, but since you're asking ... I guess I could find out my cholesterol is too high and be told to take Lipitor or some pill like that. My doc might also tell me that he strongly recommends I quit substances to avoid some kind of stroke or heart attack or something. (My relative had a heart attack at 54. That was really scary)
>
> **C:** The risks get worse until you are forced to take medication and live with the chances of a serious heart condition.
>
> **M:** Yeah, but we all take risks every day. This is one my doc, my family, and now you care to talk about.

The clinician summarizes the Decision-Making Guide discussion. The clinician then reassesses the patient's readiness to stop using the readiness ruler. If there is a shift, the clinician should evoke from the patient their thoughts and feelings about the shift. The clinician can then shift the discussion by asking the patient in an open-ended manner, what they intend to do around their use. If interest in any degree of change is stated, negotiate a plan for reduction of use or stopping altogether.

Review and Conclude

There are several possible outcomes after this motivational enhancement change talk discussion. If remaining undecided, the patient may be encouraged to continue exploration and remain in treatment until reaching a clear decision. The clinician might ask them to try "sampling a sobriety period" or suggest continuing to raise self-awareness and committing to accurately monitoring use to identify any easy targets of change or places to make reductions in use. If the patient commits to stopping use of substances, the clinician can introduce change plan tools from Sessions 1 and 2.

Session 8. Making Important Life Decisions Handouts

202 | *Orientation to Clinical Interventions Addressing Cannabis Use Disorder*

Clinician's Quick Reference to Session 8

1) Welcome the patient and continue to build rapport.
   - Check in on past week
   - Follow up on between-session challenge
2) Share the session agenda and rationale.
   - Discuss the decision of concern, the benefits, and any consequences.
   - Review the between-session challenge(s).
   - Review the daily check-in and supporter plan completion.
3) Introduce motivational strategy involving readiness for change.
   - Reintroduce the readiness ruler.
   - Elicit the patient's readiness score regarding specific concern.
   - Seek elaboration and outcomes.
   - Discuss the history of patient's life prior to use or in relationship to current concern.
   - Discuss real and potential future for patient without change and with change.
4) Introduce and teach decision-making steps:
   - Discuss concept of decision-making, normalizing ambivalence as part of the process.
   - Provide a rationale for focusing on decision-making.
   - Introduce idea that certain steps can make the decision-making process less overwhelming and potentially more clear.
   - Introduce how clarity of personal values helps guide decision-making.
   - Emphasize that while these steps can be used for any decision, today's session focus will be on the decision whether to continue to use.
   - Give patient Decision-Making Guide and review steps 1 through 5.
5) Complete steps 1 through 3 of the Decision-Making Guide for decision regarding use.
   - Elicit from patient what the decision topic is and from which options the patient can choose.
   - Using Decision-Making Guide, explore pros and cons of each choice, including how the choice relates to patient's short- and long-term goals and what feelings each decision evokes.
   - Review relevant history of patient's life.

Clinician's Quick Reference to Session 8 | 203

- Discuss real and potential future for patient without change and with change.
- Elicit the patient's top three statements in each category; end with the benefits of changing.

6) Using the readiness ruler in the Decision-Making Guide, ask the patient to reassess their readiness.
  - Summarize the change talk discussions, emphasizing any change in readiness: Illustrate any increased readiness or continued ambivalence.
  - Have patient complete step 5 of the Decision-Making Guide.
  - If appropriate, assign a between-session challenge and elicit a specific commitment to complete the challenge:
  - If appropriate, discuss and help patient develop a specific plan such as: reduction target, "sampling sobriety period," or stop date (if the patient has not already stopped using).
  - If the patient is not ready to make changes but is willing to engage in continued exploration: If change is substance specific, suggest committing to accurately monitoring use to identify any possibility of change or reduction.
  - If the patient has made a decision, affirm the patient's efforts to date and end in a positive fashion. It may be useful to ask the patient to think it over, talk about it with a significant other, and then call with a final decision in a day or two.

7) Conclude the session.

MI Skills and Strategies

Motivational Interviewing (MI) Spirit	Responding to Change Talk
Interviewing	Reflection
Collaboration	Elaboration questions
Guiding	Summary
MI principles	Affirmation
Express empathy	Elicit-Provide-Elicit
Develop discrepancy	Menu of options
Roll with resistance	Dealing with resistance
Support self-efficacy	Simple reflections
Fundamental skills	Amplified reflections
Open-ended questions	Double-sided reflections and
Affirmations	shifting focus
Reflections	Agreement with a twist
Summarizations	Coming alongside
Change talk	Reframing
Desire to change	Emphasizing personal control
Ability	Disclosing feelings
Reason	Traps
Need	Premature focus
Commitment	Labeling
Eliciting change talk	Question/answer
Importance/confidence ruler	Confrontation/denial
Querying extremes	Expert
Looking back; looking forward	Blaming
Evocative questions	
Decisional balance	
Goals/values exploration	
Elaboration	

Readiness-to-Change Ruler

The Readiness-to-Change Ruler is used to assess a person's willingness or readiness to change, determine where they are on the continuum between "not prepared to change" and "already changing," and promote identification and discussion of perceived barriers to change. The ruler represents a continuum from "not prepared to change" on the left to "already changing" on the right.

The Readiness-to-Change Ruler may be used as a quick assessment of a person's present motivational state relative to changing a specific behavior and serve as the basis for motivation-based interventions to elicit behavior change. Readiness to change should be assessed regarding a specific activity, such as reducing use of cannabis, since persons may differ in their stages of readiness to change for different behaviors.

Administration

1) Indicate the specific behavior to be assessed on the Readiness-to-Change Ruler form. Ask the person to mark on a linear scale from 0 to 10 their current position in the change process. A 0 on the left side of the scale indicates "not prepared for change," and a 10 on the right side of the scale indicates "already changing."
2) Question the person about why they did not place the mark further to the left, which elicits motivational statements.
3) Question the person about why they did not place the mark further to the right, which elicits perceived barriers.
4) Ask the person for suggestions about ways to overcome identified barriers and actions that might be taken.

Interview Questions

"Could we talk for a few minutes about your interest in making a change?"
"On a scale from 1 to 10, with 1 being not ready at all and 10 being completely ready, how ready are you to make any changes in your cannabis use?"
"You marked (or said) [____]. That's great. That means you are [____] percent ready to make change."
"Why did you choose that number and not a lower one such as a 1 or a 2? Sounds like you have some important reasons for change."

206 | *Orientation to Clinical Interventions Addressing Cannabis Use Disorder*

Values Exploration

In this simple exercise have your patient place the "My Values" sheet in front and take a minute to review the list of values. Have your patient without major deliberation write five or six values that they hold most important today. Note today is important. In successive rings add five more and five more. Reflect and explore with your patient on each of the values at the center. Ask—Why are these of greatest importance? How aligned with these are you today? Where might you choose to make a change and why? This exploration will better prepare your patient and you for decision-making and action planning.

List of Values

- Acceptance
- Achievement
- Adventure
- Helping others
- Attentiveness
- Balance
- Beauty
- Caring
- Charity
- Courage
- Connection (Connecting w/others)
- Competence
- Creativity
- Curiosity
- Determination
- Discipline
- Friendliness
- Friendship Fun
- Generosity
- Grace
- Gratitude
- Honesty
- Hopefulness
- Humility
- Humor

- Independence
- Integrity
- Introspection
- Joy
- Justice
- Kindness
- Knowledge
- Leadership
- Learning and growth
- Love
- Loyalty
- Nature (appreciation of)
- Open-mindedness
- Openness with others
- Optimism/being positive
- Peace
- Philanthropy
- Play/Playfulness
- Reason/Logic
- Reliability
- Respect
- Responsibility—keeping promises
- Self-control
- Spirituality/Faith
- Stability/Security support
- Teamwork
- Thoughtfulness
- Trustworthiness
- Wisdom
- Wonder
- Work
- Others

My Values

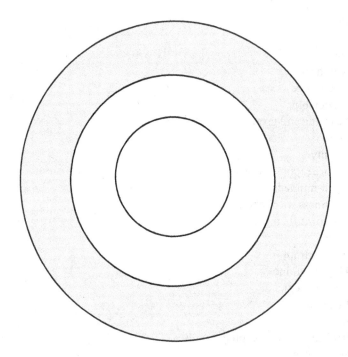

Instructions: This is a direct way to better understand your values. In the center include five or six values **most** important to you today. Your true north. In the next ring include values that are important. In the third ring include those that have some importance in life.

It's important to remember that values can and will shift in priority over time.

Values Exploration Questions

1) What is it like seeing your values laid out before?
2) Anything that you are surprised isn't here?
3) Which values are you living out to the best of your ability?
4) Which values are you struggling with right now?

Decision-Making Guide | **209**

Decision-Making Guide

Why create this decision-making guide?

This will help you think about the choices you are being presented with so you can calmly and logically identify and consider the ***Good Things*** and the ***Not-So-Good Things*** about each choice. While you are being asked to complete this sheet around your choice as to whether to continue using or abstain, it can be a helpful strategy when making other important life decisions. Weighing the ***Good Things*** and the ***Not-So-Good Things*** helps people make decisions. For example, while smoking may sometimes help people relax, it could also cause problems with family or work. Ask yourself, "What are the good things and the not-so-good things about my current use?" "What are the good things and the not-so-good things about changing my use?"

STEP 1: Define what decision you have to make, including options.	Decision Topic:		
STEP 2: Brainstorm the good and not-so-good things about **continuing** the behavior. Reflect on core values.	Option 1 (continuing behavior):		
STEP 3: Brainstorm the good and not-so-good things about **changing** the behavior. Reflect on values.	Option 2 (changing behavior):		
Continuing Behavior		Changing Behavior	
Cost	Benefits	Cost	Benefits
1.	1.	1.	1.
2.	2.	2.	2.
3.	3.	3.	3.
4.	4.	4.	4.

How will continuing the behavior help me act in accord with my values and reach my goals? EP 1: Define what decision you have to make, including options.	How will changing the behavior help me help me act in accord with my values and reach my goals?

STEP 4: Assess how ready you are to make a change in your behavior using the readiness ruler below.

Orientation to Clinical Interventions Addressing Cannabis Use Disorder

Not at all 0cm 1 2 3 4 5 6 7 8 9 10 Very

STEP 5: Write down your decision below, including how you are going to act on your decision and when you want to look back and consider how well it is working.

I intend to:

I will do this by:

I will evaluate my decision and how it is working in (*time frame*):

Decision-Making Guide Example

Why create this decision-making guide?

This will help you think about the choices you are being presented with so you can calmly and logically identify and consider the good things and the not-so-good Things about each choice. While you are being asked to complete this sheet around your choice as to whether to continue using or abstain, it can be a helpful strategy when making other important life decisions. Weighing the good things and the not-so-good things helps people make decisions. For example, while smoking may sometimes help people relax, it could also cause problems with family or work. Ask yourself, "What are the good things and the not-so-good things about my current use?" "What are the good things and the not-so-good things about changing my use?"

Here's an example from another individual. Remember, every person has different reasons for wanting to change use.

STEP 1: Define what decision you have to make, including options.	Decision Topic: My cannabis use
STEP 2: Brainstorm the good and not-so-good things about **continuing** the behavior.	Option 1 (continuing behavior): Keep smoking the way I have been—5 days a week, three to four smokes per day.
STEP 3: Brainstorm the good and not-so-good things about **changing** the behavior.	Option 2 (changing behavior): Stop smoking altogther.
Good things about my use	Good things about changing my use
More relaxed Will not have to think about my problems for a while More comfortable with my friends smoking.	More control over my life Support from family and friends Less legal trouble Better health

Not-so-good things about my use	Not-so-good things about changing my use
Disapproval from family and friends Can't get as much work done Costs too much money I'm late for class I argue with my roommate	More stress or anxiety Feel more depressed Feel inhibited with people I don't know Harder to socialize at parties
How will continuing the behavior help me reach my goals?	How will changing the behavior help me reach my goals?
Helps me handle my problems in the moment so I can keep going and get through the day.	Maybe my problems will get better, so I won't feel so stressed out and down all the time. I will have more money and do better at work and school, which will help me to stay independent.

STEP 4: Assess how ready you are to make a change in your behavior using the readiness ruler below.

Not at all 0cm 1 2 3 4 5 6 7 8 9 10 Very

STEP 5: Write down your decision below, including how you are going to act on your decision and when you want to look back and consider how well it is working.

I intend to:

I intend to stop smoking entirely.

I will do this by:

I will do this by not going to the bar, asking my friends and family for support, coming to treatment, and reminding myself why I am doing this.

I will evaluate my decision and how it is working in *(time frame)*:

I will evaluate my decision and how it is working in 1 week.

Thinking About My Use Option 3

Use this page to complete your own thinking exercise about cannabis/drug use. Remember, everyone is different, and your exercise will be uniquely yours.

Good things about my use	Good things about changing my use
Not-so-good things about my use	Not-so-good things about changing my use

Session 9. Enhancing Self-awareness

Introduction

Session 9 focuses on helping the patient to build self-awareness. Patients often view themselves and their behavior as somewhat of a mystery. They may feel puzzled and confused about what they do and why they do it. By helping a patient take greater notice of how things are happening in life, with specific focus on cannabis and substances or mood, the clinician provides a powerful tool and builds the important capacities for reflection and self-awareness.

There are many ways to increase self-awareness. The CBT approach makes use of "functional analysis," a way to carefully examine the patterns of cannabis and cannabis use. Even if a patient has been involved with substances for a long time and sees themself as highly self-aware, the person may be surprised by what is revealed during an in-depth inquiry.

The clinician is encouraged to discuss with the patient many aspects of use patterns. It is helpful to learn about the conditions where the patient is more or less likely to use. Conditions may be external (e.g., being with particular people or in certain places), and they may be internal (e.g., feelings, thoughts, general states of mind, associations).

The Patient's Experience

In Session 9, the patient is able to explore patterns of use in a nonjudgmental atmosphere. They are encouraged to share many aspects of experience with cannabis or other substances, such as when, where, and under what circumstances use is likely. The patient is also supported in discussing the positive and negative impacts of use to develop better self-knowledge and a fuller picture for the clinician. The patient may begin to identify potentially useful coping strategies to reach goals in relation to cannabis use.

Clinician Preparation

CBT Session 9. Enhancing Self-Awareness	
Materials • Cannabis Use Awareness Record • Personal Awareness Form • Learning New Coping Strategies/ Menu of Options • Future Self Letter • Relaxation Training	**Total Time** 1 hour **Delivery Method** CBT-focused individual or group therapy
Strategies • OARS (Open-ended questions, Affirmations, Reflections, Summary) • Support self-efficacy • Demonstrate skill, role-play • Follow CBT skills session reminders	
Goals for This Session • Begin to learn and practice skills that enhance self-awareness. • Introduce the patient to the rationale for coping skills training. • Examine the patient's high-risk situations, triggers, and coping strategies.	

Session 9 Outline and Overview

1) Build rapport and review:
   - Welcome the patient; check in about the week in general.
   - Review the patient's cravings, recent use experiences, and successes.
   - Review the between-session challenge.
   - Attend to the therapeutic alliance and address any obstacles, concerns.
   - Assess motivational factors and change readiness.
2) Explore the development of addictive patterns:
   - Provide rationale, such as the learned or associative nature of addiction (pairing with alterations in thinking and feeling).
   - Using the patient's own experiences, illustrate how using cannabis or other substances can change one's feelings; if the patient has not stated any examples, provide examples that are appropriate to their situation.
   - From the patient's stated use situations, identify examples of environmental triggers for use; ask the patient for other triggers they have experienced.
   - Elicit examples of feelings, beliefs, or automatic thoughts people may have about substances; use examples provided by the patient, and ask the patient for more examples.
   - Suggest that the patient start the process of change by understanding their behavior; ask, "Does this make sense to you?"
3) Empower through self-knowledge; understand high-risk situations and triggers. Explore with the patient—
   - Typical use situations (places, people, activities, time, days).
   - Triggers for use.
   - A recent use situation.
   - Thoughts and feelings at use times (tense, bored, stressed, etc.).
   - Complete *Knowledge Is Power* and summarize the list.
4) Put the pieces together: draw connections, consider new roads, and build coping strategies:
   - Emphasize the importance of coping strategies.
   - Reintroduce Learning New Coping Strategies.
   - Introduce a drawing connection exercise and identify new pathways toward desired outcomes.

Session 9 Outline and Overview | **217**

- Ask patient to identify strategies they have tried and those that might work best.
5) Develop or elicit a specific between-session challenge that incorporates material from the session.

Session Protocol

The clinician welcomes the patient and provides an overview of the session. In this session, the clinician draws on information from previous sessions to increase the patient's understanding about use patterns.

Building Rapport and Review

To continue building rapport with the patient, begin the session by eliciting information about life during the past week. Initially, try to focus on nonproblem areas. This is an opportunity to learn about the patient's interests and strengths. Such information can be used later to develop strategies for addressing the patient's cannabis use. The clinician continues to use MI skills to do this and always expresses genuine curiosity about the patient's life.

"How have things been since we last met?" Or, *"Tell me about something enjoyable you did during the past week?"*

If the patient cannot think of anything enjoyable during the past week, ask about interests and activities the person is likely to engage in, even if not during the past week.

"Tell me about some of your interests or hobbies?" Or, *"What kinds of things do you like to do in your free time?"*

Continue by asking the patient how they have been doing over the past week regarding cannabis and/or drug use.

"Tell me about your [drug(s) of choice] use during the past week?" Or, *"What has your use been like since we last met?"* Or, *"What thoughts have you had about your use since we last spoke?"*

Guidelines

Listen for possible changes in the patient's behaviors, thoughts, and feelings regarding use. Try to refrain from asking many questions. Let the patient tell you how they have been doing regarding their use or abstinence. Respond with reflective comments, and attempt to elicit the patient's own motivation-enhancing statements. Affirm any efforts made to reduce use and look for opportunities to support the patient's sense of self-efficacy. If there has been little or no change in the patient's use, look for opportunities to develop discrepancy through the use of double-sided reflections, exploring pros and cons, and seeking elaboration.

Explore the Development of Addictive Patterns

The clinician asks the patient to look closely at their behavior, environment, and beliefs to identify addictive patterns. See the sample language provided.

We think of repeated cannabis use as learned behavior. When people start to use cannabis or other substances a lot, they learn that it changes the way they feel. For example, some people use it like a tranquilizer to help them cope with stressful situations. Some use it when they feel blue. Others expect it to enhance positive feelings. Some think it makes them more confident. And some use it to avoid thinking about troublesome things. How does that fit with your experience? [Waits for answer.]

After a while, things in the environment can trigger use, sometimes without your even realizing it. The environment can trigger cravings. Things in the environment that can trigger use include seeing or smelling cannabis or other substances, being around people who are using, or being in stressful situations. During the assessment session, we talked about the connection you've noticed between getting paid on Fridays and buying cannabis. Are there other connections like that for you?

People often develop beliefs about substances they are using. These are ideas or "automatic thoughts" you've come to believe about you and your cannabis use. I've heard you say things in previous sessions like, "I can't be creative or work effectively without it," "I can't take the way I feel when I've tried to quit," "I need to change, but it's not worth the effort." What other beliefs do you have about you and [____]?

Substances can change the way a person feels, acts, and thinks. To help you avoid or cope with the situations in which you smoke and to help you find things you can do instead of using, let's start by working on understanding your behavior. Does this make sense to you?

Session 9 Outline and Overview | **219**

High-Risk Situations, Triggers, and Patient Empowerment through Self-Knowledge

The clinician explains that cannabis use behavior is learned over time. The patient's understanding of their use patterns can help the patient change those patterns. Understanding high-risk situations can help the patient avoid or cope with those situations. See the sample language provided.

> *If using cannabis or other substances changes the way a person acts, thinks, and feels, it's helpful to begin by identifying use patterns and habits. Once your patterns are identified, you may find it easier to change your behavior. You can find ways to cope with your high-risk situations without using. Change involves learning specific skills and strategies. Once you know about the situations and problems that contribute to your using, you can look for other ways to handle those situations. What do you think about that?*

The clinician focuses on the patient's behaviors and high-risk situations. See the sample language provided.

> *In what situations do you use cannabis/substances (e.g., places, people, activities, specific times, days)?*
>
> *What are your triggers for using (e.g., when you're in a social situation, when you've had a tense day, when you're faced with a difficult problem, when you want to feel relaxed)?*
>
> *Can you describe a recent situation when you used (e.g., a recurrence of use story)?*
>
> *Can you remember your thoughts and feelings at the time you used (e.g., tense, bored, depressed, stressed, overwhelmed, angry)?*
>
> *What were the consequences of using?*

Guidelines

Knowing what affects someone's own use gives more personal awareness (power) to decide whether to use or not use. Looking at the pros and cons of what happens after use also increases understanding and helps the individual make the decision about use in the future.

Hence, the name of the worksheet for understanding more about triggers is *Knowledge Is Power.*

Provide the patient with the Knowledge Is Power handout. Walk through the form as the patient fills it out as it relates to personal use from the previous week or a recent use episode.

220 | *Orientation to Clinical Interventions Addressing Cannabis Use Disorder*

Can you describe in detail the last time you used or had an opportunity to use? As you recall the incident, see if you can identify the triggers, thoughts, and feelings, decision to use, and pros and cons of your use.

Ask the patient to read the columns in the Knowledge Is Power handout and follow up with a series of questions to help generate statements for each required column. Get the patient to verbalize responses to each section of the handout before writing it down. This enables offering feedback/suggestions before anything is put on paper. The patient is less likely to feel criticized this way.

For example: "Many people report that a common trigger is a negative situation such as a fight with others and the bad feelings that arise as a result." Has this happened to you recently? Generate a discussion with the patient regarding personal triggers. Then, have the patient fill in the Knowledge Is Power handout.

"Now that we've filled in your Knowledge Is Power worksheet, I'd like you to read it aloud." To emphasize nonuse decisions, it is also good to ask, "Can you give me an example of a time when the same trigger did not result in your using?"

Indicate that this situational analysis—via the Knowledge Is Power worksheet—is something you hope the patient will continue using between sessions to help support decisions and steps toward reducing use and improving future wellness.

For example: "We think self-awareness and self-knowledge are essential to breaking the cycle of negative habits (such as automatically smoking cannabis) that some people get into. Instead, using the Knowledge Is Power worksheet makes us take a moment to think about all the elements prior and after our actions. This will help us understand how to avoid, replace, and cope with the thoughts, feelings, and situations in new ways."

The clinician asks the patient about alcohol/cannabis use behavior using MI techniques (e.g., reflection, expressing empathy) while learning important information about the patient's use environment. See the sample language provided.

> **Clinician (C):** In what situations do you find yourself using?
> **Doug (D):** When things get hectic at home. Between my wife and my son, it seems as if everyone is out to get me. When I smoke, I can cope with them.

Session 9 Outline and Overview | **221**

C: Using helps you cope with stress at home. Are there other situations when you smoke?

D: Not right now. When I go home, I should be able to relax, but with all the nagging, I end up using to escape.

C: You want your home to be peaceful, but conflicts over your using push you to smoke.

D: Yeah; sounds crazy, doesn't it?

C: Your situation is difficult. Things you identify that lead you to smoke are called triggers. You've said that conflicts at home trigger you to smoke. What are your thoughts and feelings during times of conflict at your house, right before you light up?

D: I'm thinking that if everyone would get off my back, I might be able to quit using. But they don't, and it's the only way I know how to relax.

C: You find yourself in a bind. Let's use the Knowledge Is Power document [presents it] to list the things we're talking about. You said using [____] helps you relax. What else does it do for you?

D: It helps me sleep. When I don't get high, it's hard getting to sleep. I used to enjoy the high a lot more than I do now. I keep using, but I don't even get that high anymore.

C: Sounds as if you're listing the negative parts of using. Are there others?

Together the clinician and patient fill out the Knowledge Is Power handout. Complete for two recent experiences (one internal, one external, if possible), or one use and one nonuse example.

Putting the Pieces Together: Draw Connections, Consider New Roads, and Build Coping Strategies
Identify Positive Effects

The patient will likely have discussed some positive effects in the course of identifying triggers and listing consequences. Summarize these and ask the patient to identify other desired effects of cannabis use.

I have already learned about some affects you look forward to when you smoke, like feeling some relief from stress and forgetting about the day. I am wondering what other effects of smoking you enjoy?

Use of evocative questions can be helpful for eliciting multiple effects. Both positive reinforcement (e.g., euphoria, drug effects) and the negative reinforcement (e.g., numb feelings, stop worrying) that may result from cannabis use should be considered as factors that maintain cannabis use.

What else?
If you stopped using cannabis today, what would you miss most?
Does smoking make some things in your life more tolerable?
What is the feeling you are looking for when you have your first smoke of the night?

Directive questions can also be used as needed:

You mentioned smoking in some social circumstances. What do you think cannabis does for you in that type of situation?

Summarize Effects

It sounds like we have gotten most of these. Let me read back what we have come up with so far. Some of the desirable effects of smoking that you see include reducing stress, forgetting about the day, feeling more socially confident, being able to stand up for yourself, feeling some excitement, feeling rewarded, and relieving boredom. Does that sound about right? This probably accounts for most of the effects that you are looking for when you smoke but perhaps not all. If you think of something else, we can always add it later.

Draw Connections

The clinician should help the patient make a connection between the triggers and the effects on the New Roads Worksheet (see, Figure 2).

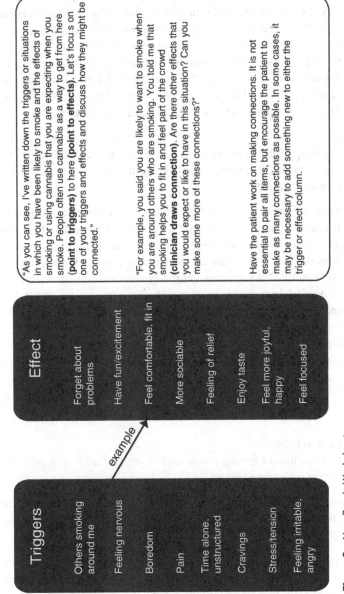

Figure 2 New Roads Worksheet.

Discuss Psychological Dependence

The relationship between triggers and effects is a good representation of how the patient has come to rely on substances to achieve a desired effect or to cope with some unpleasant circumstances. Attempting to cut back or quit using substances often causes an increase in discomfort for the patient, and without other options to manage the distress, continued cannabis use is more probable. This psychological dependence on substances will persist until the patient has addressed the deficit in coping skills and found more adaptive means for achieving these effects.

You have mapped this out well. One thing I noticed right away is that almost every trigger leads to this effect of "feeling relaxed." It is clear that feeling relaxed is an important effect for you, and smoking is how you get there most of the time.

What we have here is a map of how you have come to depend on cannabis in your life. If cannabis dependence were just a physical problem, you could get a three-day detox and come out never wanting to use again. In some way, this is a map of what keeps you using cannabis even when you may not want to. This is psychological dependence. Over time you have come to depend on cannabis to achieve these positive effects. When you stop smoking, you may begin to feel uncomfortable, not because of any physical withdrawal, but because you are not finding a way to get from this side (point to triggers) to this side (point to effects). Breaking the psychological dependence involves finding another way to get from the trigger to the effect that does not involve cannabis. If you can find ways to achieve some of these effects without smoking, I think you are going to have a lot less desire for cannabis. What do you think?"

Consider New Roads

Introduce the idea of finding a new road or path for achieving desirable outcomes in each trigger situation.

So, I am curious. As you look at all these triggers and the desired effects, can you think of any way you could get a similar effect you are looking for without cannabis as a new road or path?

If the patient has trouble identifying any alternative coping strategies, reminding the patient of alternative strategies that they talked about in previous sessions may be helpful for moving the discussion forward.

Earlier you told me that watching TV is a good escape from reality for the moment. This is one way to get this effect of forgetting about problems. Can you think of any other ways?

As the patient discusses current coping strategies and possible new means for achieving the desired effects, reflect and affirm as needed.

Exercise has worked for you in the past when you are feeling stressed, and it may be something that could help you again now. These are great ideas you are coming up with. What else can you imagine would help you get from any of these triggers to the desired effects without smoking?

The clinician keeps a detailed account of the new roads the patient identifies over the course of this discussion, and when the patient has run out of ideas, the clinician summarizes the patient's strategies.

You have really done a great job coming up with other ways to achieve these effects without needing to smoke to get there. You have things you have been using for a while that work in some of these situations. You also have some ideas about new strategies you could try for a few of these trigger situations, such as exercise, distracting yourself, and leaving your house when you are bored. These are all great ideas.

The clinician emphasizes the importance of coping strategies. See the sample language provided.

We've talked about your high-risk situations and triggers, and we have started to make connections between several important things. This is important because many people are unaware of how they put themselves at risk for using. Now we'll focus on coping with these situations in ways that will help you resist the urge to use. You've already read the (Menu of Options) Learning New Coping Strategies (presents Session 2 handout again). Let's take a few moments to go through it and identify the strategies you've tried and others that might work. Remember, some strategies involve things you can do or specific actions you can take, some involve ways of thinking, and some involve other people or your surroundings.

Assign a Between-Session Challenge

The clinician gives the patient a blank copy of Knowledge Is Power and asks the patient to document episodes of craving or desire for substances

226 | *Orientation to Clinical Interventions Addressing Cannabis Use Disorder*

between this session and the next one. The clinician chooses an appropriate assignment from among the following and reviews the instructions with the patient:

- Write a future letter to self
- Practice relaxation training

Review and Conclude

The clinician reviews the content of the session, asks the patient for feedback, responds empathically to their comments, and troubleshoots any difficulties. The clinician explains that the patient will report back on their efforts to complete the between-session exercises at the next session. The clinician prepares the patient for the upcoming session by briefly describing the topic and how the skill addressed will support the patient's needs. This emphasizes and builds a positive expectation for the upcoming work.

Session 9. Enhancing Self-Awareness Handouts

228 | *Orientation to Clinical Interventions Addressing Cannabis Use Disorder*

Clinician's Quick Reference to Session 9

1) Building Rapport and Review
   - Welcome the patient; check in about the week in general.
   - Review the patient's cravings, recent use experiences, and successes.
   - Review the between-session challenge.
2) Explore the Development of Addictive Patterns
   - Provide rationale, such as the learned or associative nature of addiction (pairing with alterations in thinking and feeling).
   - Using the patient's own experiences, illustrate how using cannabis or other substances can change one's feelings; if the patient has not stated any examples, provide examples that are appropriate to their situation.
   - From the patient's stated use situations, identify examples of environmental triggers for use; ask the patient for other triggers they have experienced.
   - Elicit examples of feelings, beliefs, or automatic thoughts people may have about substances; use examples provided by the patient, and ask the patient for more examples.
   - Suggest that the patient start the process of change by understanding their behavior; ask, "Does this make sense to you?"
3) Empowerment Through Self-Knowledge: Understanding High-Risk Situations and Triggers
   - Explore with the patient—
     - Typical use situations (places, people, activities, time, days).
     - Triggers for use.
     - A recent use situation.
     - Thoughts and feelings at use times (tense, bored, stressed, etc.).
     - Complete Knowledge Is Power and summarize the list.
4) Putting the Pieces Together: Draw Connections, Consider New Roads, and Build Coping Strategies
   - Emphasize the importance of coping strategies.
   - Reintroduce Learning New Coping Strategies.
   - Introduce a drawing connection exercise and identify new pathways toward desired outcomes.
   - Ask patient to identify strategies they have tried and those that might work best.
5) Develop or Elicit a Specific Between-Session Challenge That Incorporates Material from the Session

Alcohol/Cannabis Use Awareness Record

As a way to increase awareness about your patterns of use, we'll use this form to identify the kinds of situations, thoughts, feelings, and consequences that are associated with your alcohol/cannabis use. It may be difficult initially, but once you get accustomed to paying more attention, you will become skilled at discovering the ways in which you typically use alcohol/substances.

Trigger (What types of events tend to make you want to use? For example, an argument, disappointment, loss, or frustration; spending time with friends who use; having alcohol/substances easily available to you; recalling positive memories of past use.)

1 _____

2 _____

Thoughts, Feelings, and Beliefs (What were you thinking or how were you feeling in relation to the triggers you have identified? For example, thinking you were incompetent or stupid or that you could never achieve a particular goal; feeling angry, sad, frightened, or glad.)

1 _____

2 _____

Behavior (What did you actually do when you were thinking and feeling in these ways? For example, used [____], went out to dinner, isolated yourself from people.)

1 _____

2 _____

Positive Consequences (What good came out of your response to the situation? For example, I felt much better for a short period.)

1 _____

2 _____

230 | *Orientation to Clinical Interventions Addressing Cannabis Use Disorder*

Negative Consequences (What negative things happened as a result of your response? For example, I felt bad about myself for using; I couldn't complete the work I needed to finish.)

1 _____

2 _____

Alcohol/Cannabis Use Awareness Record (continued)

As a way to increase awareness about your patterns of use, use this form to identify the kinds of situations, thoughts, feelings, and consequences that are associated with your alcohol/cannabis use.

Describe Incident:

Trigger	Thoughts, Feelings, and Beliefs	Intensity of Craving	Behavior	Positive Results	Negative Results
(What sets me up to be more likely to use alcohol or drugs?)	(What was I thinking? What was I feeling? What did I tell myself?)	Low–high, 1–10	(What did I do then?)	(What good things happened?)	(What bad things happened?)

Date and Time: _____

Alcohol/Cannabis Use Awareness Record Example

As a way to increase awareness about your patterns of use, use this form to identify the kinds of situations, thoughts, feelings, and consequences that are associated with your alcohol/cannabis use. Below is an example of how the form might be used.

Describe Incident: Spent evening with my friend smoking weed and drinking beer.

Trigger	Thoughts, Feelings, and Beliefs	Intensity of Craving	Behavior	Positive Results	Negative Results
(What sets me up to be more likely to use alcohol or drugs?)	(What was I thinking? What was I feeling? What did I tell myself?)	Low–high, 1–10	(What did I do then?)	(What good things happened?)	(What bad things happened?)
Friend called and invited me to get high with him. Nothing else to do.	"I want to reward myself." "I'm bored." "Felt good about going 15 days without using, so felt OK about getting high today."		Went out with friend and used.	Had fun. Felt good to get high, having gone 15 days without.	Broke the 15-day abstinence (although wasn't too worried about this). Didn't get as much done. Didn't feel as healthy.

Future Self Letter

Sometime during the next week, imagine that a year has passed and that you haven't used cannabis/substances for a year. Making believe that it's next year, write a letter to yourself (the old you). Write about your life as it has become. Include the reasons why you stopped a year earlier, what your lifestyle is like in the new year, and the benefits you enjoy from not using. Mention in your letter any problems you faced during the past year in giving up cannabis/cannabis use. Describe yourself without cannabis substances as clearly as you can. As you visualize yourself in the future without cannabis/substances, it may help to think about friendships, self-esteem, health, employment, recreational activities, and general lifestyle satisfaction. If you prefer, draw, sketch, or paint a picture of this image of yourself in the future, rather than depicting it in writing. Choose a medium that will allow you to see another possibility for yourself.

This exercise is extremely useful. It helps you visualize your journey and your goal. Having a clear picture of where you're going, why, and how you're going to get there will be useful in the months ahead. At our next session, we'll talk about the future you foresee for yourself.

Relaxation Practice Exercise

Arrange to spend some quiet time in a room where you will not be interrupted. Try to practice this relaxation technique at least three times during the next week. Proceed through the eight groups of muscles in the list below, first tensing each for 5 seconds and then relaxing each for 15 to 20 seconds. Settle back as comfortably as you can, take a deep breath, and exhale very slowly. You may feel most comfortable if you close your eyes. Notice the sensations in your body; you will soon be able to control those sensations. Begin by focusing your attention on your hands and forearms.

- Squeeze both hands into fists, with arms straight. Then relax hands.
- Flex both arms at the elbows. Then relax arms.
- Shrug shoulders toward head. Tilt chin toward chest. Then relax shoulders and neck.
- Clench jaw, gritting your teeth together. Then relax jaw.
- Close your eyes tightly. Then relax eyes.
- Wrinkle up your forehead and brow. Then relax these muscles.
- Harden your stomach muscles, as if expecting someone to punch you there (continue to breathe slowly as you tense your stomach). Then relax stomach.
- Stretch out both legs, point your toes toward your head, and press your legs together. Then relax legs.

Self-Rating Task

Each day that you engage in this exercise, rate your relaxation level before and after, using the following guide: *0 = highly tense; 100 = fully relaxed*.

Day	Time	Before	After

Session 10. Mindfulness, Meditation, and Stepping Back

Introduction

Session 10 introduces the patient to the practice of mindfulness, which has been found effective in the treatment of substance abuse, depression, anxiety, and other health and psychological difficulties and has existed within the wisdom traditions for thousands of years [155].

Meditation

Meditation is a well-established practice and part of many religious philosophies, particularly in the East. It has been incorporated into the Western world as a therapeutic and health strategy because of its broad appeal, relative accessibility, demonstrated efficacy, and lack of adverse consequences. Meditation is incorporated into ICBT because it is a highly accessible, easily learned (though not necessarily easily practiced) strategy, and has been used successfully in the treatment of many physical and emotional health conditions. It has been used in the treatment of substance abuse and incorporated into CBT interventions for the treatment of depression.

While the learning and practice of meditation could itself be the subject of an entire treatment guide, it is included here as one of the skills-building sessions in hopes the information will encourage the patient to engage in further study and practice beyond the time involved with ICBT. There are many different types of meditation, from very formal to informal. Given the brevity of the clinician's contact with each patient, an informal approach to teaching meditation is encouraged, rather than one tied to the tenets of a particular religious faith. Meditation is offered as one strategy that may be helpful in reducing or stopping use of cannabis and other substances. Patients may also look into classes in the community as a way to learn more and as a strategy for prosocial connections. Patients may also check online for free resources related to both meditation and mindfulness. Public sites such as YouTube have dozens of examples.

Mindfulness

Mindfulness refers to the practice of increasing one's capacity to remain in the present moment and accept experience without judgment. The strategy recognizes our minds are busy, distracted, and reactive to events, situation, thoughts, and feelings. Building a capacity for mindfulness involves becoming increasingly aware of one's moment-to-moment experience and approaching the present moment with acceptance. The intended outcome is a move toward "present-centered"-ness, which creates greater clarity about the nature of one's struggles, builds capability for accepting situations and feelings as they are, and sheds light on new pathways for recovery and growth.

There are numerous ways to increase mindfulness or the ability to stay in the present moment, and it is easy to recognize how often one becomes "non-mindful." Meditation is one method, which can involve sitting (or lying down) and focusing on a single point of concentration (e.g., the breath, a mantra, a word or phrase, a nonword). There are other ways, such as engaging in daily activities like washing dishes or driving to work, but with extra attention on staying present, self-aware, and connected to the here and now.

Why Might Increasing Mindfulness Be Helpful for Change?

One important reason mindfulness can be useful in addressing cannabis use problems is because individuals tend to use substances to escape from difficult emotions or experiences. Cannabis and other substances may serve as "affective regulators," and the individual may have few other tools or options when faced with overwhelming sadness, fear, anger, etc. Building a capacity for mindfulness (for example, through meditation) may help patients learn how to withstand and "stay with" difficult internal states, rather than automatically opting for substances.

When conducting the session on enhancing self-awareness during Session 9, the clinician may have learned about high-risk situations for the patient, such as feeling a certain way (e.g., powerless, discouraged). The information from the functional analysis can be helpful in teaching the patient about mindfulness and meditation. The clinician might remind the patient about certain high-risk or trigger emotions and suggest how mindfulness could help handle the feelings differently. For example, when meditating for any length of time, one becomes acutely aware of the transient nature of internal states. And yet, most people are likely to feel "attached" to these states. We feel as though our thoughts and feelings are ours that they belong to us. If one can approach a particularly disturbing thought and note, "Oh, it's just a thought," this can change the way one feels and reacts.

Similarly, if one can step back from an intense emotional experience and observe, "Oh, that's dissatisfaction," or, "That's just longing," this ability can be tremendously empowering because one no longer has to act or do something about a particular thought or feeling. It is also not necessary to continue to feel bad about a certain kind of thought because thoughts are not necessarily true. The individual comes to see themself as more than, or at least separate from, any particular emotional state, thought, or idea.

The Patient's Experience

In this session, the patient is introduced to the concept of mindfulness and the practice of meditation as strategies for achieving a state of non-judgmental acceptance of the present moment. The patient is encouraged to develop an attitude of curiosity and interest in moment-to-moment experiences. This is seen as a mechanism for achieving important goals related to alcohol or other cannabis use. Mindfulness is seen as consistent with the overall objectives of cultivating self-awareness and self-acceptance. The exercises during this session may be novel and seem strange to the patient, and it is important for the clinician to both normalize this reaction and to encourage the patient to give them a try. The patient should have the experience of feeling more present and connected, and more aware of the feelings and thoughts that occupy consciousness. The patient may become aware of difficult or unpleasant emotions that tend to distract, and this information can be useful to the clinician in building coping skills during this session and later sessions.

Clinician Preparation

CBT Session 10. Mindfulness, Meditation, and Stepping Back	
Materials • Mindfulness Exercise • Meditation Instructions • Meditation Exercise: On the Riverbank (Session 9 handout)	**Total Time** 1 hour **Delivery Method** CBT-focused individual or group therapy
Strategies • OARS (Open-ended questions, Affirmations, Reflections, Summary) • Support self-efficacy • Demonstrate skill, role-play • Follow CBT skills session reminders	
Goals for This Session • Introduce the patient to the concept of mindfulness. • Teach the patient about meditation and different approaches for focusing awareness. • Provide several experiential exercises demonstrating mindfulness and meditation.	

Source: Steinberg Gallucci, Damon, & McRee, 2012

Session 10 Outline and Overview | **239**

Session 10 Outline and Overview

1) Build rapport and review:
   - Check in with the patient on recent experiences.
   - Attend to the therapeutic alliance and address any obstacles or concerns.
   - Assess motivational factors and change readiness.
2) Clinician introduces concept of mindfulness:
   - Awareness and acceptance of present moment.
   - Connection to alcohol/cannabis use.
   - Role of mindfulness in regulating internal states.
3) Clinician conducts experiential exercises demonstrating mindfulness:
   - Mindfulness exercise (e.g., eating raisin).
   - Process patient's experience and reaction.
4) Clinician discusses meditation:
   - Can be part of religious practice but is also incorporated into non-religious health practices.
   - Strategy for increasing mindfulness.
   - Strategy for managing difficult emotions and thoughts.
   - Approach for coping with alcohol or other cannabis use.
5) Clinician conducts experiential meditation exercise:
   - Breathing meditation.
   - Clinician processes patient's experience.
6) Clinician provides the following to the patient:
   - Provides meditation instructions.
   - Provides alternate meditation exercise (*On the Riverbank*).
   - Encourages daily practice.
7) Clinician closes session.

Session Protocol

The clinician greets the patient and elicits information about life during the previous week. The clinician asks about any between-session exercises such as journaling, thought records, and self-awareness charts. Inquire about the patient's current feelings, change readiness, and progress on goals related to quitting or cutting back use of cannabis or other substances. The clinician continues to use MI skills, always expressing genuine curiosity. Following are some examples of how to initiate such interaction with the patient.

"How have things been since we last met?" Or, "Tell me about something enjoyable you did during the past week."

If the patient cannot think of anything enjoyable during the past week, ask about interests and activities, even if they did not engage in them during the past week. Continue by asking the patient how they have been doing over the past week regarding cannabis or drug use.

"Tell me about your [patient's drug of choice] use during the past week." Or, "What has your use been like since we last met?" Or, "What thoughts have you had about your use since we last spoke?"

Guideline. Listen for possible changes in the patient's behaviors, thoughts, and feelings regarding use. Try to refrain from asking many questions. Let the patient tell you how they have been doing. Respond with reflective comments, and attempt to elicit the patient's own motivation-enhancing statements. Affirm any efforts made to reduce use and look for opportunities to support the patient's sense of self efficacy. If there has been little or no change in the patient's use, look for opportunities to develop discrepancy through the use of double-sided reflections, exploring pros and cons, and seeking elaboration.

Provide Overview of Session and Description of Mindfulness

Introduce the topic with brief descriptions of mindfulness and meditation. It might be helpful to begin by asking whether the patient has heard of or been exposed to these ideas and what the experience has been.

Well, I am pleased to talk to you today about an important concept called "mindfulness." Have you ever heard this term before? Mindfulness is simply trying to stay focused on the present moment, what's happening with you right now. You know how everyone is so busy in this world, between our computers, cell phones, televisions, rushing here to there. Well, often people don't even have time to enjoy a simple meal. Or they are so distracted by all the things they have to get done that they don't even know how they feel or what they might like to do if they had a free moment. Does this sound familiar to you?

Some people think that using cannabis or substances is a way for them to just slow down, relax, or feel better in the face of all the stress they have. Is that how you tend to think about your cannabis use? But there are other ways to do this that don't have the harmful consequences that substances can. I want to teach you about mindfulness and some specific ways to increase this ability, which we all have.

Mindfulness can be increased in a variety of ways but the overall purpose is to help you to become more "present"—that is, more aware of your experience of the present moment. It is a way to help you feel less distracted and pulled in many directions. It is a way to help you perhaps feel more grounded, focused, calm. Increasing mindfulness has been found effective for people struggling with mood, anxiety, and cannabis use problems. I think this could be very helpful to you as you try to make these important changes in your use of [_____]. For example, you told me during our first meeting that you have a hard time "shutting off your brain" and that [substance] seems to help you do this. Developing skills related to mindfulness may help you manage when you are feeling uncomfortable without using any substances. Are you willing to give it a try? Great!

The clinician leads the patient in several experiential exercises involving mindfulness and/or meditation. The focus of these exercises is to help the patient become more aware of how they experience the present moment.

The Raisin Exercise

Give the patient (or each group member) one raisin, piece of chocolate, or other small item of food. (Ask beforehand if there are any foods that might be problematic.) Have the patient put the food item in the mouth, and ask them not to chew or swallow it right away. Then ask the individual to focus on various aspects, such as the taste, texture, feeling in the mouth. Ask to notice more complex experiences (e.g., the chocolate seems at first sweet, but then slightly salty), and ask about thoughts and feelings experienced while eating this small morsel. Eventually, the

242 | *Orientation to Clinical Interventions Addressing Cannabis Use Disorder*

person may finish eating. Then inquire about any interesting observations (e.g., many people are astounded to realize how one small raisin can be quite satisfying when one is fully present in the moment to experience and enjoy it).

Okay, here is our first exercise in mindfulness. This may seem a little silly, but just bear with me. I want you to take this raisin. Now, first look at it and notice what you see. Okay, now you can place it in your mouth, but don't eat it right away. I just want you to see what happens when you stay present to eating this one, small raisin, rather than doing the automatic thing we all do of swallowing food and not even paying attention to the experience of eating. So put it in your mouth and just let it sit on your tongue ... what do you notice? (You don't have to answer out loud. I'm just going to toss out questions for you to think about if you can.)

What sensations are there? What is the flavor? How does it feel to just sit there and not chew it right away? What happens when you think about where this raisin came from and how it got to this place so you could eat it? What is the actual texture? Does it change? How about the flavor? What do you notice about yourself as you are eating this raisin in this much slower way? Is it frustrating? Enjoyable? How does it compare to how you usually eat? Okay, now you can start to chew and swallow the raisin. Pay close attention to this as well. Notice each moment and how you feel as you eat the raisin. Are you feeling more or less hungry after this exercise? More or less satisfied? Anything else you noticed?

The clinician discusses the patient's experience with this exercise and how it compares to their usual approach toward daily activities. Try to address the following points:

- Is this a significant departure from the way the patient is living?
- Discuss how making efforts to be more mindful—when it comes to eating, working, doing laundry, or spending time with friends or family—could have the effect of reducing the desire for cannabis or substances.
- Using substances actually takes one away from the present moment and may contribute to feelings of disconnection or being emotionally numb.
- One may have the belief that the substances are helping with difficult feelings; however, they often have the opposite effect since they serve to move one away from actual experiences and feelings.

- Disconnecting from feelings, or trying to get past them quickly, does not generally help one to work through difficult emotions in an effective way.
- Mindfulness-based activities such as meditation can teach one that they are capable of experiencing and getting through even very painful feelings.

These may be new concepts for patients. Acknowledge and explore skepticism or reluctance to consider this new way of approaching lived experience. Indicate that a goal of this treatment is to help patients learn valuable tools that can assist them in making the changes they want for themselves. Not every tool or strategy will be appealing to every patient. They can choose or focus on the ones that seem most credible, helpful, and useful. However, ask that they be open to learning new strategies, even if they seem strange at first, or unlikely to be of benefit.

Clinician Discusses Meditation

Following the mindfulness exercise, discuss meditation as a technique or practice that can also improve mindfulness, or an ability to remain present in the moment. Inquire about the patient's previous experience, understanding, and/or perspective related to meditation approaches. If the patient has little or no background, provide a general introduction. Then conduct a demonstration to practice a short breathing meditation.

The clinician can explain that meditation has been practiced for thousands of years. It is part of many religions, such as Hinduism and Buddhism, particularly in the Eastern part of the world. Many view meditation as a viable path to enlightenment, or a heightened state of being. Meditation has also been adopted in the Western world because it is seen to have many health benefits. For example, there is evidence that people who meditate can reduce their blood pressure, require less anesthesia for surgery, and improve their sleep, among other things. Meditation also seems to be beneficial in reducing depression and anxiety and helping with substance-related problems. Meditation may seem very simple, and learning it is simple. It is the consistent practice that can be challenging. It can also be difficult for some people to "just sit" or "do nothing" because this runs counter to our societal value that we should also be productive and engaged in some kind of activity. The idea of "stopping" or sitting with one's thoughts and feelings without acting on them may be quite novel. Some sample language follows.

I'd like you to give this a try because I think it has great potential value in relation to your goals for this treatment. You won't be graded on how well you do meditation. I'd just like you to try it. Many times people who develop cannabis or drug difficulties become accustomed to "reacting" to difficult emotional states by using. It seems in the moment that this will solve the problem, or get them past the feeling they don't want to experience. However, it is this kind of avoidance of painful states that can lead to harmful patterns and habits and contribute to beliefs about ourselves that are not constructive (for example, thinking that cannabis or drug use is the only way to deal with a particular problem or feeling). Among the benefits of meditation is the developing awareness that our thoughts and feelings are actually quite transitory. There is a sense of impermanence in that everything changes, in a dynamic state of flux. This can be unsettling for those of us who are seeking "ground" or a sense of permanence and security. However, if we accept that things are in fact changing all the time, including us, that makes it possible to fashion our own future, at least in the next moment. It can help us to be hopeful in seeing that we are capable of many, many things, despite what we may have come to believe through some unfortunate conditioning.

Meditation Involving the Breath

Meditation can mean many things. In this treatment, we want to teach you a simple and straightforward meditation technique that involves sitting and focusing on your breathing for a specific period of time. You can sit in the chair or on the floor [if there's carpet, not hard floor] and cross your legs. With either position, try and keep your back straight. It's better not to lie down or become overly relaxed. This is not a relaxation exercise, although we will learn about those later. What I'd like you to do is simply turn your attention to the in and out of your breath. You don't need to change your breathing in any way. Just pay attention to it. You can close your eyes, or keep them open with a "soft focus" (for example, on the carpet a few feet in front of you).

I'm going to signal the start of our meditation with this sound [e.g., bell, tap, other gentle sound]. We will sit for 10 minutes. If you have never done this before, this will feel like a very long time. All I ask you to do is try to focus your attention on your breathing. Just noticing it. The in and out of it. It is inevitable your mind will wander. It will be difficult to stay focused on your breathing for this entire time. You may become aware of things you have to do, things you are happy or upset about, different sensations in your body such as hunger, discomfort, feelings of boredom or anxiety. This is totally normal. It does not mean you're doing it wrong, not trying, or that it can't help you to do this. When you notice your mind has gone astray, just gently bring your attention back to the breath. You can also make an observation to yourself such as, "Oh, thinking," and come back to focusing on your breath. At the end of the 10 minutes, I will make a signal for us to stop. Do you have any questions before we start?

The clinician conducts the 10-minute meditation. When it's complete, inquire about the patient's experiences. It is typical for someone who has never tried meditation to be astonished at how long the 10 minutes seem. The person may report becoming sleepy or physically uncomfortable (especially if sitting cross-legged) or being unable to focus on breathing. The person may report not feeling any better or different after the exercise. Reassure the patient that all these feelings are normal and typical of what most others say after meditating for the first time. Indicate that one generally does not feel better immediately after a meditation session. It is something that accrues benefits over time with repeated practice. Just like any other skill, it is something that takes some discipline and willingness to invest energy in to become proficient or notice clear benefit. Explain there are many benefits from meditation for those who practice regularly. If it seems appropriate, give examples such as lowering blood pressure, reducing cardiovascular risk, reducing anxiety and depression, improving focus and attention, and changing use of substances. Ask the patient to try over the next week to find a time of day to practice this new skill. The individual may want to designate a space at home with less likelihood of distraction and a time of day that can be built into practice most comfortably. For example, some find first thing in the morning is a good time to meditate. Ask if there are any questions or concerns.

Review and Conclude

Thank the patient for being open to hearing about these concepts and for trying the exercises, especially if there was some disinclination initially. Provide the session handouts on meditation, mindfulness, and instructions for practice. Ask the patient to try the skills over the next week each day at a convenient time and to record the experience in a journal (e.g., day, length of sitting, overall experience). Discuss the next session planned for the patient and how the topic chosen and skills learned will be valuable on the path toward wellness.

Session 10. Mindfulness, Meditation, and Stepping Back Handouts

Clinician's Quick Reference to Session 10

1) Build rapport and review
   - Check in on past week
   - Follow up on between-session challenges
2) Clinician introduces mindfulness and provides rationale
   - Awareness and acceptance of present moment
   - Connection to alcohol/cannabis use
   - Role of mindfulness in regulating internal states
3) Clinician conducts experiential exercises demonstrating mindfulness
   - Mindfulness exercise (e.g., eating raisin)
   - Process patient's experience and reaction
4) Clinician discusses meditation
   - Can be part of religious practice, but also incorporated into nonreligious health practices
   - Strategy for increasing mindfulness
   - Strategy for managing difficult emotions and thoughts
   - Approach for coping with alcohol/cannabis use
5) Clinician conducts experiential meditation exercise
   - Breathing meditation
   - Clinician processes patient's experience
6) Clinician provides the following to the patient
   - Provides meditation instructions
   - Provides alternate meditation exercise (*On the Riverbank*)
   - Encourages daily practice
7) Clinician closes session

Mindfulness Meditation Instructions

1) Find a quiet, comfortable location, with few distractions.
2) Choose a time of day that increases the chance you will be able to sit quietly with few distractions.
3) Sit on a cushion (cross-legged if not difficult) or chair. Try to keep back straight, but do not hold tension there to do this (i.e., do not try too hard).
4) Maintain a soft gaze.
5) Have a timer and signal for starting and stopping.
6) Choose a single point of focus (e.g., the breath, a word or phrase, a nonmeaningful word, an image or picture).
7) Sit quietly for 10 minutes and maintain focus.
8) Observe distracting sounds, thoughts, and feelings with mild disinterest and attempt to return to focus. This may happen many times during one sitting. Try not to be discouraged but, rather, recognize this is how our minds are.
9) Try to practice this daily, and journal or record in a log.

Source: Steinberg Gallucci, Damon, & McRee, 2012

Meditation Exercise: On the Riverbank

For this variation on a standard meditation, find a quiet place with few distractions. Begin by focusing on your breathing and trying to slow it down to increase a sense of peace and relaxation. Count slowly with each inhalation and exhalation, increasing from 1 to 10 so your breathing rate slows considerably. Imagine yourself sitting on a riverbank on a beautiful, sunny day, watching the water flow by. You may notice fish, stream currents; a small boat may sail by from time to time. Imagine that as you sit at the bank, observing what is happening, these objects passing by are your thoughts, feelings, and sensations that arise in the course of your meditation. Consider that with each object, each representing an experience of yours, you may choose how to relate to it.

For example, you can get into a boat of "worry" and ride downstream for a while. Or you can decide to let that boat pass you by. Perhaps you see a school of fish representing your thoughts that you will never be able to accomplish this or that. Do you decide to swim with those fish, or sit back and take notice saying, "Ah ... doubt?"

For each thought, feeling, or interpretation that threatens to derail or take you off track, recognize you have the capacity to swim, sail, or sit back and watch it come and go. They are "just thoughts" or "just feelings." They are not necessarily true, good, or bad. They just are. Perhaps they do not even belong to you but are merely finding a host, temporarily, to attach to. You can become attached to them and their "stories," own them, hide from them, and live in fear of them. Or you can simply take notice as you might a sailboat passing by on a summer's day, but not go for a ride. And simply wait for the next interesting entity to pass your way. Keep your focus.

Source: Steinberg Gallucci, Damon, & McRee, 2012

References

1 Cosgrove, B. (2013, January 23). *What America's war on drugs looked like in 1969*. TIME, Time USA, LLC. https://time.com/3688343/what-americas-war-on-drugs-looked-like-in-1969

2 Smith, A. (2012, November 8). *Colorado, Washington legalize recreational Marijuana use*. CNN, Cable News Network. https://money.cnn.com/2012/11/07/news/economy/marijuana-legalization-washington-colorado

3 Jones, J. M. (2019, October 23). *U.S. support for legal Marijuana steady in past year*. Gallup. https://news.gallup.com/poll/267698/support-legal-marijuana-steady-past-year.aspx

4 Swift, A. (2013, October 22). *For first time, Americans Favor legalizing Marijuana*. Gallup. https://news.gallup.com/poll/165539/first-time-americans-favor-legalizing-marijuana.aspx

5 Bienstock, R. (2020). *Pot sounds: The 20 greatest weed-themed songs of All time, Rolling Stone*. Rolling Stone. Available at: https://wdoneww.rollingstone.com/music/music-lists/pot-sounds-the-20-greatest-weed-themed-songs-of-all-time-627951/dangelo-brown-sugar-1995-2-628129. Accessed October 7, 2022.

6 Bures, B. (2019) *It's official: Weed's not cool anymore, Observer*. Observer. Available at: https://observer.com/2019/01/pot-weed-marijuana-not-cool-anymore. Accessed 7 October 2022.

7 [r/AskReddit] Cannabis users of Reddit, how did it help change your health, mentality or overall life? (2019, February 16). Reddit, Advance Publications. www.reddit.com/r/AskReddit/comments/ara97r/cannabis_users_of_reddit_how_did_it_help_change. Accessed October 7, 2022.

A Practitioner's Guide to Cannabis, First Edition. Win Turner and Joseph Hyde.
© 2023 John Wiley & Sons, Inc. Published 2023 by John Wiley & Sons, Inc.

References | **251**

8 *Daily use of high potency marijuana linked to higher rates of psychosis, study finds* (2019). NBCNews.com. NBCUniversal News Group. Available at: https://www.nbcnews.com/storyline/legal-pot/daily-use-high-potency-marijuana-linked-higher-rates-psychosis-study-n985151. Accessed October 7, 2022.

9 Colorado Department of Public Health and Environment. (n.d.). *Healthy Kids Colorado Survey data tables and reports*. https://cdphe. colorado.gov/healthy-kids-colorado-survey-data-tables-and-reports

10 Bonini, S. A., Premoli, M., Tambaro, S., Kumar, A., Maccarinelli, G., Memo, M., & Mastinu, A. (2018). Cannabis sativa: A comprehensive ethnopharmacological review of a medicinal plant with a long history. *Journal of Ethnopharmacology, 227*, 300–315. https://doi.org/10.1016/j. jep.2018.09.004.

11 Zuardi, A. W. (2006). History of cannabis as a medicine: A review. *Brazilian Journal of Psychiatry, 28*, 153–157.

12 Russo, E. B., Jiang, H. E., Li, X., Sutton, A., Carboni, A., del Bianco, F., Mandolino, G., Potter, D. J., Zhao, Y. X., Bera, S., Zhang, Y. B., Lü, E. G., Ferguson, D. K., Hueber, F., Zhao, L. C., Liu, C. J., Wang, Y. F., & Li, C. S. (2008). Phytochemical and genetic analyses of ancient cannabis from Central Asia. *Journal of Experimental Botany, 59*(15), 4171–4182. https://doi.org/10.1093/jxb/ern260.

13 Warf, B. (2014). *High points: An historical geography of cannabis. Geographical Review, 104*. https://doi.org/10.1111/j.1931-0846.2014.12038.x.

14 Siff, S. (2014). The illegalization of marijuana: A brief history. *Origins, 7* (2014), 8. http://origins.osu.edu/article/illegalization-marijuana-brief-history

15 Grinspoon, L. (2005). *History of cannabis as a medicine [White paper]*. DEA Administrative Law Judge hearing. August 16, 2005. https://maps. org/research-archive/mmj/grinspoon_history_cannabis_medicine.pdf

16 Bridgeman, M. B., & Abazia, D. T. (2017). Medicinal cannabis: History, pharmacology, and implications for the acute care setting. *Pharmacy and Therapeutics, 42*(3), 180. https://www.ncbi.nlm.nih.gov/pmc/articles/PMC5312634

17 Downs, D. (2016, April 16). *The science behind the DEA's long war on marijuana*. Scientific American. April 2016 Issue https://www. scientificamerican.com/article/the-science-behind-the-dea-s-long-war-on-marijuana

18 Martin, S. C. (2016). A brief history of Marijuana law in America. TIME. Magazine https://time.com/4298038 [Preprint].

19 Bradford, A. C., & Bradford, W. D. (2017). Factors driving the diffusion of medical marijuana legalisation in the United States. *Drugs: Education, Prevention and Policy, 24*(1), 75–84. https://doi.org/10.3109/0 9687637.2016.1158239.

20 Maciag, M. (2012, November 7). *State Marijuana laws in 2019 map* [updated 2019, June 25]. Governing.com. https://www.governing.com/gov-data/ safety-justice/state-marijuana-laws-map-medical-recreational.html.

21 Felson, J., Adamczyk, A., & Thomas, C. (2019). How and why have attitudes about cannabis legalization changed so much? *Social Science Research, 78*, 12–27. https://doi.org/10.1016/j.ssresearch.2018.12.011.

22 O'Brien, P. K. (2013). Medical Marijuana and social control: Escaping criminalization and embracing medicalization. *Deviant Behavior, 34*(6), 423–443. https://doi.org/10.1080/01639625.2012.735608.

23 Nathan, D. L., Clark, H. W., & Elders, J. (2017). The physicians' case for marijuana legalization. *American Journal of Public Health, 107*(11), 1746. https://doi.org/10.2105/AJPH.2017.304052.

24 American Civil Liberties Union. (2013). The War on Marijuana in black and white. https://www.aclu.org/files/assets/aclu-thewaronmarijuana-rel2.pdf.

25 New York Times Editorial Board. (2016, November 25). *Race and Marijuana arrests.* https://www.nytimes.com/2016/11/25/opinion/ race-and-marijuana-arrests.html?_r=0.

26 Drug Policy Alliance. (2016, August). *It's not legal yet: Nearly 500,000 Californians arrested for marijuana in last decade.* http://www.drugpolicy. org/sites/default/files/California_Marijuana_Arrest_Report_081816.pdf.

27 Compton, W. M., & Han, B. (2018). The epidemiology of Cannabis use in the United States. In *The complex connection between Cannabis and Schizophrenia* (pp. 9–36). Academic Press. https://doi.org/10.1016/ B978-0-12-804791-0.00002-1.

28 ElSohly, M. A., Mehmedic, Z., Foster, S., Gon, C., Chandra, S., & Church, J. C. (2016). Changes in cannabis potency over the last 2 decades (1995–2014): Analysis of current data in the United States. *Biological Psychiatry, 79*(7), 613–619. https://doi.org/10.1016/ j.biopsych.2016.01.004.

29 Hanuš, L. O., Meyer, S. M., Muñoz, E., Taglialatela-Scafati, O., & Appendino, G. (2016). Phytocannabinoids: A unified critical inventory. *Natural Product Reports, 33*(12), 1357–1392. https://doi.org/10.1039/ c6np00074f.

References | 253

30 Andre, C. M., Hausman, J. F., & Guerriero, G. (2016). Cannabis sativa: The plant of the thousand and one molecules. *Frontiers in Plant Science, 7*(February 2016), 19. https://doi.org/10.3389/fpls.2016.00019.

31 American Chemistry Society. (2014, May 1). *Cannabis chemistry 101* [Webinar]. https://www.acs.org/content/dam/acsorg/events/popular-chemsitry/Slides/2014-05-01-cannabis-101.pdf.

32 Whiting, P. F., Wolff, R. F., Deshpande, S., Di Nisio, M., Duffy, S., Hernandez, A. V., Keurentjes, J. C., Lang, S., Misso, K., Ryder, S., Schmidlkofer, S., Westwood, M., & Kleijnen, J. (2015). Cannabinoids for medical use: A systematic review and meta- analysis. *JAMA, 313*(Number 15), 2456–2473. https://doi.org/10.1001/jama.2015.6358.

33 Pacher, P., Kogan, N. M., & Mechoulam, R. (2020). Beyond THC and endocannabinoids. *Annual Review of Pharmacology and Toxicology, 60,* 637–659. https://doi.org/10.1146/annurev-pharmtox-010818-021441.

34 Russo, E. B., & Marcu, J. (2017). Cannabis pharmacology: The usual suspects and a few promising leads. *Advances in Pharmacology, 80,* 67–134. https://doi.org/10.1016/bs.apha.2017.03.004.

35 Russo, E. B. (2011). Taming THC: Potential cannabis synergy and phytocannabinoid-terpenoid entourage effects. *British Journal of Pharmacology, 163*(7), 1344–1364. https://doi.org/10.1111/j.1476-5381.2011.01238.x.

36 Booth, J. K., Page, J. E., & Bohlmann, J. (2017). Terpene synthases from Cannabis sativa. *PLoS One, 12*(3), e0173911. https://doi.org/10.1371/journal.pone.0173911.

37 Tait, R. J., Caldicott, D., Mountain, D., Hill, S. L., & Lenton, S. A systematic review of adverse events arising from the use of synthetic cannabinoids and their associated treatment. *Clinical Toxicology (Philadelphia), 54*(1), 1–13. doi:10.3109/15563650.2015.1110590. Epub 2015 Nov 15. PMID: 26567470.

38 Zaurova, M., Hoffman, R. S., Vlahov, D., & Manini, A. F. (2016). Clinical effects of synthetic cannabinoid receptor agonists compared with Marijuana in emergency department patients with acute drug overdose. *Journal of Medical Toxicology: Official Journal of the American College of Medical Toxicology, 12*(4), 335–340. https://doi.org/10.1007/s13181-016-0558-4.

39 Kemp, A. M., Clark, M. S., Dobbs, T., Galli, R., Sherman, J., & Cox, R. (2016, March). Top 10 facts you need to know about synthetic cannabinoids: Not so nice spice. *The American Journal of Medicine,*

254 | *References*

129(3), 240–4.e1. doi:10.1016/j.amjmed.2015.10.008. Epub 2015 Oct 30. PMID: 26522795.

40 https://www.google.com/search?rlz=1C1CHBD_ enUS860US860&sxsrf=ALiCzsY-kkLfpqPyNChWd3uNov4uyVmyLQ:16 65250242120&q=Walton,+A.+G.+(2015,+March+23).+New+study+s hows+how+marijuana+potency+has+changed+over+time.+Forbes.+ https://www.forbes.com/sites/alicegwalton/2015/03/23/pot-evolution- how-the-makeup-of-marijuana-has-changed-over-time/%2350d8763959 e5&spell=1&sa=X&ved=2ahUKEwjn15LJlNH6AhXqFFkFHRlxAxgQB SgAegQIHxAB.

41 Freeman, T. P., Groshkova, T., Cunningham, A., Sedefov, R., Griffiths, P., & Lynskey, M. T. (2019). Increasing potency and price of cannabis in Europe, 2006–16. *Addiction, 114*(6), 1015–1023. https://doi.org/10.1111/ add.14525.

42 Substance Abuse and Mental Health Services Administration. (2019). Key substance use and mental health indicators in the United States: Results from the 2018 National Survey on Drug Use and Health (HHS Publication No. PEP19-5068, NSDUH Series H-54). Center for Behavioral Health Statistics and Quality, Substance Abuse and Mental Health Services Administration.

43 National Institute on Alcohol Abuse and Alcoholism. (2015, October 21). Prevalence of marijuana use among U.S. adults doubles over past decade [News release]. https://www.niaaa.nih.gov/news-events/ news-releases/ prevalence-marijuana-use-among-us-adults-doubles-over-past-decade.

44 Hasin, D. S., Kerridge, B. T., Saha, T. D., Huang, B., Pickering, R., Smith, S. M., Jung, J., Zhang, H., & Grant, B. F. (2016, June 1). Prevalence and correlates of DSM-5 cannabis use disorder, 2012–2013: Findings from the national epidemiologic survey on alcohol and related conditions-III. *American Journal of Psychiatry, 173*(6), 588–599. doi: 10.1176/appi.ajp.2015.15070907. Epub 2016 Mar 4. PMID: 26940807; PMCID: PMC5026387.

45 Carliner, H., Brown, Q. L., Sarvet, A. L., & Hasin, D. S. (2017). Cannabis use, attitudes, and legal status in the U.S.: A review. *Preventive Medicine, 104*, 13–23. https://doi.org/10.1016/j.ypmed.2017.07.008.

46 Johnston, L. D., Miech, R. A., O'Malley, P. M., Bachman, J. G., & Schulenberg, J. E. (2016). *Teen use of any illicit drug other than marijuana at new low, same true for alcohol.* University of Michigan News Service: Ann Arbor, MI, 2016. http://www.monitoringthefuture.org.

47 Dilley, J. A., Richardson, S. M., Kilmer, B., Pacula, R. L., Segawa, M. B., & Cerdá, M. (2019). Prevalence of cannabis use in youths after legalization in Washington state. *JAMA Pediatrics, 173*(2), 192–193.

48 Cerdá, M., Wall, M., Feng, T., Keyes, K. M., Sarvet, A., Schulenberg, J., … Hasin, D. S. (2017). Association of state recreational marijuana laws with adolescent marijuana use. *JAMA Pediatrics, 171*(2), 142–149. https://doi.org/10.1001/jamapediatrics.2016.3624.

49 Compton, W. M., Han, B., Jones, C. M., Blanco, C., Hughes, A. (2016 October). Marijuana use and use disorders in adults in the USA, 2002–14: Analysis of annual cross-sectional surveys. *Lancet Psychiatry, 3*(10), 954–964. doi:10.1016/S2215-0366(16)30208-5. Epub 2016 Aug 31. PMID: 27592339.

50 Davenport, S. (2018). Falling rates of marijuana dependence among heavy users. *Drug and Alcohol Dependence, 191*(October 1), 52–55. doi:10.1016/j.drugalcdep.2018.06.025. Epub 2018 Jul 25. PMID: 30077891.

51 Compton, W. M., Han, B., Jones, C. M., & Blanco, C. (2019). Cannabis use disorders among adults in the United States during a time of increasing use of cannabis. *Drug and Alcohol Dependence, 204*, 107468. https://doi.org/10.1016/j.drugalcdep.2019.05.008.

52 Sahlem, G. L., Tomko, R. L., Sherman, B. J., Gray, K. M., & McRae-Clark, A. L. (2018). Impact of cannabis legalization on treatment and research priorities for cannabis use disorder. *International Review of Psychiatry, 30*(3), 216–225. https://doi.org/10.1080/09540261.2018.1465398.

53 Hall, W., & Weier, M. (2015, June). Assessing the public health impacts of legalizing recreational cannabis use in the USA. *Clinical Pharmacology & Therapeutics, 97*(6), 607–615. doi:10.1002/cpt.110. Epub 2015 Apr 17. PMID: 25777798.

54 Hasin, D. S., Saha, T. D., Kerridge, B. T., Goldstein, R. B., Chou, S. P., Zhang, H., … Grant, B. F. (2015). Prevalence of marijuana use disorders in the United States between 2001–2002 and 2012–2013. *JAMA Psychiatry, 72*(12), 1235–1242.

55 Cerdá, M., Wall, M., Keyes, K. M., Galea, S., & Hasin, D. (2012). Medical marijuana laws in 50 states: Investigating the relationship between state legalization of medical marijuana and marijuana use, abuse and dependence. *Drug and Alcohol Dependence, 120*(1–3), 22–27. https://doi.org/10.1016/j.drugalcdep.2011.06.011.

56 American Psychiatric Association. (2013). *Diagnostic and statistical manual of mental disorders* (5th ed.). https://doi.org/10.1176/appi.books.9780890425596.

References

57 Ferland, J. M. N., & Hurd, Y. L. (2020). Deconstructing the neurobiology of cannabis use disorder. *Nature Neuroscience, 23*(5), 600–610. https://doi.org/10.1038/s41593-020-0611-0.

58 Winhusen, T., Theobald, J., Kaelber, D. C., & Lewis, D. (2019). Regular cannabis use, with and without tobacco co-use, is associated with respiratory disease. *Drug and Alcohol Dependence, 204*(November 1), 107557. doi:10.1016/j.drugalcdep.2019.107557. Epub 2019 Sep 16. PMID: 31557578; PMCID: PMC6878136.

59 Bartoli, F., Crocamo, C., & Carrà, G. (2019). Cannabis use disorder and suicide attempts in bipolar disorder: A meta-analysis. *Neuroscience & Biobehavioral Reviews, 103*(August), 14–20. doi:10.1016/j.neubiorev.2019.05.017. Epub 2019 May 20. PMID: 31121199.

60 Silins, E., Horwood, L. J., Patton, G. C., Fergusson, D. M., Olsson, C. A., Hutchinson, D. M., Spry, E., Toumbourou, J. W., Degenhardt, L., Swift, W., Coffey, C., Tait, R. J., Letcher, P., Copeland, J., Mattick, R. P., & Cannabis Cohorts Research Consortium. (2014, September). Young adult sequelae of adolescent cannabis use: an integrative analysis. *Lancet Psychiatry, 1*(4), 286–293. doi:10.1016/S2215-0366(14)70307-4. Epub 2014 Sep 10. PMID: 26360862.

61 Adkisson, K., Cunningham, K. C., Dedert, E. A., Dennis, M. F., Calhoun, P. S., Elbogen, E. B., ... Kimbrel, N. A. (2019). Cannabis use disorder and post-deployment suicide attempts in Iraq/Afghanistan-Era veterans. *Archives of Suicide Research, 23*(4), 678–687. https://doi.org/10.1080/13811118.2018.1488638.

62 Liang, D., Wallace, M. S., & Shi, Y. (2019). Medical and non-medical cannabis use and risk of prescription opioid use disorder: Findings from propensity score matching. *Drug and Alcohol Review, 38*(6), 597–605. https://doi.org/10.1111/dar.12964.

63 Gunn, J. K., Rosales, C. B., Center, K. E., Nuñez, A., Gibson, S. J., Christ, C., & Ehiri, J. E. (2016, April 5). Prenatal exposure to cannabis and maternal and child health outcomes: a systematic review and meta-analysis. *BMJ Open, 6*(4), e009986. doi:10.1136/bmjopen-2015-009986. PMID: 27048634; PMCID: PMC4823436.

64 Shen, J. J., Shan, G., Kim, P. C., Yoo, J. W., Dodge-Francis, C., & Lee, Y. J. (2019). Trends and related factors of cannabis-associated emergency department visits in the United States: 2006–2014. *Journal of Addiction Medicine, 13*(3), 193–200. https://doi.org/10.1097/ADM.0000000000000479.

65 Charilaou, P., Agnihotri, K., Garcia, P., Badheka, A., Frenia, D., & Yegneswaran, B. (2017, June). Trends of cannabis use disorder in the inpatient: 2002 to 2011. *The American Journal of Medicine, 130*(6),

678–687.e7. doi:10.1016/j.amjmed.2016.12.035. Epub 2017 Feb 2. PMID: 28161344.

66 Richards, J. R., Bing, M. L., Moulin, A. K., Elder, J. W., Rominski, R. T., Summers, P. J., & Laurin, E. G. (2019). Cannabis use and acute coronary syndrome. *Clinical Toxicology*, *57*(10), 831–841. https://doi.org/10.1080/15563650.2019.1601735.

67 Stuyt, E. (2018). The problem with the current high potency THC marijuana from the perspective of an addiction psychiatrist. *Missouri Medicine*, *115*(6), 482–486.

68 Smart, R., Caulkins, J. P., Kilmer, B., Davenport, S., Midgette, G. (2017, December). Variation in cannabis potency and prices in a newly legal market: Evidence from 30 million cannabis sales in Washington state. *Addiction*, *112*(12), 2167–2177. doi:10.1111/add.13886. Epub 2017 Jul 4. PMID: 28556310; PMCID: PMC5673542.

69 Meier, M. H., Docherty, M., Leischow, S. J., Grimm, K. J., & Pardini, D. (2019, September). Cannabis concentrate use in adolescents. *Pediatrics*, *144*(3), e20190338. doi:10.1542/peds.2019-0338. PMID: 31451609.

70 Struble, C. A., Ellis, J. D., & Lundahl, L. H. (2019). Beyond the bud: Emerging methods of cannabis consumption for youth. *Pediatric Clinics*, *66*(6), 1087–1097. https://doi.org/10.1016/j.pcl.2019.08.012.

71 Jones, C. B., Meier, M. H., & Pardini, D. A. (2018). Comparison of the locations where young adults smoke, vape, and eat/drink cannabis: Implications for harm reduction. *Addictive Behaviors Reports*, *8*, 140–146. https://doi.org/10.1016/j.abrep.2018.09.002.

72 Budney, A. J., Sargent, J. D., & Lee, D. C. (2015, November). Vaping cannabis (marijuana): parallel concerns to e-cigs? *Addiction*, *110*(11), 1699–1704. doi:10.1111/add.13036. Epub 2015 Aug 12. PMID: 26264448; PMCID: PMC4860523.

73 Troutt, W. D., & DiDonato, M. D. (2017, November). Carbonyl compounds produced by vaporizing cannabis oil thinning agents. *The Journal of Alternative and Complementary Medicine*, *23*(11), 879–884. doi:10.1089/acm.2016.0337. Epub 2017 Mar 29. PMID: 28355118.

74 Loflin, M., & Earleywine, M. (2014, October). A new method of cannabis ingestion: The dangers of dabs? *Addictive Behaviors*, *39*(10), 1430–1433. doi:10.1016/j.addbeh.2014.05.013. Epub 2014 May 28. PMID: 24930049.

75 Meier, M. H. (2017). Associations between butane hash oil use and cannabis-related problems. *Drug and Alcohol Dependence*, *179*(October

258 | References

1), 25–31. doi:10.1016/j.drugalcdep.2017.06.015. Epub 2017 Jul 14. PMID: 28750253.25–31.

76 Keller, C. J., Chen, E. C., Brodsky, K., & Yoon, J. H. (2016, July–September). A case of butane hash oil (marijuana wax)-induced psychosis. *Substance Abuse, 37*(3), 384–386. doi:10.1080/08897077.2016.1141153. Epub 2016 Jan 28. PMID: 26820171.

77 Russo, E. B. (2019). The case for the entourage effect and conventional breeding of clinical cannabis: No "strain," no gain. *Frontiers in Plant Science, 9*(January 9), 1969. doi:10.3389/fpls.2018.01969. PMID: 30687364; PMCID: PMC6334252.

78 Camí, J., Guerra, D., Ugena, B., Segura, J., & Torre, R. D. L. (1991). Effect of subject expectancy on the THC intoxication and disposition from smoked hashish cigarettes. *Pharmacology Biochemistry and Behavior, 40*(1), 115–119. https://doi.org/10.1016/0091-3057(91)90330-5.

79 Hill, K. P. (2015). Medical marijuana for treatment of chronic pain and other medical and psychiatric problems: A clinical review. *JAMA, 313*(24), 2474–2483. https://doi.org/10.1001/jama.2015.6199.

80 Hill, K. P. (2015). *Marijuana: The unbiased truth about the world's most popular weed.* Hazelden Publishing.

81 Budney, A. J., Sofis, M. J., & Borodovsky, J. T. (2019). An update on cannabis use disorder with comment on the impact of policy related to therapeutic and recreational cannabis use. *European Archives of Psychiatry and Clinical Neuroscience, 269*(1), 73–86. https://doi.org/10.1007/s00406-018-0976-1.

82 Metrik, J., Rohsenow, D. J., Monti, P. M., McGeary, J., Cook, T. A., de Wit, H., ... Kahler, C. W. (2009). Effectiveness of a marijuana expectancy manipulation: Piloting the balanced-placebo design for marijuana. *Experimental and Clinical Psychopharmacology, 17*(4), 217. https://doi.org/10.1037/a0016502.

83 Boden, M. T., McKay, J. R., Long, W. R., & Bonn-Miller, M. O. (2013). The effects of cannabis use expectancies on self-initiated cannabis cessation. *Addiction, 108*(9), 1649–1657. https://doi.org/10.1111/add.12233.

84 Green, B., Kavanagh, D., & Young, R. (2003, December). Being stoned: a review of self-reported cannabis effects. *Drug and Alcohol Review, 22*(4), 453–460. doi:10.1080/09595230310001613976. PMID: 14660135.

85 Osborne, G. B., & Fogel, C. (2008). Understanding the motivations for recreational marijuana use among adult Canadians. *Substance Use &*

Misuse, 43(3–4): 539–572. Discussion 573–579, 585–587. doi:10.1080/10826080701884911. PMID: 18365950.

86 Atakan, Z. (2012). Cannabis, a complex plant: different compounds and different effects on individuals. *Therapeutic Advances in Psychopharmacology, 2*(6), 241–254. https://doi.org/10.1177/2045125312457586.

87 Mechoulam, R., & Parker, L. A. (2013). The endocannabinoid system and the brain. *Annual Review of Psychology, 64*(1), 21–47. https://doi.org/10.1146/annurev-psych-113011-143739. Epub 2012 Jul 12. PMID: 22804774.

88 Borodovsky, J. T., & Budney, A. J. (2018). Cannabis regulatory science: Risk–benefit considerations for mental disorders. *International Review of Psychiatry, 30*(3), 183–202. https://doi.org/10.1080/09540261.2018.1454406.

89 Mashhoon, Y., Sagar, K. A., & Gruber, S. A. (2019, December). Cannabis use and consequences. *Pediatrics Clinics of North America, 66*(6), 1075–1086. doi:10.1016/j.pcl.2019.08.004. PMID: 31679598.

90 National Institute on Alcohol Abuse and Alcoholism. National epidemiologic survey on alcohol and related conditions-III (NESARC-III). Available online: https://www.niaaa.nih.gov/research/nesarc.

91 Hasin, D., & Walsh, C. (2021). Cannabis use, cannabis use disorder, and comorbid psychiatric illness: A narrative review. *Journal of Clinical Medicine, 10*(1), 15. https://dx.doi.org/10.3390/jcm10010015.

92 Agosti, V., Nunes, E., & Levin, F. (2002). Rates of psychiatric comorbidity among U.S. residents with lifetime cannabis dependence. *The American Journal of Drug and Alcohol Abuse, 28*(4), 643–652. https://doi.org/10.1081/ADA-120015873.

93 Green, B. O. B., Young, R., & Kavanagh, D. (2005). Cannabis use and misuse prevalence among people with psychosis. *The British Journal of Psychiatry, 187*(4), 306–313. https://doi.org/10.1192/bjp.187.4.306. PMID: 16199787.

94 Lev-Ran, S., Le Foll, B., McKenzie, K., George, T. P., & Rehm, J. (2013). Cannabis use and cannabis use disorders among individuals with mental illness. *Comprehensive Psychiatry, 54*(6), 589–598. https://doi.org/10.1016/j.comppsych.2012.12.021.

95 Belendiuk, K. A., Baldini, L. L., & Bonn-Miller, M. O. (2015). Narrative review of the safety and efficacy of marijuana for the treatment of commonly state-approved medical and psychiatric disorders. *Addiction Science & Clinical Practice, 10*(1), 1–10. https://doi.org/10.1186/s13722-015-0032-7.

96 Ware, M. A., Martel, M. O., Jovey, R., Lynch, M. E., & Singer, J. (2018). A prospective observational study of problematic oral cannabinoid use. *Psychopharmacology*, *235*(2), 409–417. https://doi.org/10.1007/s00213-017-4811-6.

97 (2017, October). Committee Opinion No. 722: Marijuana use during pregnancy and lactation. *Obstetrics & Gynecology*, *130*(4), e205–e209. doi:10.1097/AOG.0000000000002354. PMID: 28937574.

98 Volkow, N. D., Han, B., Compton, W. M., & Blanco, C. (2017). Marijuana use during stages of pregnancy in the United States. *Annals of Internal Medicine 2017*, *166*(10), 763–764. https://doi.org/10.7326/L17-0067.

99 Rodriguez, C. E., Sheeder, J., Allshouse, A. A., Scott, S., Wymore, E., Hopfer, C., Hermesch, A., Metz, T. D. (2019, November). Marijuana use in young mothers and adverse pregnancy outcomes: A retrospective cohort study. *BJOG*, *126*(12), 1491–1497. doi:10.1111/1471-0528.15885. Epub 2019 Aug 25. PMID: 31334907; PMCID: PMC8051186.

100 Young-Wolff, K. C., Sarovar, V., Tucker, L. Y., Conway, A., Alexeeff, S., Weisner, C., Armstrong, M. A., & Goler, N. (2019). Self-reported daily, weekly, and monthly cannabis use among women before and during pregnancy. *JAMA Network Open*, *2*(7), e196471. https://doi.org/10.1001/jamanetworkopen.2019.6471.

101 Conner, S. N., Bedell, V., Lipsey, K., Macones, G. A., Cahill, A. G., & Tuuli, M. G. (2016, October). Maternal marijuana use and adverse neonatal outcomes: A systematic review and meta-analysis. *Obstetrics and Gynecology*, *128*(4), 713–723. doi:10.1097/AOG.0000000000001649. PMID: 27607879.

102 Gunn, J. K., Rosales, C. B., Center, K. E., Nuñez, A., Gibson, S. J., Christ, C., & Ehiri, J. E. (2016, April 5). Prenatal exposure to cannabis and maternal and child health outcomes: a systematic review and meta-analysis. *BMJ Open*, *6*(4), e009986. doi:10.1136/bmjopen-2015-009986. PMID: 27048634; PMCID: PMC4823436.

103 Metz, T. D., & Borgelt, L. M. (2018, November). Marijuana use in pregnancy and while breastfeeding. *Obstetrics and Gynecology*, *132*(5), 1198–1210. doi:10.1097/AOG.0000000000002878. PMID: 30234728; PMCID: PMC6370295.

104 Hartman, R. L., & Huestis, M. A. (2013). Cannabis effects on driving skills. *Clinical Chemistry*, *59*(3), 478–492. https://doi.org/10.1373/clinchem.2012.194381.

105 Berning, A., Compton, R., & Wochinger, K. (2015, February). Results of the 2013–2014 national roadside survey of alcohol and drug use by drivers. (Traffic Safety Facts Research Note. Report No.DOT HS 812 118). National Highway Traffic Safety Administration.

106 Lane, T. J., & Hall, W. (2019, May). Traffic fatalities within US states that have legalized recreational cannabis sales and their neighbours. *Addiction, 114*(5), 847–856. doi:10.1111/add.14536. Epub 2019 Feb 4. PMID: 30719794.

107 Rogeberg, O. (2013). Correlations between cannabis use and IQ change in the Dunedin cohort are consistent with confounding from socioeconomic status. *PNAS Proceedings of the National Academy of Sciences of the United States of America, 110*(11), 4251–4254. https://doi.org/10.1073/pnas.1215678110.

108 Zalesky, A., Solowij, N., Yücel, M., Lubman, D. I., Takagi, M., Harding, I. H., Lorenzetti, V., Wang, R., Searle, K., Pantelis, C., & Seal, M. (2012, July). Effect of long-term cannabis use on axonal fibre connectivity. *Brain, 135*(Pt 7), 2245–2255. doi:10.1093/brain/aws136. Epub 2012 Jun 4. PMID: 22669080.

109 Scott, J. C., Slomiak, S. T., Jones, J. D., Rosen, A. F. G., Moore, T. M., & Gur, R. C. (2018, June 1). Association of cannabis with cognitive functioning in adolescents and young adults: A systematic review and meta-analysis. *JAMA Psychiatry, 75*(6), 585–595. doi:10.1001/jamapsychiatry.2018.0335. PMID: 29710074; PMCID: PMC6137521.

110 National Academies of Sciences, Engineering, and Medicine. (2017). *The health effects of Cannabis and Cannabinoids: The current state of evidence and recommendations for research.* The National Academies Press. https://doi.org/10.17226/24625.

111 de Lago, E., Moreno-Martet, M., Cabranes, A., Ramos, J. A., & Fernández-Ruiz, J. (2012, June). Cannabinoids ameliorate disease progression in a model of multiple sclerosis in mice, acting preferentially through CB1 receptor-mediated anti-inflammatory effects. *Neuropharmacology, 62*(7), 2299–2308. doi:10.1016/j.neuropharm.2012.01.030. Epub 2012 Feb 8. PMID: 22342378.

112 Corey-Bloom, J., Wolfson, T., Gamst, A., Jin, S., Marcotte, T. D., Bentley, H., & Gouaux, B. (2012). Smoked cannabis for spasticity in multiple sclerosis: A randomized, placebo-controlled trial. *CMAJ: Canadian Medical Association Journal = journal de l'Association medicale canadienne, 184*(10), 1143–1150. https://doi.org/10.1503/cmaj.110837.

262 | References

113 Ribeiro, L., & Ind, P. W. (2018, September). Marijuana and the lung: Hysteria or cause for concern? *Breathe (Sheff), 14*(3), 196–205. doi:10.1183/20734735.020418. PMID: 30186517; PMCID: PMC6118880.

114 Touriño, C., Zimmer, A., & Valverde, O. (2010). THC prevents MDMA neurotoxicity in mice. *PLoS ONE, 5*(2), Article e9143. https://doi.org/10.1371/journal.pone.0009143.

115 Piper, B. J., Beals, M. L., Abess, A. T., Nichols, S. D., Martin, M., Cobb, C. M., & DeKeuster, R. M. (2017). Chronic pain patients' perspectives of medical cannabis. *Pain, 158*(7), 1373. https://doi.org/10.1097/j.pain.0000000000000899.

116 Treede, R. D., Rief, W., Barke, A., Aziz, Q., Bennett, M. I., Benoliel, R., Cohen, M., Evers, S., Finnerup, N. B., First, M. B., Giamberardino, M. A., Kaasa, S., Kosek, E., Lavand'homme, P., Nicholas, M., Perrot, S., Scholz, J., Schug, S., Smith, B. H., ... Wang, S. J. (2015). A classification of chronic pain for ICD-11. *Pain, 156*(6), 1003–1007. https://doi.org/10.1097/j.pain.0000000000000160.

117 Johnson, J. R., Burnell-Nugent, M., Lossignol, D., Ganae-Motan, E. D., Potts, R., & Fallon, M. T. (2010, February). Multicenter, double-blind, randomized, placebo-controlled, parallel-group study of the efficacy, safety, and tolerability of THC:CBD extract and THC extract in patients with intractable cancer-related pain. *Journal of Pain and Symptom Management, 39*(2), 167–179. doi:10.1016/j.jpainsymman.2009.06.008. Epub 2009 Nov 5. PMID: 19896326.

118 Ware, M. A., Wang, T., Shapiro, S., Collet, J. P., & COMPASS study team. (2015, December). Cannabis for the management of pain: Assessment of safety study (COMPASS). *The Journal of Pain, 16*(12), 1233–1242. doi:10.1016/j.jpain.2015.07.014. Epub 2015 Sep 16. PMID: 26385201.

119 Abrams, D. I., Couey, P., Shade, S. B., Kelly, M. E., & Benowitz, N. L. (2011). Cannabinoid–opioid interaction in chronic pain. *Clinical Pharmacology & Therapeutics, 90*(6), 844–851. Wiley Online Library https://doi.org/10.1038/clpt.2011.18.

120 Carter, G. T., Javaher, S. P., Nguyen, M. H., Garret, S., & Carlini, B. H. (2015). Re-branding cannabis: The next generation of chronic pain medicine? *Pain Management, 5*(1), 13–21. doi:10.2217/pmt.14.49. PMID: 25537695.

121 Banerjee, S., & McCormack, S. (2019). Medical cannabis for the treatment of chronic pain: A review of clinical effectiveness and

guidelines. [Internet]. Canadian Agency for Drugs and Technologies in Health. https://www.ncbi.nlm.nih.gov/books/NBK546424.

122 Hill, K. P. (2015). Medical marijuana for treatment of chronic pain and other medical and psychiatric problems: A clinical review. *JAMA, 313*(24), 2474–2483. https://doi.org/10.1001/jama.2015.6199.

123 Russo, E. B. (2017, May) Cannabis and epilepsy: An ancient treatment returns to the fore. *Epilepsy & Behavior, 70*(Pt B), 292-297. doi:10.1016/j.yebeh.2016.09.040. Epub 2016 Dec 15. PMID: 27989385.

124 Friedman, D., & Devinsky, O. (2015). Cannabinoids in the treatment of epilepsy. *The New England Journal of Medicine, 373*(11), 1048–1058. https://doi.org/10.1056/NEJMra1407304.

125 *Originally drafted in 2014, updated in 2018, updated in 2020 by Dominic Fee, MD, FAAN; Dan Freedman, DO; Anup D. Patel, MD, FAAN, FAES; Korak Sarkar, MD; Sarah Song, MD, MPH, FAAN. Approved by the AAN Board of Directors September 9, 2020.*

126 Devinsky, O., Marsh, E., Friedman, D., Thiele, E., Laux, L., Sullivan, J., Miller, I., Flamini, R., Wilfong, A., Filloux, F., Wong, M., Tilton, N., Bruno, P., Bluvstein, J., Hedlund, J., Kamens, R., Maclean, J., Nangia, S., Singhal, N. S., Wilson, C. A., Patel, A., & Cilio, M. R. (2016, March). Cannabidiol in patients with treatment-resistant epilepsy: an open-label interventional trial. *The Lancet Neurology, 15*(3), 270–278. doi:10.1016/S1474-4422(15)00379-8. Epub 2015 Dec 24. Erratum in: Lancet Neurol. 2016 Apr;15(4):352.PMID: 26724101.

127 Caffarel, M. M., Andradas, C., Pérez-Gómez, E., Guzmán, M., & Sánchez, C. (2012, November). Cannabinoids: a new hope for breast cancer therapy? *Cancer Treatment Reviews, 38*(7), 911–918. doi:10.1016/j.ctrv.2012.06.005. Epub 2012 Jul 7. PMID: 22776349.

128 Orellana-Serradell, O., Poblete, C. E., Sanchez, C., Castellón, E. A., Gallegos, I., Huidobro, C., Llanos, M. N., Contreras, H. R. (2015, April). Proapoptotic effect of endocannabinoids in prostate cancer cells. *Oncology Reports, 33*(4), 1599–1608. doi:10.3892/or.2015.3746. Epub 2015 Jan 21. PMID: 25606819; PMCID: PMC4358087.

129 Huang, Y. H., Zhang, Z. F., Tashkin, D. P., Feng, B., Straif, K., & Hashibe, M. (2015, January). An epidemiologic review of marijuana and cancer: An update. *Cancer Epidemiology, Biomarkers & Prevention, 24*(1), 15–31. doi: 10.1158/1055-9965.EPI-14-1026. PMID: 25587109; PMCID: PMC4302404.

130 Zhang, L. R., Morgenstern, H., Greenland, S., Chang, S. C., Lazarus, P., Teare, M. D., Woll, P. J., Orlow, I., Cox, B., Cannabis and Respiratory

Disease Research Group of New Zealand, Brhane, Y., Liu, G., & Hung, R. J. (2015, February 15). Cannabis smoking and lung cancer risk: Pooled analysis in the International Lung Cancer Consortium. *International Journal of Cancer, 136*(4), 894–903. doi:10.1002/ijc.29036. Epub 2014 Jun 30. PMID: 24947688; PMCID: PMC4262725.

131 Abrams, D. I. (2016, March). Integrating cannabis into clinical cancer care. *Current Oncology, 23*(2), S8–S14. doi:10.3747/co.23.3099. Epub 2016 Mar 16. PMID: 27022315; PMCID: PMC4791148.

132 Zuardi, A. W., Crippa, J. A. S., Hallak, J. E. C., Bhattacharyya, S., Atakan, Z., Martin-Santos, R., ... Guimaraes, F. S. (2012). A critical review of the antipsychotic effects of cannabidiol: 30 years of a translational investigation. *Current Pharmaceutical Design, 18*(32), 5131–5140. https://doi.org/10.2174/138161212802884681.

133 Kosiba, J. D., Maisto, S. A., & Ditre, J. W. (2019). Patient-reported use of medical cannabis for pain, anxiety, and depression symptoms: Systematic review and meta-analysis. *Social Science & Medicine, 233*(July), 181–192. doi:10.1016/j.socscimed.2019.06.005. Epub 2019 Jun 8. PMID: 31207470.

134 Khoury, J. M., Neves, M. C. L. D., Roque, M. A. V., Queiroz, D. A. B., Corrêa de Freitas, A. A., de Fátima, Â., Moreira, F. A., & Garcia, F. D. (2019, February). Is there a role for cannabidiol in psychiatry? *The World Journal of Biological Psychiatry, 20*(2), 101–116. doi:10.1080/156 22975.2017.1285049. Epub 2017 Feb 20. PMID: 28112021.

135 Bobitt, J., Qualls, S. H., Schuchman, M., Wickersham, R., Lum, H. D., Arora, K., ... Kaskie, B. (2019). Qualitative analysis of cannabis use among older adults in Colorado. *Drugs & Aging, 36*(7), 655–666. https://doi.org/10.1007/s40266-019-00665-w.

136 Black, N., Stockings, E., Campbell, G., Tran, L. T., Zagic, D., Hall, W. D., ... Degenhardt, L. (2019). Cannabinoids for the treatment of mental disorders and symptoms of mental disorders: A systematic review and meta-analysis. *The Lancet Psychiatry, 6*(12), 995–1010.

137 Gardiner, K. M., Singleton, J. A., Sheridan, J., Kyle, G. J., & Nissen, L. M. (2019). Health professional beliefs, knowledge, and concerns surrounding medicinal cannabis–a systematic review. *PLoS One, 14*(5), e0216556. https://doi.org/10.1371/journal.pone.0216556.

138 Rahm, A. K., Boggs, J. M., Martin, C., Price, D. W., Beck, A., Backer, T. E., & Dearing, J. W. (2015). Facilitators and barriers to implementing screening, brief intervention, and referral to treatment (SBIRT) in primary care in integrated health care settings. *Substance Abuse, 36*(3),

281–288. doi:10.1080/08897077.2014.951140. Epub 2014 Aug 15. PMID: 25127073.0.

139 Miller, P. M., Ravenel, M. C., Shealy, A. E., & Thomas, S. (2006). Alcohol screening in dental patients: The prevalence of hazardous drinking and patients' attitudes about screening and advice. *The Journal of the American Dental Association, 137*(12), 1692–1698.

140 Groves, P., Pick, S., Davis, P., Cloudesley, R., Cooke, R., Forsythe, M., & Pilling, S. (2010). Routine alcohol screening and brief interventions in general hospital in-patient wards: Acceptability and barriers. *Drugs: Education, Prevention and Policy, 17*(1), 55–71. https://doi.org/10.3109/09687630802088208.

141 Budney, A. J., Roffman, R., Stephens, R. S., & Walker, D. (2007). Marijuana dependence and its treatment. *Addiction Science & Clinical Practice, 4*(1), 4–16. https://doi.org/10.1151/ascp07414.

142 Kopak, A. M., Proctor, S. L., & Hoffmann, N. G. (2014). The elimination of abuse and dependence in DSM-5 substance use disorders: What does this mean for treatment? *Current Addiction Reports, 1*(3), 166–171. https://doi.org/10.1007/s40429-014-0020-0.

143 Esser, M. B., Hedden, S. L., Kanny, D., Brewer, R. D., Gfroerer, J. C., & Naimi, T. S. (2014). Prevalence of alcohol dependence among US adult drinkers, 2009–2011. *Preventing Chronic Disease, 11*(November 20), E206. doi:10.5888/pcd11.140329. PMID: 25412029; PMCID: PMC4241371.

144 Williams, E. C., Bryson, C. L., Sun, H., Chew, R. B., Chew, L. D., Blough, D. K., ... Bradley, K. A. (2012). Association between alcohol screening results and hospitalizations for trauma in Veterans Affairs outpatients. *The American Journal of Drug and Alcohol Abuse, 38*(1), 73–80.

145 Miller, W. R., & Rollnick, S. (2012). *Motivational interviewing: Helping people change.* Guilford press.

146 Miller, W. R., Yahne, C. E., Moyers, T. B., Martinez, J., & Pirritano, M. (2004, December). A randomized trial of methods to help clinicians learn motivational interviewing. *Journal of Consulting and Clinical Psychology, 72*(6), 1050–1062. doi:10.1037/0022-006X.72.6.1050. PMID: 15612851.

147 D'Onofrio, G., Bernstein, E., & Rollnick, S. (1996). Motivating patients for change: A brief strategy for negotiation. In E. Bernstein & J. Bernstein, *Emergency medicine and the health of the public* (pp. 51–62). Jones and Bartlett.

References

148 Miller, W. R., & Rollnick, S. (2012). *Motivational interviewing: Helping people change* (3rd ed.). Guilford Press.

149 Magill, M., & Ray, L. A. (2009, July). Cognitive-behavioral treatment with adult alcohol and illicit drug users: a meta-analysis of randomized controlled trials. *Journal of Studies on Alcohol and Drugs, 70*(4), 516–527. doi:10.15288/jsad.2009.70.516. PMID: 19515291; PMCID: PMC2696292.

150 Carroll, K. M. (1996, February). Relapse prevention as a psychosocial treatment: A review of controlled clinical trials. *Experimental and Clinical Psychopharmacology, 4*(1), 46–54. [Google Scholar].

151 Marlatt, G. A. (1996, December). Taxonomy of high-risk situations for alcohol relapse: Evolution and development of a cognitive-behavioral model. *Addiction, 91*(Suppl), S37–S49.PMID: 8997780.

152 Monti, P. M., Kaden, R., Rohsenow, D. J., Cooney, N., & Abrams, D. (2002). *Treating Alcohol Dependence: A coping skills training guide* (2nd ed.). Guilford Press.

153 Moyers, T. B., & Huck, J. (2011). Combining motivational interviewing with cognitive-behavioral treatments for substance abuse: Lessons from the COMBINE Research Project. *Cognitive and Behavioral Practice, 18*(1), 38–45.

154 Carroll, K. M., & Onken, L. S. (2005). Behavioral therapies for drug abuse. *The American journal of psychiatry, 162*(8), 1452–1460. https://doi.org/10.1176/appi.ajp.162.8.1452.

155 Bowen, S., Chawla, N., Collins, S. E., Witkiewitz, K., Hsu, S., Grow, J., Clifasefi, S., Garner, M., Douglass, A., Larimer, M. E., & Marlatt, A. (2009). Mindfulness-based relapse prevention for substance use disorders: A pilot efficacy trial. *Substance Abuse, 30*(4), 295–305. https://doi.org/10.1080/08897070903250084.

Index

a

abstinence   111, 132, 157, 182
 cravings and   169
activities and actions
 clinician-led *see* clinician-led
  activities
 new/replacement   86, 126,
  136–149
 pleasurable *see* pleasurable
  activities
 session 1   85–86
addiction and dependence   12, 216,
 218, 228
 psychological   17, 224
administration/delivery (methods)
 risks related to   24–26
 screening and   43, 46–47
adolescents and young adults   10,
 21, 24–25, 33–34, 38, 46
adverse effects *see* safety issues
aggressive communication   115,
 122, 124–125
alcohol (drinking)   96–97, 111, 132,
 152, 229–232
 dependence   224

driving and   33
future self letter   233
screening   42, 43
Alcohol/Cannabis Use Awareness
 Record   229–232
 example   105, 232
 session 2   91–93, 98, 100,
  104–105
 session 3   109
 session 4   129
 session 6   152, 154–155
 session 7   169, 172
 session 9   229–232
alpha-pinene   15
ambivalence (about change)   95
anger   77, 87
Ansliger, Harry   8
appetite stimulation   29
assertiveness   107–125
 assertive communication
  115–116, 123, 124–125
 benefits   110, 116, 123
 handouts   120–125
automatic thoughts   167, 216,
 218, 228

A Practitioner's Guide to Cannabis, First Edition. Win Turner and Joseph Hyde.
© 2023 John Wiley & Sons, Inc. Published 2023 by John Wiley & Sons, Inc.

268 | *Index*

avoidance 85, 179
awareness (enhancing) 89,
    102–106
  of need to change 95–96
  situational 89–90, 102–106
  of use 89, 92
  see also Alcohol/Cannabis Use
    Awareness Record;
    self-awareness

b

behavior(s) 176–177
  in Alcohol/Cannabis Use
    Awareness Record 98,
    104–105, 229, 231–232
  change in *see* change
  learned 218
beliefs 228
  addictive patterns and 218
  in Alcohol/Cannabis Use
    Awareness Record 98,
    104–105, 229, 231–232
between-session challenges
    60–62, 66–67
  negotiating and
    preparing 66–67, 74, 92,
    99–100, 110, 119, 131,
    134–135, 141–142, 154,
    161–162, 171, 185
  session 1 and 66–67, 74–76
  session 2 and 89, 91–92, 95–96,
    99–100, 103
  session 3 and 108–112, 118–119,
    121, 124, 125
  session 4 and 128–129, 131,
    132–134
  session 5 and 138, 144
  session 6 and 152, 154–156,
    161–162, 164

  session 7 and 169, 171–173, 185,
    188
  session 8 and 196, 202–203
  session 9 and 217, 225–226, 228
body
  cannabinoids and 18–19
  physical sensations 176,
    190–191
body language 117, 124
Boggs Act (1951) 9
brain
  development
    (neurodevelopment) 23, 32
  reward and *see* reward
    mechanisms
brainstorming 153, 158–160, 165
  clinician-led 159–160
    to identify real-world
      application 140–141
  in decision-making 209, 211
breast cancer 38
breath in meditation 244–245
brief intervention (BI) 43–45, 49,
    54
  see also SBIRT
brief motivational interviewing for
    misuse 54–55
Brief Negotiated Interview
    (BNI) 54–55
brief treatment (BT) 49, 55, 57
Britain and United Kingdom 7,
    7–8

c

California 9–10
cancer 38
  chemotherapy 35, 37–38
cannabichromene (CBC) 14
cannabidiol (CBD) 5, 14–15, 18–19

Index 269

therapeutic use 31, 37–39
cannabigerol (CBG) 14
cannabinoids 5, 13–19
  endogenous
    (endocannabinoids) 14,
    17–18, 32, 34
  human body and 18–19
  receptors 14–18
    partial agonist 16, 18
  synthetic 15–17, 19
cannabinol (CBN) 14–15
cannabis (marijuana)
  abuse 48–50
  chemistry 5, 13–19
  history 1–2, 5–10
  as medication 31, 35–41
  misuse *see* misuse
  psychoactivity *see* psychoactivity
  screening *see* screening
  use *see* use
  user's experience *see* experiences
Cannabis Intervention Screener
    (CIS) 4, 44–52, 55
  development 45–46
  Impact Questions Alignment 49
  Impact Scale Scores 49
  implications from
    findings 51–52
  summary of findings 46–48
Cannabis sativa 5, 14
  seizure treatment 38
cannabis use disorder
    (CUD) 20–24
  CIS and 49
  comorbid mental health
    illnesses 30
  interventions 4, 53–63
CBC (cannabichromene) 14
CBD *see* cannabidiol

CBG (cannabigerol) 14
CBN (cannabinol) 14–15
CDC 16, 22–23
Center for Disease Control
    (CDC) 16, 22–23
Central America 6–7
change (incl. change plan) 78–88
  ambivalence 95
  being not ready 67, 196, 203,
    205
  handouts 78–88
  readiness (to proceed) with *see*
    readiness
  session 1 66–67, 73–76, 77, 84
  session 2 91, 95–96, 100
    change talk 89
  session 3 111–112
  session 6 155–156, 158–159
  session 8 195–198, 200,
    202–203, 205
    change talk 196, 198, 200,
      203–204
  session 9 228
  session 10 236–237
chemistry 5, 13–19
chemotherapy 35, 37–38
chronic pain 36–37
clinician-led activities
  brainstorming *see* brainstorming
  demonstration/role play 62,
    91–92, 98–99, 110, 117, 153,
    160–161, 170, 172, 183
clinician preparation
  session 1 65
  session 2 90
  session 3 108
  session 5 137
  session 6 151
  session 7 168

270 | *Index*

session 8   194
session 9   215
session 10   238
cognitive behavioural therapy (CBT
    and ICBT)   55–63
    functional analysis and   54–55,
        58, 89, 192, 214, 220, 236
    meditation incorporated
        into   235
    self-awareness and   214
    sessions *see* sessions
cognitive impairment   32–33
Colorado   1, 10, 19, 21, 33
commitment, eliciting   59, 63, 79
    session 1   66, 74, 76
    session 2   92, 100
    session 3   110, 119
    session 4   126, 131, 134
    session 5   139, 142
    session 6   154, 162
    session 7   171, 185
    session 8   194, 196, 203
communication styles   108, 110,
    122–124
comorbid mental health illnesses
        with cannabis use disorder
        (CUD)   23, 30
Compassionate Use Act (1996)   10
Comprehensive Drug Abuse
        Prevention and Control Act
        (1970)   9
compromise, willingness   117, 124
concentrates   24–26
concentration (mental)
    increased   29
    in meditation   236
conflict, interpersonal   77, 87
connections, drawing   216, 222,
    228

see also disconnection
consumption, risks related to
        methods if   24–26
coping strategies (and learning new
        ones)   85–88
    *Coping with Cravings and
        Discomfort* (handout)   170,
        174–175, 178, 184, 187–188
    handouts   85–88, 187–188
    Learning New Coping Strategies
        (handout)   85–88, 199
    session 1   67, 75, 85–88
    session 2   91, 94–95
    session 3   111
    session 6   150, 155
    session 7   170, 179–180, 184,
        187, 189
    session 9   216, 221–222,
        224–225, 228
core values   193
cost, medicinal cannabis   41
cravings *see* urges
creativity   29
criminalization and criminal justice
        (US)   9
    reforms   11
cues *see* triggers and cues
cultural aspects   2, 4, 11

d

dabs/dabbing   24–26, 47
Daily Record of Urges to Use   171,
    185, 188, 189
DAST (Drug Abuse Screening
        Test)   43, 45–46
decision-making (life
        decisions)   192–213
    decisional balance form   95–96,
        193

Index | **271**

Decision-Making Guide   195–196, 198–200, 202–203, 209–210
  example   211–212
  introducing and teaching steps in   195–196
decriminalization *see* legalization
delivery *see* administration/delivery
delta-9-tetrahydrocannabinol *see* tetrahydrocannabinol
demonstration, clinician-led   62, 91–92, 98–99, 110, 117, 153, 160–161, 170, 172, 183
dependence *see* addiction and dependence
Diagnostic and Statistical Manual of Mental Disorder 5th edition (DSM-5)   23, 43, 48–49
discomfort *see* urges/cravings/discomfort
disconnection (feelings of)   243
distraction   85–86, 180
District of Columbia (Washington D.C.)   1–2, 20–21
dopamine   18, 127
double-sided reflection   193, 195
drinking *see* alcohol
driving   33
Drug Abuse Screening Test (DAST)   43, 45–46
Drug Enforcement Agency and Administration   9–10, 19, 35
DSM-5 (Diagnostic and Statistical Manual of Mental Disorder 5th edition)   23, 43, 48–49

e

EDARS   65, 90, 108, 128, 194
edibles   24–25, 47

embrace strategies   170, 180–181
emergency department visits   23, 45
emotions   176–178
  negative   77, 87
empowerment   237
  through self-knowledge   216, 219–220, 228
endocannabinoids (endogenous cannabinoids)   14, 17–18, 32, 34
energy, low   77, 87
entourage effect   15, 27
epilepsy   38
escape   85, 179–180
Europe, historical aspects   6
exercise (physical activity)   86, 225
experiences incl. recent ones   27–28, 39–41
  negative *see* negative experiences
  positive *see* positive experiences
  session 1   66, 67
  session 2   89, 92, 94, 98–100
  session 3   111
  session 4   132
  session 5   136
  session 6   155
  session 7   172–173, 175–176
  session 8   193
  session 9   214, 216, 221, 228
  session 10   237
external situations as urges/triggers   178–179

f

family   71–72
  communication styles   114, 122
fatigue   77
fear and assertiveness   117

federal (national) government and law 1, 8–10, 30, 35, 41

feelings 228
Alcohol/Cannabis Use Awareness Record 98, 104, 105, 229, 231, 232
see also emotions

fetal development 23, 32

friends, non-smoking 87

frustration 77, 87

functional analysis 54–55, 58, 89, 192, 214, 220, 236

future self letter 233

g

geographical origins 6–7

goals
session 1 64–65
session 2 89–90
session 3 107–108, 111
session 4 126–128
session 5 136
session 6 150–151
session 7 167–168
session 8 194
session 9 215
session 10 238

good
good things and not-so-good things in decision-making 209
planning and strategies to feel 106, 140, 180, 199

h

health care providers 3–4, 11–12, 17, 19, 27

Healthy Kids Colorado Survey 3

healthy replacement (new) activities 86, 136–149

hemp 5–7, 14

high-risk or tempting situations
session 1 77, 87
session 9 219–222
session 10 236

highway safety 33

history 1–2, 5–10

hospital inpatient management 23–24

i

ICBT sessions *see* sessions

imagery and/or visualization 86, 181

India 6, 7

inpatient (hospital) management 23–24

insomnia 77, 87

internet-based CBT sessions *see* sessions

interpersonal conflict 77, 87

interpersonal skills training 57–58

interventions (treatment/therapy)
cannabis use disorder (CUD) 4, 53–63
screener *see* Cannabis Intervention Screener
sessions *see* sessions
see also treatment information handout

intrapersonal skills training 57

Iowa 45

I-SOLVE model 96, 150, 157–162, 165, 169, 172

k

Knowledge is Power (worksheet) 119, 216, 219–221, 225

l

law (and legislation; regulations), US 8–12
  federal/national government 1, 8–10, 30, 35, 41
  state government *see* state law/ legalization *see also* criminalization; legalization
law of thirds 59–63
  session 1 66–67
  session 2 91–93
  session 3 109–110
  session 4 129–131
  session 5 138–139
  session 6 152–154
  session 7 169–171
learned behavior 218
Learning New Coping Strategies (handout) 85–88, 199
legalization and decriminalization (US) 1–2, 9–12, 21, 45
  factors influencing 10–12
  potential effects 20–22
legislation *see* criminalization; law; legalization
life decisions *see* decision-making
life movie, eliciting 64–66, 69–75
  handouts 64, 78–87
limonene 15
lung cancer 38

m

marijuana *see* cannabis
Marijuana Tax Act (1937) 8
mastery activities 103, 132, 138, 140–141, 148–149
medical (therapeutic) use 3, 10, 14, 35–41
  history (US) 7–10, 22
  for mental health problems 31, 39, 50
  self-medication 3
  user's experience 39–41
meditation 235–249
  breath in 244–245
  discussing 239, 243–244, 247
  handouts 246–249
  mindful *see* mindfulness
  riverbank exercise 249
meetings *see* sessions
mental health disorders (psychiatric problems)
  cannabis as medication with 31, 39, 50
  comorbid, in cannabis use disorder 23, 30
mindfulness 57, 180, 235–249
  change and 236–237
  description of 250–251
  handouts 246–249
  instructions for practice 248
  introduction to concept of 237, 239
misuse (cannabis) 48–50
  brief motivational interviewing for 54–55
motivational enhancement therapy (MET) 53–56
  session 2 90
  session 8 194, 200
motivational interviewing (MI) 43, 53–55, 56, 59, 61, 67, 71, 95
  brief, for misuse 54–55
  life movie 81–83
  skills and strategies 62, 204
motivational strategies 89, 195, 200, 202
multiple sclerosis 36
myrcene 15

274 | *Index*

n

Narcotic Control Act (1956) 9
national (federal) government and
law 1, 8–10, 30, 35, 41
negative emotions 51, 77, 87
negative experiences (and
consequences/impact/
outcomes/results) 43, 48,
117, 152, 159, 181, 214, 230
in Alcohol/Cannabis Use
Awareness Record 98, 104,
105, 230, 231–232
with medicinal cannabis 41
screening of use impacts 48–51
neurochemicals 127
neurodevelopment (brain
development) 23, 32
neurologic signs and symptoms 16
new roads 224–225, 228
New Roads worksheet 178, 223
New Roads worksheet 178, 223

o

OARS 65, 90, 108, 128, 137, 151,
194, 215, 238
oils (hash) 15, 19, 24–26
O'Shaughnessy, William Brooke 7
overdose 16–18, 23

p

pain, chronic 36–37
passive-aggressive
communication 114–115,
122–125
passive communication 114, 122–123
patient-led practice 62, 92, 99, 118,
134, 153, 161, 170, 182
physical activity (exercise) 86, 225
physical sensations 176, 190–191

α-pinene (alpha-pinene) 15
pleasurable/pleasant activities 76,
132, 135, 136, 138, 140–141,
148, 149
list of 148
sexual pleasure 29
poisoning (synthetic cannabinoids),
clinical features 16
see also safety issues
positive experiences (and
consequences/effects/
outcomes/results) 156, 159,
176–177, 214, 221–222
Alcohol/Cannabis Use Awareness
Record 98, 104–105, 229,
231, 232
with medicinal cannabis 40
post-traumatic stress disorder
(PTSD) 31, 40
potency 30–31
increased/high 12, 19, 24–26
interventions and 44
power *see* empowerment;
Knowledge is Power
practice exercises 79–80
assertiveness 124–125
future self letter 233
problem solving 165–166
relaxation 234
pregnancy 23, 31–34
present moment (in
mindfulness) 235–237, 241
substances taking one away
from 242
problem-solving 150–166
brainstorming *see*
brainstorming
handouts 163–166

Index **275**

I-SOLVE model 96, 150,
    157–162, 165, 169, 172
progress (review/assessment
    of) 59, 60
  session 1 66, 68
  session 2 91, 94–96, 103
  session 3 109, 111, 121
  session 4 129, 132
  session 5 144
  session 6 152, 155–156, 164
  session 7 169, 172
propylene glycol and polyethylene
    glycol 24
prostate cancer 38
protocol (with scripts)
  session 1 68–77
  session 2 94–101
  session 3 111–119
  session 4 132–135
  session 5 140–142
  session 6 155–162
  session 7 172–185
  session 8 197–200
  session 9 217–226
  session 10 240–245
psychiatric problems *see* mental
    health disorders
psychiatric signs and symptoms 16
psychoactivity 5, 13–15, 24
  history 6, 8
psychological dependence 17, 224
PTSD (post-traumatic stress
    disorder) 31, 40

r

raisin exercise (awareness
    raising) 241–243
rapport, establishing/building/
    strengthening 59

session 1 66, 68
session 2 91, 94
session 3 109, 111
session 4 129, 132
session 6 152, 155
session 7 169, 172
session 8 202
session 9 216–218, 228
session 10 239, 247
rationale, providing 61
  session 1 (and eliciting life
    movie) 66, 69–70
  session 2 91, 96–97
  session 3 109, 112–113
  session 4 130, 134–135
  session 5 136, 138, 140
  session 6 152, 156–157
  session 7 169, 173–174
  session 8 202
  session 9 216, 228
  session 10 247
readiness (to proceed with/make)
    change (incl. change plan)
  session 1 66–67, 73–74
  session 2 95–96
  session 8 195, 196, 202, 205
    readiness rulers 193, 196–198,
      200, 203, 209, 212
real-world application,
    identifying 62
  session 2 92, 99
  session 3 110, 118–119
  session 4 134
  session 5 139, 140–141
  session 6 153, 161
  session 7 171, 184, 185
recovery (aiding) 126–149
  new/replacement activities 86,
    126, 136–149

276 | *Index*

social support 126–135
recreational use 10, 14, 21, 24, 29–31
 historical 6–7
Reddit cannabis subgroups 28, 35, 39
referral to treatment 24, 42, 49, 53
 see also SBIRT
reflection, double-sided 193, 195
relationships *see* family; friends; significant others
relaxation
 with cannabis 29
 practice exercises 234
replacement (new) activities, healthy 86, 136–149
reward mechanisms/centers (brain) 138
 neurochemicals 127
risks *see* safety issues
riverbank exercise 249
role-play, clinician-led 62, 91–92, 98–99, 110, 117, 153, 160–161, 170, 172, 183
route of administration *see* administration/delivery

s

safety issues (incl. risks, adverse/ side effects and toxicity) 22–26, 31–34
 delivery methods and potency 24–26
 driving 33
 medical cannabis patients 41
 pregnancy 23, 32
 screening and 48–50
 synthetic cannabinoids 16–17
SBIRT (screening, brief intervention, and referral to treatment) model 42–43, 45, 53

schizophrenia 30
screening 42–52
 Cannabis Intervention Screener (CIS) 4, 44–52, 55
 common tools 43
 rational for screener 43–44
 SBIRT (screening, brief intervention, and referral to treatment) model 42–43, 45, 53
scripts, protocol with *see* protocol
seizures 38
self-awareness 214–234
 handouts 227–234
self-image 77, 87
self-knowledge 220
 empowerment through 216, 219–220, 228
self-medication 3
self-talk 86, 116, 119, 181–183
serotonin 127
sessions (CBT/ICBT)
 challenges between *see* between-session challenges
 law of thirds *see* law of thirds
 regularity and structure of meeting 79
 session 1 58, 64–88
 session 2 58, 89–106
 session 3 58, 107–125
 session 4 58, 126–135
 session 5 58, 126–127, 136–139
 session 6 58, 150–166
 session 7 58, 167–191
 session 8 192–213
 session 9 178, 214–234
 session 10 178, 235–249
sexual pleasure 29
side effects *see* safety issues
significant others 81

Index | **277**

situational awareness 89–90, 102–106
skills
  assertiveness, guidelines 116–117
  motivational interviewing, and strategies 62, 204
  teach session 62
    session 2 91, 98
    session 3 109–110, 113–114
    session 5 142
    session 6 153, 157
    session 7 170, 174–178
skills application 62
  real world *see* real world application
skills training 56
  interpersonal 57–58
  intrapersonal 57
skills transfer 61, 62
  patient-led practice 62, 92, 99, 118, 134, 153, 161, 170, 182
sleeplessness (insomnia) 77, 87
smoking (cannabis) and the Cannabis Intervention Screener 47
social activity/social environment 29, 86–87
  social pressure 77, 87
  supportive 126–135, 145–147
    how to ask for support 130–131, 145
    Plan for Seeking Support handout 147
    types of support 130, 145
social atom 146
South America 6–7
state (US) law/legalization 17
  criminalization 8

decriminalization/legalization 9–11, 21, 41
stepping back 236
stigma, medicinal cannabis 41
Substance Abuse and Mental Health Service Administration 20, 42
substance use disorders (SUDs) 23
  universal screening 42–48
synthetic cannabinoids 15–17, 19

t

tempting situations *see* high-risk or tempting situations
tension relief 77, 87
terpenes and terpenoids 13, 15, 27
tetrahydrocannabinol (THC; delta-THC; Δ⁹) 5, 14–15, 18, 24
  risks and concentration of 24–25
  therapeutic use 14, 36–37
tetrahydrocannabivarin (THCV) 14–15
THC *see* tetrahydrocannabinol
THCV(tetrahydrocannabivarin) 14–15
therapeutic use *see* medical use
therapy *see* interventions
thinking *see* thoughts
thoughts 176
  in Alcohol/Cannabis Use Awareness Record 98, 104–105, 229, 231, 232
  assertiveness and 117
  automatic 167, 216, 218, 228
  challenging and changing them 181
  new 86
  stopping 86
  use and thinking about it 21

278 *Index*

time-out   77, 87

toxicity *see* safety issues

treatment information
handout   69
see also interventions

triage (Cannabis Intervention Screener)   44–46, 55

triggers or cues   98
session 2   98, 104, 105
session 7 (urges/cravings)
coping strategies   170, 179–180, 187–188
identifying/recognizing   177–178
session 9   216, 219–222, 228–229, 231–232

u

UK and Britain   7–8

Uniform State Narcotic Act (1937)   8

United Kingdom and Britain   7–8

United States   5, 7–12
legalization   1–2, 9–12
legislation *see* law
screening *see* screening
use in   20–26

urges/cravings/discomfort   167–191
handouts   186–191
recognizing   175–176
role in use   174–175
session 1   77, 85, 87–88
session 2   98, 104–105
session 7   167–191
session 9   231–232
triggers *see* triggers or cues

urge surfing   167–168, 170–171, 180–181, 183–185, 190–191

US *see* United States

use (cannabis)   20–26, 48–50
awareness *see* awareness
medical *see* medical use
methods *see* administration
recreational   10, 14, 21, 24, 29–31
session 1 and   79
open discussion   67
session 3 and   111
session 4 and   132
session 6 and   152
session 7 and thinking about   213
urges to *see* urges

user's experience *see* experiences

v

values   192, 206–208
core   193
list of   206–207

vaping and vaporizing   18, 25–26, 47

Vermont   2, 26, 42, 45

visualization and/or imagery   86, 181

w

Washington D.C. (District of Columbia)   1–2, 20–21

Washington state   1, 21, 24, 33, 45

Western Medicine   8

y

young adults and adolescents   10, 21, 24–25, 33–34, 38, 46